Parallel Curriculum Units for

Language Arts

Grades 6–12

Parallel Curriculum Units for Language Arts

Grades 6–12

Jeanne H. Purcell | **Jann H. Leppien**

EDITORS

CORWIN

A SAGE Company

For information:

Corwin
A SAGE Company
2455 Teller Road
Thousand Oaks, California 91320
(800) 233-9936
Fax: (800) 417-2466
www.corwinpress.com

SAGE India Pvt. Ltd.
B 1/I 1 Mohan Cooperative Industrial Area
Mathura Road, New Delhi 110 044
India

SAGE Ltd.
1 Oliver's Yard
55 City Road
London EC1Y 1SP
United Kingdom

SAGE Asia-Pacific Pte. Ltd.
33 Pekin Street #02-01
Far East Square
Singapore 048763

Printed in the United States of America

Library of Congress Cataloging-in-Publication Data

Parallel curriculum units for language arts, grades 6–12/Jeanne H. Purcell and Jann H. Leppien, editors.
    p. cm.
Includes bibliographical references and index.
ISBN 978-1-4129-6537-8 (cloth)
ISBN 978-1-4129-6538-5 (pbk.)
    1. Language arts (Secondary)—Curricula. 2. Gifted children—Education—Curricula.
3. Curriculum planning. I. Purcell, Jeanne H. II. Leppien, Jann H. III. Title.

LB1631.P25 2009
428'.0071'2—dc22   2009014366

This book is printed on acid-free paper.

09 10 11 12 13 10 9 8 7 6 5 4 3 2 1

Acquisitions Editor:	David Chao
Editorial Assistant:	Brynn Saito
Production Editor:	Amy Schroller
Copy Editor:	Trey Thoelcke
Typesetter:	C&M Digitals (P) Ltd.
Proofreader:	Charlotte Waisner
Indexer:	Jean Casalegno
Cover Designer:	Rose Storey

Contents

About the Editors

 **Jeanne H. Purcell** provides leadership for Advanced Placement and gifted and talented education at the Connecticut State Department of Education. Prior to her work at the State Department of Education, she was an administrator for Rocky Hill Public Schools, where she was a K–8 curriculum coordinator and conducted a three-year staff development initiative on curriculum differentiation; a program specialist with the National Research Center on the Gifted and Talented (NRC/GT), where she worked collaboratively with other researchers on national issues related to the achievement of high-achieving young people; and a staff developer to school districts across the United States and Canada. She was an English teacher, grades 7–12, for eighteen years in Connecticut school districts.

She is the author of five books and has published many articles that have appeared in *Educational Leadership, Educational and Psychological Measurement, National Association of Secondary School Principals' Bulletin, Our Children: The National PTA Magazine, Gifted Child Quarterly, Parenting for High Potential,* and *Journal for the Education of the Gifted.* Her special interests include curriculum and instruction, with a particular interest in differentiation for all learners.

 **Jann H. Leppien** is an associate professor at the University of Great Falls in Great Falls, Montana, where she teaches course work in curriculum and instruction, gifted education, assessment and learning, educational research, and methods in social sciences. Additionally, she teaches curriculum courses and thinking-skills courses online and in the Three Summers Program at the University of Connecticut. Before joining the faculty at the University of Great Falls, she worked as a research assistant for the NRC/GT. She has been a classroom teacher, enrichment specialist, and coordinator of a gifted education program in Montana. She is the coauthor of *The Multiple Menu Model: A Practical Guide for Developing Differentiated Curriculum,* and *The Parallel Curriculum: A Design to Develop High Potential and Challenge High-Ability Students.* She conducts workshops for teachers in the areas of differentiated instruction, curriculum design and assessment, thinking skills, and program development.

About the Contributors

Kristen Donegan has a love for reading, writing, and the art of teaching and learning. She began teaching language arts to middle grades in Weld County School District 5 in Greeley, Colorado. When she met Dr. Poole, Principal at Sky Vista Middle School in Cherry Creek School District and discussed the Parallel Curriculum Model (PCM), she knew she had found a unique place to teach and learn. After teaching sixth-grade language arts there, she transitioned to the new role of teacher librarian. She loves the interaction with students (soaking up their enthusiasm, energy, and knowledge) and the craft of planning and teaching with the innovative and reflective teachers in her school.

Lee-Ann Hayen is the Staff Development Coordinator at Sky Vista Middle School in Aurora, Colorado. As Staff Development Coordinator, Lee-Ann works with teachers on planning and implementing PCM units for all students at Sky Vista Middle School. Before moving into this position, she taught eighth grade language arts. She received her Bachelor's degree in English Education from Colorado State University and her Master's degree in Curriculum and Instruction from the University of Phoenix. Lee-Ann is currently working on her administrative license.

Judith Walsh has a bachelor's degree in English from the College of William and Mary and a master's degree in English from Trinity College. Her career in education includes twenty-eight years at Tolland High School in Tolland, Connecticut, where she served as the English Department chairperson for twenty-one of those years. In Tolland, she designed and taught several elective courses, including AP English Language and Composition. She also developed guidelines, activities, and assessment devices for core English courses in line with state and national standards. Following her retirement from classroom teaching, she worked at the Connecticut State Department of Education as an editor for a Javits curriculum writing project. Presently she is volunteering in the Durham, Connecticut, school district and is preparing to teach a course at the Middlesex Institute for Lifelong Education.

INTRODUCTION TO THE PARALLEL CURRICULUM MODEL

A Brief History of the Parallel Curriculum Model (PCM)

When *The Parallel Curriculum: A Design to Develop High Potential and Challenge High-Ability Learners* was published (Tomlinson, et al., 2002), the six of us who authored the work knew we had found ideas in the model to be interesting, challenging, and worthy of a great deal more thought and articulation. Since the original book's publication more than six years ago, we have spent a great deal of time talking among ourselves and with other practitioners about the Parallel Curriculum Model (PCM). These colleagues were as passionate as we were about the nature of high-quality curriculum and the increasing need for such learning experiences for all students. Our colleagues offered us invaluable viewpoints, opinions, suggestions, and probing questions. We surely benefitted in countless ways from their expertise and insights.

Our conversations led to the publication of two new books about PCM in 2006. The first, *The Parallel Curriculum in the Classroom: Essays for Application Across the Content Areas, K–12,* featured articles that we hope clarified and expanded on selected aspects of the model. We continue to hope that it helps educators think more deeply about important facets of the model and some of its "nonnegotiable" components.

The second book, *The Parallel Curriculum in the Classroom: Units for Application Across the Content Areas, K–12,* invited readers to consider eight curriculum units that were designed using PCM. As we compiled the units, we sought to answer the question: "What is necessary in the design process of any Parallel Curriculum unit?"

We did not consider these units as off-the-shelf selections that a teacher might pick up and teach. Rather, we viewed the eight units as professional development tools helpful to any educator who wanted to reflect on one way of creating thoughtful curriculum.

Over the past two years, we continued to engage in conversations about the nature of curriculum models and how they can be used to create rigorous learning opportunities for students. As before, these conversations ultimately led us to two additional projects. The first was to create an updated version of the original publication. This second edition was completed in spring 2008, and is called, *The Parallel Curriculum: A Design to Develop Leaner Potential and Challenge Advanced Learners* (Tomlinson, et al., 2008). The second edition extends our understanding of how this framework for curriculum development can be used to create, revise, or adapt curriculum to the needs of *all* students. In addition, it explores the concept of Ascending Intellectual Demand for all learners in today's heterogeneous classrooms.

The second project was the creation of a series of curriculum units, based on PCM, that could be used by practitioners. To address the varying needs of teachers across the K–12 grade span—as well as different content areas—we decided to create a series of five publications. The first publication is dedicated to the elementary grades, K–5. It features lessons and curriculum units that have been designed to address the needs of primary and elementary learners.

The other four publications span the secondary grades, 6–12. Each of the four publications focuses on a different content area: English/Language Arts, Social Studies/History, Science, and Mathematics. It is our hope that the lessons in each not only underscore important and discipline-specific content, but also illuminate the four parallels in unique and enduring ways.

We could not have completed these tasks without the invaluable assistance of two new team members. Cindy Strickland contributed to both publications in 2006, and she also created *The Parallel Curriculum Multimedia Kit*. Marcia Imbeau is also a long-time user and trainer in PCM. She edited the K–5 book in this series.

THE PARALLEL CURRICULUM MODEL: A BRIEF OVERVIEW[1]

A wonderfully illuminating fable exists about seven blind men who encountered an elephant. Because each man felt a different part of the beast, none was able to figure out the true nature of the gigantic creature.

Did you ever stop to think that students' perceptions about their learning experiences might be as limited as the perceptions the blind men had about the nature of the elephant? Perhaps, like the blind men, students learn only bits and pieces of the curriculum over time, never seeing, let alone understanding, the larger whole that is mankind's accumulated knowledge.

What if we were able to design curriculum in a multifaceted way to ensure that all learners understand: (1) the nature of knowledge, (2) the connections that link humankind's knowledge, (3) the methodology of the practitioner who creates knowledge, and (4) the "fit" between the learner's values and goals and those that characterize practicing professionals? How would classrooms be different if the focus of curriculum was *qualitatively differentiated curriculum* that prompts learners not only to accumulate information, but also to experience the power of knowledge and their potential role within it?

The Parallel Curriculum Model suggests that all learners should have the opportunity to experience the elephant and benefit "from seeing the whole." Moreover, as students become more expert in their understanding of all the facets of knowledge, the curriculum should support students' developing expertise through "ascending levels

---

1. *Source:* Reprinted from *Teaching for High Potential* (Vol. IV, No. 1, April 2002), published by the National Association for Gifted Children, Washington, DC. www.nagc.org

of intellectual demand." This overview of PCM will provide readers with a very brief summary of the model and an opportunity to see how the sum of the model's component parts can be used to create qualitatively differentiated curriculum for *all* students.

THE PARALLEL CURRICULUM: A UNIQUE CURRICULUM MODEL

What is a curriculum model? Why are there so many models to choose from? A curriculum model is a format for curriculum design developed to meet unique needs, contexts, goals, and purposes. To address specific goals and purposes, curriculum developers design or reconfigure one or more curriculum components (see Figure I.1) to create their models. The Parallel Curriculum Model is unique because it is a set of four interrelated, yet parallel, designs for organizing curriculum: Core, Connections, Practice, and Identity.

Figure I.1 Key Curriculum Components

Curriculum Component	Definition
Content	The knowledge, essential understandings, and skills students are to acquire
Assessment	Tools used to determine the extent to which students have acquired the content
Introduction	A precursor or foreword to a lesson or unit
Teaching Methods	Methods teachers use to introduce, explain, model, guide, or assess learning
Learning Activities	Cognitive experiences that help students acquire, rehearse, store, transfer, and apply new knowledge and skills
Grouping Strategies	The arrangement of students
Resources	Materials that support learning and teaching
Products	Performances or work samples that constitute evidence of student learning
Extension Activities	Enrichment experiences that emerge from representative topics and students' interests
Differentiation Based on Learner Need, Including Ascending Levels of Intellectual Demand	Curriculum modifications that attend to students' need for escalating levels of knowledge, skills, and understanding
Lesson and Unit Closure	Reflection on the lesson to ensure that the point of the learning experience was achieved or a connection to the unit's learning goal was made

Reprinted from *Teaching for High Potential* (Vol. IV, No. 1, April 2002), published by the National Association for Gifted Children, Washington, DC. www.nagc.org

THE FOUR CURRICULUM PARALLELS

Let's look at these parallel designs through the eyes of Lydia Janis, a Grade 5 teacher, who develops expertise in using the four parallels over several years. We will focus on one curriculum unit, Lydia's Civil War unit, in order to illuminate how it changes, or transforms, to accommodate the goals and purposes of each parallel. For the sake of our discussion, we treat each parallel as a separate unit. In reality, teachers use the parallels fluidly to address students' talent development needs. At the end of this summary, we will speak directly to when and how these parallels are used. Readers wishing for a more detailed analysis of Lydia's work are referred to Chapters 4 through 7 in both editions of *The Parallel Curriculum.*

The Core Curriculum

Lydia Janis sat at her kitchen table and looked over her textbook objectives for the Civil War unit, as well as her state frameworks. She was troubled. She realized that the textbook objectives were low level; they simply called for students to identify and describe facts, such as "Describe how the Civil War began," and "Identify the differences between the North and South." Her frameworks, on the other hand, required different kinds of knowledge and understandings: "Explain reasons for conflicts and the ways conflicts have been resolved in history," and "Understand causal factors and appreciate change over time."

Lydia realized that the content embedded in her frameworks—concepts and principles—lay at the heart of history as a discipline. These key understandings were vastly more powerful, enduring, and essential to the discipline than the facts in the textbook objectives. She decided to keep her textbook and use it as a resource, however. After all, the information was right there on her shelf, she was familiar with the contents, and the topics covered were fairly well aligned with her state frameworks. But Lydia decided to replace the more simplistic objectives found in the text with the objectives found in the state frameworks.

Lydia realized that the change in *content* would necessitate changes in other curriculum components. Her *assessments* would need to match the content. Her assessment tools would need to measure—both pre and post—students' conceptual understanding in addition to basic facts about the time period. Her *introduction* would need to be retooled to prepare students for the various roles they would assume during the unit as analyzers of documents, data, maps, and events, and to lead them to the powerful understandings she had targeted.

Lydia's *teaching methods* would no longer be strictly didactic, such as lecture and direct instruction, but more inductive to support students as they constructed their own understanding of the time period. Her *learning activities* invited students to think about and draw conclusions about maps, documents, and related data. She supplemented the textbook with other *resources,* such as primary source documents, college textbooks, and the video series, *The Civil War.* She imagined that she would have students who wanted to pursue *extension activities.* She gathered a few books about the Underground Railroad, Abraham Lincoln, and strategic battles. Finally, because she knew already that her students were at different stages in their ability to understand materials and content, she gathered print materials that varied in complexity, from song lyrics and easy-to-decipher documents to several "dense" primary source documents, so that *all* students could work at *ascending levels of intellectual demand.*

Lydia also altered the *products* that students created. In a variety of *grouping* arrangements, they completed document analysis worksheets, ongoing concept maps, and time lines to chronicle their deepening understandings about conflict and the causal relationships of events that led up to the Civil War.

Lydia reflected on her work. She had made significant changes to her teaching and student learning, and she was confident in her improvements. She felt the power of the Core Curriculum as a foundational curriculum.

The Curriculum of Connections

Later in Lydia's career, she became aware of initiatives for interdisciplinary teaching. She was puzzled by some of the units that were labeled "interdisciplinary." A unit on Mexico, completed recently by fourth graders, came to mind. Students learned and performed the Mexican Hat dance, held a fiesta during which they broke a piñata and ate tacos, viewed a display of Mexican money, and drew maps of the migration route of monarch butterflies. "Yikes," she thought to herself, "this unit is an illusion. It *looks* integrated, but it lacks a powerful theme to tie the activities together!"

Lydia sat looking at the Core Curriculum unit on the Civil War that she had created a few years ago. She thought about the concept that earlier had focused her work: conflict. It reminded her that history repeats itself across people, time periods, and cultures: the Vietnam War, women's suffrage, the civil rights movement, and the civil war in Bosnia. This principle, "history repeats itself," held so much power. She realized that she could use the macroconcept, conflict, and the generalization, "history repeats itself," as the content centerpiece to help students build authentic and powerful "bridges" between their understanding of the American Civil War and other times, events, cultures, and people.

Lydia made preliminary plans for her Curriculum of Connections unit. She prepared some assessment prompts, with accompanying rubrics, to assess students' understanding of conflict and the idea that "history repeats itself." She developed a preassessment and essential questions for the introduction to clarify the focus for this unit: "What is a war? Do all conflicts have a resolution? Does history repeat itself?" She knew that her teaching strategies would need to help students make their own "bridges" for the connections among the American Civil war and other events and time periods. She decided to emphasize synectics, metaphorical thinking, Socratic questioning, problem-based learning, and debriefing. Her learning activities emphasized analytic thinking skills to help students in the comparisons and contrasts they needed to make and to encourage analogy making. Her supplemental resources were more varied and covered more events, cultures, and time periods than the resources she had used in her old Core unit, and the materials that she developed to scaffold student thinking included many more graphic organizers, such as Venn diagrams and reader response questions. She was pleased when she realized that the products, grouping strategies, and extension activities would remain similar to those she had used in the Core Curriculum.

For students needing support with this unit, she developed more detailed graphic organizers; for those needing increasing levels of ascending intellectual demand, she thought of several unfamiliar contexts to which students could apply their new learning, such as the Irish conflict and additional revolutionaries like Nelson Mandela and Elizabeth Cady Stanton. She tucked away these ideas for later use.

Lydia reflected on the modifications she had made. "This unit will benefit all my students, especially my abstract thinkers, students who value the 'big picture,' and my scholars," she thought. "It holds so much promise . . . much different than the Mexican Hat Dance unit," she mused.

The Curriculum of Practice

That summer, Lydia realized she could polish the same unit even more. Even though she had seen her students engaged and learning deeply about the Civil War, she began thinking more about how talent develops, specifically how students become acquainted with and skillful in the use of methodologies. "Now that students have the important ideas within and across disciplines, they need to learn how to act like a practitioner," she thought to herself.

So began Lydia's journey through the Curriculum of Practice. She sought out her state and national frameworks to identify the standards related to the role of the historian. To address them, she decided to invite students to read historical novels set during the mid 1800s and record the characters' feelings, images, perspectives, as well as note how they changed throughout the story. Second, she would deepen students' understandings of these historical perspectives by asking them to read related primary source documents and find evidence to support the characters' feelings and attitudes.

In order for students to complete these tasks, she decided to focus her teaching on the skills of the historian: the steps of historical research, taking notes, determining bias, and analyzing point of view, to name a few. She decided to demonstrate or model these skills for students and then use more indirect teaching methods, such as Socratic questioning, to help students construct their own analyses of primary source material. To help students focus on the methodology of the field, she decided to invite a local museum curator to take part in the introduction of the unit.

Lydia subsequently decided to scaffold students' work with a learning contract. The learning contract required specific learning activities and also asked students to complete several short-term products as well as a culminating project, their historical research. Lydia provided them with a rubric to guide and assess their final work. Lydia knew her grouping formats needed to be fluid to honor students' interests and acknowledge that there were times when students needed to work alone or in pairs. This fluidity would be especially important if students elected to complete extension activities around self-selected research questions.

To accommodate students with sophisticated knowledge about the historical research process, Lydia prepared a list of more complex research topics that required ascending levels of intellectual demand, such as inviting advancing students to conduct oral histories on a topic of their choice.

Lydia reviewed the lessons that now reflected the Curriculum of Practice. "Wow," she thought. "So far, I have three ways to optimize learning." Lydia compared and contrasted the three sets of revisions to the Civil War unit: Core, Connections, and Practice. "Each approach is unique and powerful," she thought. And she understood why teaching artful curriculum was a satisfying, career-long journey. "What will I discover next?" she wondered.

The Curriculum of Identity

It was a student who set Lydia on her next journey through the PCM. His name was Jacob, and she was amazed at his knowledge of American history. She envisioned this boy as a history professor, immersed in his own research about historical topics and mentoring others as they investigated questions not yet answered.

She spent time thinking about how she could "morph" her curriculum once more. The content for any Identity unit has a triple focus: her already rich Core curriculum; the ideas, attitudes, beliefs, dispositions, and life outlooks of a professional; and the learning profile of each student, including his or her interests, learning style preferences, values, and goals. Her task, she thought, would be to increase students' awareness about the degree of "fit" between their own emerging sense of self and the profile of practitioners in the field.

Lydia developed a survey of her students' abilities, interests, grouping preferences, goals, and co-curricular activities. Next, she sketched out the stages that students might go through as they went from an early awareness of and interest in history to self-actualization *through* the discipline. "This tool will help me identify where each student currently is on this continuum so I can support his or her progress," she thought.

Now familiar with the many teaching strategies available, Lydia selected visualization as an important method because students would have to move back and forth between their past self, current self, and future self. She also knew that she would use problem-based learning, simulations, and coaching to help students come to understand their place in the Civil War unit as they acted as historians, authors of historical fiction, or war correspondents.

She envisioned her students in varied grouping formats as they spent time with learning activities that required self-analysis and reflection, prediction, and goal setting, among others. Ideas for products came easily to Lydia: completed learning profiles, prompts that asked students to reflect upon and note patterns in their changing profiles, and prompts that invited students to reflect upon the fit between themselves and those of the guest speakers (i.e., a local historian and journalist), who would take part in the introduction to the unit.

Lydia anticipated several extension activities, including explorations about notable leaders from the 1860s, as well as less well-known figures, such as the girls who dressed and fought as soldiers during the Civil War. As she gathered resources to support this unit and its potential extensions, she made sure that her collection featured a variety of introspective materials that would help students understand the beliefs, values, goals, achievements, and sacrifices made by practitioners and enable students' comparisons between their own emerging beliefs and attitudes and those of the professionals.

Lydia reflected on her continuing journey with the Parallel Curriculum Model. Her journey elicited a clarity that comes only with time and persistence. She now understood deeply the model's power and promise. It held the power to awaken and support a teacher's passion and focused creativity. Equally important, it held such promise for uncovering and supporting the gifts and talents of *all* students.

Lydia imagined each of her students as a diamond (see Figure I.2). The model's four parallels—Core, Connections, Practice, and Identity—served as unique polishing tools to reveal the brilliance in each young person. The Core fostered deep understanding in a discipline, while Connections elicited the metaphoric thinking required to span the breadth of man's knowledge. Practice advanced the methodological skills required to contribute in a field, and Identity cultivated the attitudes, values, and life outlook that are prerequisites to self-actualization in a field.

THE FOUR PARALLELS: WHEN AND HOW

We began this article by talking about seven blind men, their limited perceptions about an elephant, and their ultimate realization that: "Knowing in part may make a fine tale, but wisdom comes from seeing the whole." Lydia's work with each of the parallels illustrates how different curriculum components can be modified to help students gain an understanding and appreciation for the whole of a particular discipline.

There are an infinite number of ways to draw upon the parallels. They can be used to *revise* or *design* tasks, lessons, or units. With a revised or designed unit "in

Figure I.2 Lydia's View of the PCM

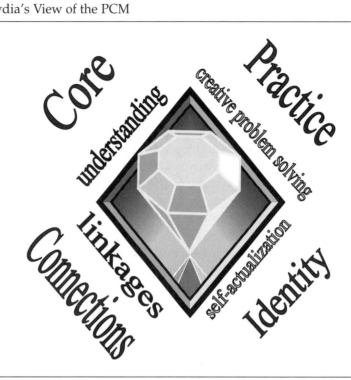

Reprinted from *Teaching for High Potential* (Vol. IV, No. 1, April 2002), published by the National Association for Gifted Children, Washington, DC. www.nagc.org

hand," a teacher can move back and forth across one, some, or all parallels in a single unit. Equally attractive, a teacher might use just one parallel to extend a Core unit.

Various individuals within a school can use the parallels differently. A classroom teacher can use the parallels separately for different purposes, or teachers can work collectively—within grade levels, across grade levels and subjects—to use the parallels to support the learning for all, some, or a few students. Furthermore, classroom teachers can use the parallels to modify learning opportunities for students who need something beyond the grade-level curriculum.

What is the driving force behind decisions about when and how to use the parallels? Decisions stem from teacher expertise, the learning goals, and, most important, the students themselves. We draw upon the parallels to make curriculum more meaningful, emotive, powerful, engaging, and more likely to advance energetically the abilities and talents of students.

The PCM holds the power to help students and teachers "see the whole" of what they are learning. It is our hope that curriculum based upon this model will optimize student learning and enhance the likelihood that all students will lead productive and fulfilling lives. We invite practitioners to read more about this model and join us on a professional journey that we believe will yield that joy and wisdom that comes from seeing the whole. The possibilities are limitless.

THE FORMAT

The curriculum books that are part of our latest initiative share four features that will provide common threads to readers as they transition among the publications. First, each unit contains a section called "Introduction to the Unit" that provides readers with a snapshot of the lessons or unit. If a series of lessons are provided—instead of a whole unit of study—the author may suggest ways to incorporate the subset of lessons into a larger unit. The author may also identify the parallel(s) he or she has elected to emphasize and his or her rationale for highlighting the Core Curriculum or the Curricula of Connections, Connections, and/or Identity. Authors may share their experiences regarding the best time to teach the unit, such as the beginning of the year or well into the latter half of the year. Finally, the author may share what students are expected to know before the unit is taught, as well as resources that would support the teaching and learning activities.

The second common element is the "Content Framework." One of the "nonnegotiables" of PCM units is that they lead students explicitly to a conceptual understanding of the topics and disciplines on which they are based. Thus, each set of lessons or unit contains a list of concepts, skills, and principles that drive the teaching and learning activities. We also included the national standards addressed in each unit and lesson.

Unit "Assessments" is the third common feature. Within this section, authors have the opportunity to describe the assessments that are included within their lessons. Some authors, especially those who supplied an entire unit of study, included preassessments that align with a performance-based postassessment. All authors have included formative assessments. Naturally, scoring rubrics are included with these assessments. In many cases, authors describe the nature of students' misconception that surface when these performance measures are used, as well as some tips on how to address students' mistaken beliefs.

The final common element is the *two-column format* for organizing the lessons. In the left-hand column, authors sequence the instruction in a step-by-step manner. In the right-hand column, readers will hear the author's voice as he or she thinks "outloud" about the introduction, teaching, and learning activities and closure. Authors provide many different kinds of information in the right-hand column including, for example: teaching tips, information about student misconceptions, and suggestions on how to differentiate for above-grade level or below-grade level students.

OUR INVITATION

We invite you to peruse and implement these curriculum lessons and units. We believe the use of these lessons will be enhanced to the extent that you:

- **Study PCM.** Read the original book, as well as other companion volumes, including *The Parallel Curriculum in the Classroom: Units for Application Across the Content Areas, K–12*, *The Parallel Curriculum in the Classroom: Essays for Application Across the Content Areas, K–12*, and *The Parallel Curriculum Multimedia Kit*. By studying the model in depth, teachers and administrators will have a clear sense of its goals and purposes.
- **Join us on our continuing journey to refine these curriculum units.** We know better than to suggest that these units are scripts for total success in the classroom. They are, at best, our most thoughtful thinking to date. They are solid evidence that we need to persevere. In small collaborative and reflective teams of practitioners, we invite you to field test these units and make your own refinements.
- **Raise questions about curriculum materials.** Provocative, compelling and pioneering questions about the quality of curriculum material—and their incumbent learning opportunities—are absolutely essential. Persistent and thoughtful questioning will lead us to the development of strenuous learning opportunities that will contribute to our students' lifelong success in the 21st century.

- **Compare the units with material developed using other curriculum models.** Through such comparisons, we are better able to make decisions about the use of the model and its related curriculum materials for addressing the unique needs of diverse learners.

THE LANGUAGE ARTS BOOK, GRADES 6–12

This volume contains four units and sets of lessons. The first is a Grade 6 writing unit, "A Writing Unit on Voice." Kristen Donegan designed this six-lesson unit to help young writers identify and analyze the factors that shape a writer's voice and personal identity. Moreover, she provides students with the opportunity to acquire the tools that writers use so that they, in turn, attain their own voice. Within the six lessons, she highlights the Curriculum of Practice, the Core Curriculum, and the Curriculum of Connections.

Lee-Ann Hayen created the second unit, "The Little Napoleon in Us All." It is designed for students in Grade 8 and focuses on literary criticism. Across the twelve lessons in this unit, Lee-Ann provides continuous opportunities for students to read carefully and patiently in order to peel back the multiple layers of meaning in *Animal Farm*, the popular allegory about the Russian Revolution. Her lessons address the Core Curriculum, the Curriculum of Connections, and the Curriculum of Practice.

The third unit, "Reacting to a Literary Model," was designed by Judy Walsh for students in Grades 9 or 10. The unit is based on Harper Lee's *To Kill a Mockingbird*, but other novels could be substituted easily, including *Of Mice and Men* or *The Adventures Huckleberry Finn*. Students are provided with opportunities to analyze the ways an author creates a believable setting, an appropriate mood, characters that become real to the reader, and important conflicts and themes that touch the reader. It contains eight lessons, including a preassessment and postassessment, and could be taught easily in several weeks. It highlights all four parallels.

The final unit—also by Judy Walsh—is called "You Be the Critic," and it is a four-week unit for students in Grades 11 and 12. In the beginning lessons, students briefly hone skills learned in earlier grades, such as analyzing characters, setting, and theme. The majority of the lessons are dedicated to helping students understand more subtle skills required of the literary critic, such as uncovering an author's tone and style. Students analyze passages of fiction and nonfiction. Their work culminates in a performance task in which they write their own criticism of a selected passage. The unit highlights all the parallels, with particular emphasis on the Core Curriculum and the Curriculum of Identity.

REFERENCES

Purcell, J. H., Burns, D. E., & Leppien, J. H. (2002). The parallel curriculum model (PCM): The whole story. *Teaching for High Potential* (4)1, 1–4.

Tomlinson, C. A., et. al. (2002). *The parallel curriculum: A design to develop high potential and challenge high-ability learners*. Thousand Oaks, CA: Corwin.

Tomlinson, C. A., et. al. (2005a). *The parallel curriculum: A multimedia kit for professional development*. Thousand Oaks, CA: Corwin.

Tomlinson, C. A., et. al. (2005b). *The parallel curriculum in the classroom: Essays for application across the content areas, K–12*. Thousand Oaks, CA: Corwin.

Tomlinson, C. A., et. al. (2005c). *The parallel curriculum in the classroom: Units for application across the content areas, K–12*. Thousand Oaks, CA: Corwin.

Tomlinson, C. A., et. al. (2008). *The parallel curriculum: A design to develop learner potential and challenge advanced Learners*. Thousand Oaks, CA: Corwin.

1

Understanding and Finding Your Author's Voice

An Intermediate Language Arts Unit

Grades 6–7

Kristen Donegan

INTRODUCTION TO THE UNIT

I've often wondered what sets writers apart from people who use writing as a tool to communicate about their discipline—be it a historian who writes her reflections about rebellions, a scientist who submits an article describing a theory about a new source of energy, or a musician commenting on her decision to use a throwback style of vocals. After much deliberation and discussion with peers, I kept coming back to the concept of voice. A writer focuses on adding the wisdom, the music, or the uniqueness of his or her voice to the huge body of literature that records our experience. Writers can transport us outside of our system of thought, or force us to look from within our community. They can help us critique and celebrate what we already know, or help us discover something new. They can create a new method of writing, or reinvent one that has already been crafted. In the end, they say something about a universal experience, the human experience, in a way that is all their own.

Background for the Unit

This unit has been designed to assist young writers in learning how to identify and analyze the factors that influence the shaping of a writer's voice and identity while simultaneously acquiring the working knowledge of the methods and tools used by writers to communicate their voice in an effective manner. I chose to use three Parallel Curriculum Model parallels to create the learning experiences for my students. I start with the Curriculum of Practice to have students examine what factors shape one's identity and how this is connected to a writer's voice. Using a series of lessons that are based on the purposes and questions of this parallel, I have created a series of rich learning experiences from which students can continue to apply as they acquire new skills and knowledge of how writing concepts become the tools of a writer. By "dropping" them into this first complex experience, I have found that my students are then interested in knowing why and how a writer constructs voice, and I use the Core Curriculum parallel to guide the development of learning experiences to accomplish these goals. Next, a smooth transition can be made to assist students in making a connection between the cross-disciplinary relationships that exist between mood and tone by using the Curriculum of Connections parallel. In the concluding lesson, students then return to the Curriculum of Practice to apply the concepts, skills, and methods of writing to a self-selected prompt. My purpose is to invite students into the writer's world by applying what they have learned through prior lessons to the completion of a written piece that reflects their understanding of the principles, concepts, and skills that serve as the framework for this discipline.

CONTENT FRAMEWORK

Organizing Concepts

Macroconcepts	Discipline-Specific Concepts	Principles
M1: Identity	C1: Voice	P1: Authors create voice by manipulating word choice, sentence fluency, content, and mechanics.
M2: Communication	C2: Mood	P2: A writer's intent and a reader's experience are interdependent in making meaning.
M3: Change	C3: Tone	P3: Voice influences the audience's reaction to the message of writing.
		P4: Writers develop unique voices that may change to suit the mode or message of the writing.
		P5: Authors use voice to create tone, mood, and a message.
		P6: Voice reflects the author's identity and his or her past experiences.
		P7: An author can communicate a message through what is said and what isn't said.

National and/or State Standards

SD1: Students apply a wide range of strategies to comprehend, interpret, evaluate, and appreciate texts. They draw on their prior experience, their interactions with other readers and writers, their knowledge of word meaning and of other texts, their word identification strategies, and their understanding of textual features (e.g., sound-letter correspondence, sentence structure, context, graphics).

SD2: Students adjust their use of spoken, written, and visual language (e.g., conventions, style, vocabulary) to communicate effectively with a variety of audiences and for different purposes.

SD3: Students employ a wide range of strategies as they write and use different writing process elements appropriately to communicate with different audiences for a variety of purposes.

SD4: Students apply knowledge of language structure, language conventions (e.g., spelling and punctuation), media techniques, figurative language, and genre to create, critique, and discuss print and nonprint texts.

SD5: Students participate as knowledgeable, reflective, creative, and critical members of a variety of literacy communities.

SD6: Students use spoken, written, and visual language to accomplish their own purposes (e.g., for learning, enjoyment, persuasion, and the exchange of information).

Skills

S1: Identify patterns in word choice, sentence fluency, content, and mechanics that create an author's voice.

S2: Analyze author's purpose and the impact it has on their own readership of text.

S3: Select an appropriate voice for the context of the writing, including the message, mood, tone, and the audience.

S4: Apply their personal experiences and unique markers of identity to create a voice that is authentic and unique.

ASSESSMENTS

Preassessment

Students will answer the following questions before beginning the unit. They will answer the questions in the form of a *think-pair-share*. The think portion will be independent and written down in a journal.

- What is voice and how is voice created?
- What are the advantages and disadvantages of being able to write in various voices?
- Does changing voice change meaning, or does changing meaning change voice? What are the implications of the relationship between those two factors?
- What are challenges that authors face when selecting the voice for a piece of writing?

- Is the voice of a writer constructed or innate?
- At what point is individual identity lost due to influencing factors? Or is it ever truly lost?
- If one uses more than one voice, is truth negated?

Formative Assessments

The following assessments will be used throughout the unit.

- Identify reactions to model texts and discuss the author's effectiveness.
- Analyze model texts using a table (with title, mode, main idea, tone, mood, and patterns used as categories) for analysis.
- Discuss the patterns and variations in the voice of a self-selected author.
- Write in the style of the self-selected author.
- Reflect on what feels natural and what feels forced about the experience of writing in the author's voice. Discuss what changes can be made to write using student's authentic and unique voice.

Postassessments

In each assessment option, students will reflect on their writing and discuss the following questions:

- Which had more of an impact, your message or your voice? Why?
- What did you do to create voice in your piece?
- How does what you did reflect your identity?

  o Option #1: Creative. Craft a scary story for an audience of your peers using your knowledge of voice, tone, and mood. Stories will be entered in a scary story contest at the local bookstore, so keep in mind the guidelines outlined in the contest rules. Turn in the various stages of writing, so that we can see the way your writing evolves.

  o Option #2: Analytical. Select a variety of texts from one author or from a group of authors who are contemporaries of each other. Then look for patterns in the ways that the author or authors create voice, tone, and mood. Turn in copies of annotated text and an expository essay in which you describe what you found to be the strategies that the author or authors use to create voice, tone, and mood.

  o Option #3: Practical. Create a graphic representation of the choices you make in your various forms of writing to create an effective voice, tone, and mood. Then apply this model to writing you do in one of your classes, in your personal life, or as part of a club or team activity. Using a copy of this writing, code the text to demonstrate your application of the model you drew to represent the choices you make in writing. Turn in your graphic representation and a copy of your coded text.

UNIT SEQUENCE, DESCRIPTION, AND TEACHER REFLECTIONS

Preassessment of Voice (Twenty Minutes)

Unit Sequence—What Is Meant by Voice?	Teacher Reflections
Before beginning the unit focused on voice, preassess students' understanding of voice and its impact on writing. Listening as students think about and discuss the following questions will indicate what students already understand about voice and the power that it has in communication:	The preassessment will provide me with an evaluation of my students' understanding of voice and its relationship with the identity of the author.
1. What is voice and how is voice created? 2. What are the advantages and disadvantages of being able to write in various voices? 3. Does changing voice change meaning, or does changing meaning change voice? What are the implications of the relationship between those two factors? 4. What are challenges that authors face when selecting the voice for a piece of writing? 5. Is the voice of a writer constructed or innate? 6. At what point is individual identity lost due to influencing factors, or is it? 7. If one uses more than one voice, is truth negated?	Through their work in this unit, students will expand on this understanding to become aware of the power that an author has to draw on personal experiences to develop characters who possess voices that are unique not only from each other, but also from the author. The students will come to understand the purposeful way that authors write to engage in an exchange with readers. Finally, students will increase their expertise as writers to include the purposeful use of memorable voices in their own writing.

Lesson 1.1: The Contributors to Identity (Two Class Periods)

Macroconcepts

M1: Identity

Discipline-Specific Concepts

C1: Voice

Principles

P6: Voice reflects the author's identity and his or her past experiences.
P7: An author can communicate a message through what is said and what isn't said.

(Continued)

(Continued)

Skills

S1: Identify patterns in word choice, sentence fluency, content, and mechanics that create an author's voice.

S3: Select an appropriate voice for the context of the writing, including the message, mood, tone, and audience.

S4: Apply their personal experiences and unique markers of identity to create a voice that is authentic and unique.

Standards

SD3: Students employ a wide range of strategies as they write and use different writing process elements appropriately to communicate with different audiences for a variety of purposes.

SD4: Students apply knowledge of language structure, language conventions (e.g., spelling and punctuation), media techniques, figurative language, and genre to create, critique, and discuss print and nonprint texts.

SD5: Students participate as knowledgeable, reflective, creative, and critical members of a variety of literacy communities.

SD6: Students use spoken, written, and visual language to accomplish their own purposes (e.g., for learning, enjoyment, persuasion, and the exchange of information).

Guiding Questions

- What is the relationship between an author's voice and his or her identity?
- Is identity constructed or innate?
- Can people have multiple identities?
- Is identity dynamic or static?
- Do multiple identities create conflict for individuals?
- What influence does identity have on writers?

Unit Sequence—Curriculum of Practice	Teacher Reflections
Introduction, Teaching Strategies, and Learning Experiences	
Group Introduction and Discussion of Identity Begin by reintroducing the question: What is the relationship between an author's voice and her identity? Ask students: Are identity and voice the same? In what instances are they the same? In what instances are they not the same? Transition the students into the group study and set a purpose for their study by informing students that they will be studying this relationship between identity and voice. Then, in homogenous groups of four (based on level of understanding demonstrated on the preassessment), have students create a web map to identify sources of input to identity. As groups finish their brainstorming, provide each group	*The Curriculum of Practice parallel has been selected to create an opportunity for students to engage in the type of analysis that scholars use when analyzing the concepts of voice and identity. The learning activities are purposeful in design to enhance understanding about how scholars begin to critically examine the structure of voice and identity in a piece of writing. These activities also provide students with a rich, problem-based, common experience from which to acquire skills and dispositions necessary as they become more fluid writers.* *Beginning the study by using the Curriculum of Practice guides the students*

Unit Sequence—Curriculum of Practice	Teacher Reflections
Introduction, Teaching Strategies, and Learning Experiences	

with a marker to create a whole-class web of contributors to identity. Ask group representatives to explain why they are adding that factor to the web. As students finish the web, ask them to consider the following questions:

1. Is identity constructed or innate?
2. Can people have multiple identities?
3. Is identity dynamic or static?
4. Do multiple identities create conflict for individuals?
5. What influence does identity have on writers?

Students may use various texts to find which innate factors such as gender, race, our biological ties to family, and other genetically coded factors help to create our sense of self. Additionally, socially constructed factors create a sense of self. These factors can be expressed in the food we eat, the things we say, the beliefs we express, shared stories, shared memories noted with photographs or shared tickets and souvenirs, and the connection we demonstrate to our homes.

Group Study of Poem

One text that explores the factors of identity is "Where I'm From" by George Ella Lyon, which can be found in Appendix 1.1 to this unit). Have students begin the study of the poem. Students may begin by looking at a slide show of images depicting unfamiliar vocabulary words. Words like *auger, restoreth,* and *carbon tetrachloride* can be unfamiliar to students. Additionally, students may need to discuss names like Imogene, Alafair, and Artemis to uncover connotations of the names and the insight they offer to the time period and region referenced in the poem. Then ask students to draw conclusions about the identity of the poet, explaining how the clue helped them to identify one aspect of the author's identity. Ask students to identify what parts of the poet's identity are constructed or created by parts of or experiences with our society. Also ask students to identify the parts of the poet's identity that are innate, or factors that are part of our identity from birth, that are present regardless of experience.

in a reflective and intimate study of the relationship between the concepts. As students work to manipulate voice, they can see firsthand how a word or a comma shapes the meaning that the audience makes from the author's words. Since the preassessment gives the teacher a snapshot of students' understanding, this grouping arrangement can assist in advancing students to the next level of understanding early on in the unit.

Modification for Student Need

Students with a basic understanding at the beginning of this unit can start by answering the first and third questions. As students demonstrate more sophisticated understandings of the concepts, they can begin to look at the other questions. Teachers can "muddy the water" by suggesting scenarios that seem to suggest a different conclusion than the ones that students pose in their group discussions.

By offering images of unfamiliar vocabulary words, teachers can begin the process of prereading. The skill of inferring will be used to begin to understand the message from the context of just a few pieces of information. This is important not only in developing reading expertise, but also in developing the habits and mind of a scholar.

Ascending Intellectual Demand (AID)

Students can extend their investigation of Lyons and confirm their inferences using biographical information about the author. Students should find confirmation that the voice of this particular poem is, in fact, a match to the voice of the poet. The books I Am Phoenix, Joyful Noise, *and* Big Talk *are excellent opportunities for students to study voice further. In these books of poems, Paul Fleischman crafts two or more voices for an almost lyrical effect in his poetry. Students who wish to extend creatively their learning may create their own poems for multiple voices. Students who are more analytically inclined*

(Continued)

(Continued)

Unit Sequence—Curriculum of Practice	Teacher Reflections
Introduction, Teaching Strategies, and Learning Experiences	

Next, have students read the poem. Ask the students how their impressions of the poet's identity changed once they had all the clues from the poem. Does the poet's voice match his or her identity? Why would a poet choose to create a dissonance between his or her identity and the voice used in the writing? The nostalgic tone of the poem may offer a lens with which to study this tone. On one hand, Lyon recalls images of the past in a voice that echoes her childhood voice. She triggers a sense of nostalgia with which each of us can hear a school-age child calling out "know-it-all." On the other hand, Lyon ends with a voice full of wisdom, recognizing that she is part of a force larger than herself, that she is part of those moments in time "snapped before I budded—leaf fall from the family tree." While the voices reflect some dissonance, they also speak to the multiple identities housed in one individual at any given time in his or her life.	*may choose to compare and contrast the mechanics and word choice that make the two voices possible.*
Individual Application of Poetry Study

Ask students to create their own poem that reflects aspects of their identity. They should begin by brainstorming various inputs to their identity using the Identity Poem Brainstorm Web in Appendix 1.2.

They may use the "Where I'm From" poem as a writing model or may compose a poem in a form all their own. | *Describing one's own identity is often more challenging than describing another's. The web provided will give students a starting place, but conversation with peers will also be invaluable to the process of brainstorming. In this step of the writing, as in each, a teacher model is a great source of inspiration and direction as well. The templates will also help students who require a more structured approach vs. those who prefer an open-ended opportunity. Remind students that through the act of writing their own poem, they will need to consider the impact of their words and punctuation on their audience.* |
| **Letter to Peer Editor**

Ask students to compose a cover letter to a peer editor. In this letter, students should address the following topics:

  1. Did you select a voice that matches your identity as you wrote your poem? Why or why not? | *Since the discussion of voice is greatly dependent on the reaction of an audience, the opportunity for students to have a dialogue about their writing helps them to target their words to an audience. Having students write letters back and forth provides students with another opportunity to write for a specific purpose, and also gives them the opportunity to* |

Unit Sequence—Curriculum of Practice	Teacher Reflections
Introduction, Teaching Strategies, and Learning Experiences	
2. What did you want your audience to understand about who you are? 3. What do you want feedback on? 4. What part of the poem makes you most proud? Why? **Response Letter from Peer Editor** Direct students to compose a response to the poet whose work they have read. In the response, students should indicate their feedback on the parts of the poem that the poet asked to have critiqued. Students should also give feedback on whether the poet achieved his or her goal in what they wanted the audience to understand. Finally, the editor should share the part that he or she found most insightful, surprising, or engaging. **Revised Writing** Students will revise their writing based on feedback from their peer editor. Students will turn in their revised copy for feedback that is provided on the Assessment Rubric (Appendix 1.3).	*distance themselves a little from the writing for objectivity. Asking the students to identify the aspects of their poem on which they would like feedback also helps narrow the focus of the reader.* *Remind students to reflect on their poems and consider what parts of their identity would have existed despite the people, objects, and places involved in their lives. Would they have been leaders even if they weren't the oldest child in their family? Would they have believed that anything was possible if they worked hard enough, if their father didn't believe this motto? Were they born with any physical traits that they really take pride in? Did their genetic makeup leave them with any traits that make them feel self conscious?*
Closure	
Group Discussion Ask students to respond to a 3-2-1 questionnaire and then share their reflections as a class. Ask the following questions: 1. What are three parts of your identity that are constructed? (Students may identify factors discussed in the study of texts such as "Where I'm From." Student responses may include our beliefs, what we say, our memories, our sense of right and wrong, or other ideas that were discussed in class discussion. They may also identify ideas of their own.) 2. What are two parts of your identity that are innate? (Like above, these may reflect class discussion, with responses such as gender, race, or biological family relations, or they may be ideas students come up with on their own.)	*It is also important to provide time for students to reflect on the meaningfulness of the activities by addressing at least two of the four following questions:* • What have we learned about the tools and methods used by writers? How has this influenced your work? • What skills are required of the writer? • What challenges do they face when they construct a piece of writing? What challenges did you face in these activities? • Are there certain traits or dispositions that a writer must have to participate in this type of work? Which of these traits did you experience?

(Continued)

(Continued)

Unit Sequence—Curriculum of Practice	Teacher Reflections
Closure	
3. Give one example of how your identity might change with a change in contexts. (Students may identify a variety of changes. A change in context may be a change from staying home to going to school, or it may be in moving from one town to another.)	

Lesson 1.2: Shaping Voice (One or Two Class Periods)

Macroconcepts

M1: Identity

Discipline-Specific Concepts

C1: Voice

Principles

P1: Authors create voice by manipulating word choice, sentence fluency, content, and mechanics.

P4: Writers develop unique voices that may change to suit the mode or message of the writing.

Skills

S1: Identify patterns in word choice, sentence fluency, content, and mechanics that create an author's voice.

S2: Analyze author's purpose and the impact it has on their own readership of text.

Standards

SD1: Students apply a wide range of strategies to comprehend, interpret, evaluate, and appreciate texts. They draw on their prior experience, their interactions with other readers and writers, their knowledge of word meaning and of other texts, their word identification strategies, and their understanding of textual features (e.g., sound-letter correspondence, sentence structure, context, graphics).

SD4: Students apply knowledge of language structure, language conventions (e.g., spelling and punctuation), media techniques, figurative language, and genre to create, critique, and discuss print and nonprint texts.

Guiding Questions

- What is the relationship between identity and voice?
- What is the relationship between audience, purpose, and voice?
- If you can express multiple voices, does your voice truly reflect your identity? What role do mechanics and grammar have in shaping voice?

Unit Sequence—Core Curriculum	Teacher Reflections
Introduction, Teaching Strategies, and Learning Experiences	

Introductory Student Examples and Discussion Hand out the Cue Cards (Appendix 1.4) to students in the class. Ask them to read a description of a person and an audience. Ask the students to perform their "voices" one at a time. Using a couple of student examples of these voices, record on the board what each student says. The class will then be asked to work in groups of two in order to punctuate the writing so that they can read it the same way that the model student read it. Ask students the following questions: 1. What is the relationship between identity and voice? 2. What is the relationship between audience, purpose, and voice? 3. If you can express multiple voices, does your voice truly reflect your identity? 4. What role do mechanics and grammar have in shaping voice? **Author Study** Using a model text (see Appendixes 1.5 and 1.6), ask students what they notice about the voice and how it is created in the piece. Have students read sample texts. Ask them to find one that really speaks to them or one that they think sounds like them. Students should identify the patterns that establish that author's voice.	*These lesson activities use the Core Curriculum parallel. It is designed to help students understand some of the fundamental concepts that shape effective writing. It is important for students to hear the difference that mechanics, sentence fluency, images, and word choice make in the writing that creates voices. It is also important that students understand the interconnectedness of why they are writing, who they are writing for, how they write their message, and the vehicle through which they get the attention of those for whom they write. Finally, students will begin to consider what impact the author's identity has on their reaction as readers to what they read.* *A collection of texts that would make wonderful model texts is* Guys Write for Guys Read. *The book houses narratives from several popular male writers. The stories are fast-paced and very engaging. The texts lend themselves well to analysis. They are fairly short and the voices are strong. It may be helpful to pair these readings with a reading that purposefully subverts personality to communicate more objectivity. Students could compare and contrast a textbook excerpt, for example, with the narratives. Students should focus on word choice, qualitative and quantitative descriptors, characters' thoughts and words, and other stylistic tools to determine the author's voice.*

Closure	

Group Discussion on Identity and Voice To conclude this section of the unit, have students list what they have learned about identity and voice. Then ask students to construct questions that they have formed or that went unanswered about the two concepts. Next, ask groups of four students who are heterogeneously arranged to return to the discussion questions from the beginning of the lesson. (See discussion format using spinners in the next column.)	*Since this lesson is early in the unit, asking students to demonstrate their understanding so far allows teachers to measure students' progress toward a deeper understanding of concepts. Students should gain an appreciation for the fluid nature of identity and therefore voice. They should also understand that voice conforms to the context; they should understand that what is appropriate or effective in one scenario does not necessarily apply to the next.*

(Continued)

(Continued)

Unit Sequence—Core Curriculum	Teacher Reflections
Closure	
1. What is the relationship between identity and voice? 2. What is the relationship between audience, purpose, and voice? 3. If you can express multiple voices, does your voice truly reflect your identity? 4. What roles do word choice, sentence structure, and mechanics have in shaping voice?	*Students will see that both audience and purpose are forces that influence voice, causing it to change. Students should also be able to see that at least some factors of our identity are dynamic, changing perhaps over time or in different social contexts.* *The discussion between students can be organized using the **Sample Spinner for Student Participation found in Appendix 1.7**. One spinner includes the same number of spaces as tables, while the second spinner includes four spaces, one for each member in a group. Students in each group number off. Then, a student can be selected to spin to indicate who shares their answer next. This system ensures that all students have an opportunity for participating, while adding the excitement of a climate of a game.*

Lesson 1.3: The Influences on Mood (One or Two Class Periods)

Discipline-Specific Concepts

C2: Mood
C3: Tone

Principles

P2: A writer's intent and a reader's experience are interdependent in making meaning.
P3: Voice influences the audience's reaction to the message of writing.
P5: Authors use voice to create tone, mood, and a message.
P7: An author can communicate a message through what is said and what isn't said.

Skills

S2: Analyze author's purpose and the impact it has on their own readership of text.

Standards

SD1: Students apply a wide range of strategies to comprehend, interpret, evaluate, and appreciate texts. They draw on their prior experience, their interactions with other readers and writers, their knowledge of word meaning and of other texts, their word identification strategies, and their understanding of textual features (e.g., sound-letter correspondence, sentence structure, context, graphics).

SD4: Students apply knowledge of language structure, language conventions (e.g., spelling and punctuation), media techniques, figurative language, and genre to create, critique, and discuss print and nonprint texts.

Guiding Question

- How do experts in a discipline communicate their ideas in a way that audiences engage and understand them?

Unit Sequence—Curriculum of Connections	Teacher Reflections
Introduction, Teaching Strategies, and Learning Experiences	

Group Listening Session to Identify Mood

Before beginning the listening and viewing portion of this lesson, help students to create a visual to demonstrate the difference between mood and tone. Students may use the Tale of Two Authors Worksheet (Appendix 1.8) to record their ideas. Teachers may want to refer to the Teacher Resource: Tale of Two Authors Worksheet before the discussion. The listening portion of the lesson will help students to explore the question: *How do experts in a discipline communicate their ideas in a way that audiences engage and understand them?* In this case, students will be connecting the concepts of communication and identity through the lens of music to those concepts through the lens of writing. After playing a variety of sound clips, ask students to identify the tone of the piece. Students should individually record the tone or tones on one color note card and then record observations about contributors to the tone on another color note card. Then, ask students (1) What created the tone of the musical piece? (2) How might writers create a similar tone? (3) Did your mood match the tone of the piece?

Author Study

To encourage students to make the connection between mood in music and in writing, arrange students into heterogeneous readiness reading groups of four with model texts found later in this unit, Post-its, and copies of Author Study Chart (Appendix 1.9). Instruct students to read the texts identifying the mood, its effect on them as readers, and the patterns of methods that these authors used to create mood.

This lesson uses the Curriculum of Connections to help students to understand the similarities of the challenges to communicate ideas in the disciplines of music and of writing. The lesson begins with a discussion of mood and tone. Often these concepts are confused with one another; this lesson will help students to distinguish the two concepts. The discussion of mood and tone should consider these questions: What control does the author have over tone? What control does the author have over mood? Will various audiences respond with the same mood? How does mood impact interest in a subject? From the discussion, students should understand that while tone is the emotional atmosphere that an author creates using words, images, sentence structure, and punctuation, mood is tied to the audience's reaction to the piece. Audiences look to stylistic choices an author makes and to the speaker of the piece to determine the mood. However, the mood is also determined by the lens through which it is viewed. Our own identities feed or hinder our openness to the tone and message of a piece.

By playing two pieces with striking contrasts in tone such as Danse Macabre *composed by Camille Saint-Saens and* Four Seasons: Spring *composed by Antonio Vivaldi. While both pieces focus on a dance of elements of nature, the tone is undoubtedly different. Students should be able to detect a difference in pacing, pitch, and volume between the pieces. Students should also be asked to be aware of what triggers emotional reactions to the music. They may cue into when their emotions changed to be able to think about why the change occurred.*

(Continued)

(Continued)

Unit Sequence—Curriculum of Connections	Teacher Reflections
Introduction, Teaching Strategies, and Learning Experiences	
	Perhaps a writer's most valuable tool is tone. Tone is often the quality of writing that readers connect emotionally to, and as such it determines a reader's readiness to hear and understand the author's message. Mood is really impacted by tone. Mood is the feeling that readers identify about the piece, and it often mirrors the mood of the protagonist. Mood is a great place to start when studying the relationship between mood and tone since readers are generally more intuitive about how they feel after reading a text than they are about what tone the writer was using. It is important to make a distinction between tone and mood because while they are complimentary, they are not always of the same description. Really skilled writers occasionally have tones and moods that do not necessarily match. For example, a tone may be ironic while a character is exhibiting earnestness. Readers may feel that the author is serious about the topic but doesn't necessarily buy into what the speaker says about the topic. A prime example of a tone and mood mismatch is Jonathan Swift's "A Modest Proposal." In addition to Swift's text, students may read Edgar Allen Poe, Washington Irving, or more contemporary authors such as Alvin Schwartz. Students code the text for words, images, sentence structures, and mechanics that elicited an emotional reaction from them.
Closure	
In journals, ask students to (1) record methods that writers use to create different moods; (2) consider how varying disciplines would use tone and mood in their writing; and (3) explain the relationship between tone and mood and its effective use in writing.	*Use these prompts to help students make the connection that tone and mood varies in different contexts.*

Lesson 1.4: Analyzing an Author's Voice (Four to Five Class Periods)

Macroconcepts

M1: Identity

Discipline-Specific Concepts

C1: Voice
C3: Tone

Principles

P1: Authors create voice by manipulating word choice, sentence fluency, content, and mechanics.

P3 : Voice influences the audience's reaction to the message of writing.

P4: Writers develop unique voices that may change to suit the mode or message of the writing.

P6: Voice reflects the author's identity and his or her past experiences.

Skills

S1: Identify patterns in word choice, sentence fluency, content, and mechanics that create an author's voice.

S2: Analyze author's purpose and the impact it has on their own readership of text.

S3: Select an appropriate voice for the context of the writing, including the message, mood, tone, and the audience.

Standards

SD1: Students apply a wide range of strategies to comprehend, interpret, evaluate, and appreciate texts. They draw on their prior experience, their interactions with other readers and writers, their knowledge of word meaning and of other texts, their word identification strategies, and their understanding of textual features (e.g., sound-letter correspondence, sentence structure, context, graphics).

SD4: Students apply knowledge of language structure, language conventions (e.g., spelling and punctuation), media techniques, figurative language, and genre to create, critique, and discuss print and nonprint texts.

SD5: Students participate as knowledgeable, reflective, creative, and critical members of a variety of literacy communities.

Guiding Questions

- What tone do the words create?
- How does pacing affect mood?
- How does the tone of a piece of writing and the mood impact the way you understand the message?

(Continued)

Unit Sequence—Curriculum of Practice	Teacher Reflections
Introduction, Teaching Strategies, and Learning Experiences	

Author Study

Introduce the text, *Seedfolks*, by Paul Fleischman to the students. This text provides a great opportunity for a reader's theatre activity. During a reader's theatre, the teacher or the students select an important part of the text and modify it so that all ideas can be read either from the perspective of one of the characters or from the perspective of a narrator. After the text is converted to a reader's theater, it is read like a script, with careful attention to inflection and tone; however, no props are used. *Seedfolks* is already written in the voices of each of the characters, with each character having his or her own chapter. As students read, ask them to record their responses to this unit's preassessment questions in a double entry journal. The journal should record not only student responses or thoughts, but also the quotes from the story that trigger or support those responses and thoughts.

Analyzing Impact of Identity

Instruct students to select a vignette from *Seedfolks* that demonstrates an effective use of voice. Have copies of various excerpts from the text for students to analyze and allow them to select from the collection. Then ask students to code the text for specific examples of decisions that the author made to construct voice. To prompt their thinking about this activity ask students the following questions:

1. What tone do the words create?

2. What sense of pacing do you have in the piece? How is this pace created? What impact does that have on your mood?

3. How does the tone of the piece and your mood impact the way you understand the message?

4. Do you notice any shifts in the tone of the piece? What are signals that the tone is shifting?

This lesson uses the work of experts in the field to help students understand the tools of a writer through the use of the Curriculum of Practice parallel. Analyzing a text such as Fleishman's Seedfolks *is a great way for students to see that one author can possess many voices that all speak to a greater message or theme. Students can see through texts such as this one the way that, sometimes, it takes a chorus of voices to help us hear the messages those individuals are speaking. The study also helps students to see the craft of creating voice in such a way that they can compare and contrast the components of writing that create uniqueness in voice, but continuity of message.*

In this activity, students are really focusing on the way that the parts create an overall impression. To see the impact of individual tools of word choice, imagery, sentence structure, punctuation, and other stylistic devices, students can color code or label the categories. Students may use various colored highlighters to create this text with each highlighter indicating a different stylistic tool. For an example, see Coded Seedfolks *Excerpt in Appendix 1.10. The area of analysis is one that is full of opportunities to differentiate. Some students are very intuitive and can identify multiple tones that exist within a piece. Others will need to be cued to look at words that are used and variations in sentence structure and length. Still other students may benefit from looking at excerpts before and after the reading to really focus on significant examples of word choice and sentence structure and length. Regardless of the path, however, students will be able to see that the words that an author uses give clues to how he or she feels about the subject and what message he or she wants the audience to understand. They will see how sentence structure can change the speed, the rhythm of a piece, giving emphasis to certain ideas.*

Unit Sequence—Curriculum of Connections	Teacher Reflections
Closure	
Metacognition of Writing Provide small, heterogeneous groups of learners with copies of interviews with Paul Fleischman about his writing and his inspiration for the voices of his characters from his own experiences (see the Teacher Resources). Ask students to respond to the following questions: 1. What are challenges that Fleischman faces when selecting the voice for a piece of writing? 2. In what ways is Fleischman's voice constructed? In what ways is it innate?	*Through the metacognition of writing, students will be exploring the role of a writer. Paul Fleischman has spoken a lot about the process of writing and his experience with this process. Paul Fleischman is the son of Sid Fleischman who also wrote many books for children. Paul talks about how he gained an appreciation for building the setting of a book with several, accurate details. He speaks with great insight into his process as a writer, making connections between the tools that a writer uses and the human experience that he records in a growing body of literature.* **Extending Learning** *The interviews may not satisfy students in their journey for understanding the relationship an author's identity and voice. Students can be encouraged to write to an author with questions that the class still wonders about.*

Lesson 1.5: Finding the Right Voice and Mood for Your Purpose (Two Class Periods)

Macroconcepts

M1: Identity
M2: Communication (Purpose, Audience, and Message)
M3: Change

Discipline-Specific Concepts

C1: Voice
C2: Mood
C3: Tone

Principles

P1: Authors create voice by manipulating word choice, sentence fluency, content, and mechanics.
P2: A writer's intent and a reader's experience are interdependent in making meaning.
P3: Voice influences the audience's reaction to the message of writing.
P7: An author can communicate a message through what is said and what isn't said.

(Continued)

(Continued)

Skills

S1: Identify patterns in word choice, sentence fluency, content, and mechanics that create an author's voice.

S2: Analyze author's purpose and the impact it has on their own readership of text.

S3: Select an appropriate voice for the context of the writing, including the message, mood, tone, and the audience.

Standards

SD1: Students apply a wide range of strategies to comprehend, interpret, evaluate, and appreciate texts. They draw on their prior experience, their interactions with other readers and writers, their knowledge of word meaning and of other texts, their word identification strategies, and their understanding of textual features (e.g., sound-letter correspondence, sentence structure, context, graphics).

SD2: Students adjust their use of spoken, written, and visual language (e.g., conventions, style, vocabulary) to communicate effectively with a variety of audiences and for different purposes.

SD3: Students employ a wide range of strategies as they write and use different writing process elements appropriately to communicate with different audiences for a variety of purposes.

SD4: Students apply knowledge of language structure, language conventions (e.g., spelling and punctuation), media techniques, figurative language, and genre to create, critique, and discuss print and nonprint texts.

SD5: Students participate as knowledgeable, reflective, creative, and critical members of a variety of literacy communities.

SD6: Students use spoken, written, and visual language to accomplish their own purposes (e.g., for learning, enjoyment, persuasion, and the exchange of information).

Guiding Question

- How do authors construct a voice that is effective for their audiences?

Unit Sequence—Curriculum of Practice	Teacher Reflections
Introduction, Teaching Strategies, and Learning Activities	
Understanding Purpose and Audience Students will use the gallery walk to consider the question: *How do authors construct a voice that is effective for their audiences?* Ask students to do a gallery walk with different samples of writing. Ask them to identify as they walk around who is the target audience and what the purpose of the writing is. Students should record this information on the Gallery Walk Through Effective Voice Handout (Appendix 1.11).	*The gallery walk gives students the opportunity to be exposed to several texts in an engaging and active manner. Often times, it is effective to create poster-sized copies of mentor texts so that students can view an excerpt of the text. You may also want to provide students with Post-it notes and allow them to post observations as they rotate through the texts. Students may look at texts such as the following:*

Unit Sequence—Curriculum of Practice	Teacher Reflections
Introduction, Teaching Strategies, and Learning Activities	

Discussion After students have had an opportunity to read and analyze several texts, convene as a class to construct knowledge through class observations. Through this discussion, students should be able to (1) identify words or persuasive techniques that the writers use to connect to audiences, and (2) provide examples of how the purpose of the text drives the use of particular tools. For example, many fiction writers focus on characterization and description to connect to audiences. Additionally, songs and speeches in particular use repetition. Humor and appeals to empathy are effective tools in almost any kind of writing.	• *Love That Dog* by Sharon Creech • *Puppies, Dogs, and Blue Northers: Reflections on Being Raised by a Pack of Sled Dogs* by Gary Paulsen • *Caves* by Stephen Kramer • *The FairyTale News* by Colin and Jacqui Hawkins *The History Channel has a collection of video and audio recordings of famous speeches that may provide ideas for resources that you can match with text versions so that you could post them on the wall for the gallery walk.* *The voice of a piece is one of the first impressions that an audience is exposed to, and it can open the audience to a message or close them off. Because of the power of this trait of writing, teaching students about how to analyze and manipulate voice can be very empowering for them as writers.*
Closure	
Distribute a sticky note to students and have them summarize two ways authors construct voices that are effective with audiences.	*These sticky notes can be posted on chart paper to remind students of the techniques that authors use.*

Lesson 1.6: Your Turn (Four to Five Class Periods)

All Concepts, Principles, Standards, and Skills

Unit Sequence—Curriculum of Practice	Teacher Reflections
Introduction, Teaching Strategies, and Learning Experiences	

A Writing Opportunity Building on the lessons acquired through the other three parallels, offer students a writing opportunity that calls on them to join the company of other writers. Read to them the requirements for the final assessment submission (see Appendix 1.12) and then ask them to identify the audience and purpose for their writing.	*By providing a creative, an analytical, and a practical option, this final assessment prompt appeals to different types of thinkers. There are many writing rubrics that would be appropriate for assessing writing. You may choose to use a six-trait rubric (see six-traits writing on the Internet from Northwest Regional Educational Lab (NWREL)), a district-created rubric, a state department of*

(Continued)

(Continued)

Unit Sequence—Curriculum of Practice	Teacher Reflections
Introduction, Teaching Strategies, and Learning Experiences	

Introduction to Establishing a Voice and Mood for a Purpose and Audience Use the following directions to introduce students to their writing assignment. *Student Directions:* Now that you have studied the way that authors, artists, and musicians create mood and voice, it's your turn to create a voice that speaks to a real audience. Carefully consider what the prompt asks you to do. Are you to entertain? Persuade? Explain? Then think about the structure of your writing and its influence on your audience. How will your structure help you to communicate mood? How will the voices of various characters align in one piece to create a unified impression of your voice as a writer? What role will grammar, mechanics, and word choice have in shaping that voice? **Small Group Support** In small groups, meet with students based on levels of expertise found in their writing to discuss the strengths and merits of their writing. Ask them to reflect on how the skills, methods of thinking, or structure of their writing mirror those of other writers they have analyzed or studied in this unit. Have each student discuss the challenges they faced as a writer and how they structured their success.	*education-approved rubric, or a teacher-created rubric. While teachers may assess other areas of writing, the bulk of the feedback and grade assessment should focus on voice. In the end, students should understand how important voice is to ensuring that their message is heard, understood, and embraced.* *This writing opportunity will require several days for students to complete. It is advised to work with students in small groups to address their concerns and challenges that they face as a writer. Each writing prompt will require varying degrees of feedback and scaffolding. The type of classroom organization that best serves this process of writing is a writer's workshop atmosphere where support and feedback are assured.* *Student meetings provide an opportunity for the teacher to gain insight to the self-efficacy level of his or her students as writers. Do students feel like writers? Have they come to understand how to improve their writing through grappling with the concepts of voice, identity, tone and mood, and purpose for writing? Do they see themselves as writers and contributors to the field? Future success in writing depends on the success they acquire during these learning experiences.*

Closure	

Writers' Symposium When students have completed and edited their writing, provide an opportunity for them to read their writing to each other in small groups. This can be structured by grouping students based on the writing prompt that they selected. Ask students to share with their peers their thoughts behind the construction of their writing. Prepare those who are listening to the author to share one new insight about their fellow writer's work that they experienced as a member of the audience.	

APPENDIX 1.1

Where I'm From

I am from clothespins,
from Clorox and carbon tetrachloride.
I am from the dirt under the back porch.
(Black, glistening
it tasted like beets).
I am from the forsythia bush,
the Dutch elm
whose lone gone limbs I remember
as if they were my own.

I'm from fudge and eyeglasses,
from Imogene and Alafair.
I'm from the know-it-alls
and pass-it-ons
from Perk up! and Pipe down!
I'm from He restoreth my soul
with a cotton ball lamb
and ten verses I can say myself.

I'm from Artemus and Billie's branch,
fried corn and strong coffee.
From the finger my grandfather lost
to the auger
the eye my father shut to keep his sight.

Under my bed was a dressbox
spilling old pictures,
a sift of lost faces
to drift beneath my dreams.
I am from those moments—
snapped before I budded—
leaf fall from the family tree.

—*George Ella Lyon*

Retrieved from http://www.georgeellalyon.com/where.html

APPENDIX 1.2

Identity Poem Brainstorm Web

Directions: Use the web below to brainstorm your identity modifiers. You may use existing categories to brainstorm or add your own. Think about what makes you who you are.

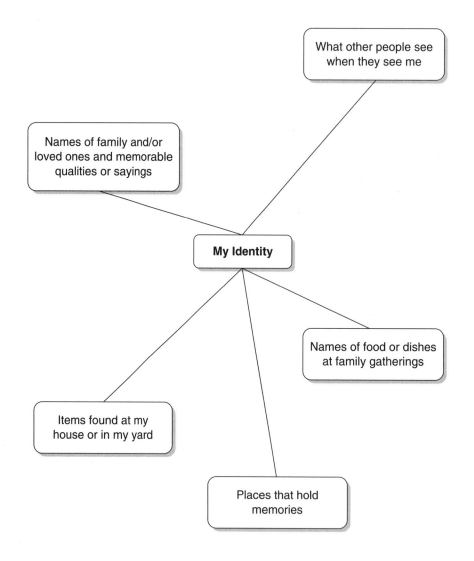

APPENDIX 1.3

Identity Poem Rubric

Overview

Students will write a poem in the style of "Where I'm From" by George Ella Lyon or a style of their own. Through the poem, students should express the factors or experiences that they feel truly shaped who they are. Students should use language artistically to create a tone and message.

Requirements

___ At least ten images of experiences or contributors to the student's identity

___ A rough draft, revisions, and a final draft of the poem

___ Correspondence between writer and a peer editor in the form of letters

Assessment Rubric

	Voice	*Word Choice*	*Mechanics*
Expert	Student uses language and images to create a poem that is unique and creative. The poem is truly an expression of the student's identity.	Student carefully selects words that add meaning and sound to his or her poem. The student's words stand out as colorful and evoke emotion.	Student writes the poem with few or no mistakes in spelling or punctuation. The writing contains a variety of simple and more complex sentence structures.
Practitioner	Student uses language or images to create a poem that is creative. The poem is an expression of the student's identity.	Student carefully selects words that add meaning and sound to his or her poem. The student's words stand out as unusual.	Student writes the poem with mistakes in spelling or punctuation. The writing contains a variety of simple and more complex sentence structures.
Apprentice	Student uses language or images to create a poem. The poem is somewhat expression of the student's identity.	Student has used his or her everyday language with ease and accuracy. The language clearly communicates the student's intended message.	Student writes the poem with many mistakes in spelling or punctuation. The writing contains several fragmented or run-on sentences.
Novice	Student uses language or images to create a poem. The poem is an expression of a young person's identity.	Student has used his or her everyday language with minor mistakes. The language somewhat communicates the student's intended message.	Student writes the poem with mistakes in spelling, punctuation, and grammar that make the meaning unclear.

APPENDIX 1.4

Cue Cards

Voice Card #1	*Voice Card #2*
Identity: Male Army Drill Sergeant	Identity: Teenage Female Movie Star
Audience: New Recruits	Audience: Reporters
Purpose: Explaining the importance of cleaning your barracks.	Purpose: Promoting your upcoming movie.
Voice Card #3	*Voice Card #4*
Identity: Teenage Male Skating Champion	Identity: Mother Shopping for Groceries
Audience: Other Teenage Male Skaters	Audience: Toddler Child
Purpose: Describing the new trick that you just mastered.	Purpose: Explaining why child cannot have a grocery item.

APPENDIX 1.5

Model Texts for Tone and Mood

Sample One: Excerpt from "The Legend of Sleepy Hollow" by Washington Irving

It was the very witching time of night that Ichabod, heavy-hearted and crestfallen, pursued his travels homewards, along the sides of the lofty hills which rise above Tarry Town, and which he had traversed so cheerily in the afternoon. The hour was as dismal as himself. Far below him the Tappan Zee spread its dusky and indistinct waste of waters, with here and there the tall mast of a sloop, riding quietly at anchor under the land. In the dead hush of midnight, he could even hear the barking of the watchdog from the opposite shore of the Hudson; but it was so vague and faint as only to give an idea of his distance from this faithful companion of man. Now and then, too, the long-drawn crowing of a cock, accidentally awakened, would sound far, far off, from some farmhouse away among the hills—but it was like a dreaming sound in his ear. No signs of life occurred near him, but occasionally the melancholy chirp of a cricket, or perhaps the guttural twang of a bullfrog from a neighboring marsh, as if sleeping uncomfortably and turning suddenly in his bed.

APPENDIX 1.6

Model Texts for Tone and Mood

Sample Two: Excerpt from "The Tell-Tale Heart" by Edgar Allen Poe

No doubt I now grew very pale;—but I talked more fluently, and with a heightened voice. Yet the sound increased—and what could I do? It was a low, dull, quick sound—much such a sound as a watch makes when enveloped in cotton. I gasped for breath—and yet the officers heard it not. I talked more quickly—more vehemently; but the noise steadily increased. I arose and argued about trifles, in a high key and with violent gesticulations; but the noise steadily increased. Why would they not be gone? I paced the floor to and fro with heavy strides, as if excited to fury by the observations of the men—but the noise steadily increased. Oh God! what could I do? I foamed—I raved—I swore! I swung the chair upon which I had been sitting, and grated it upon the boards, but the noise arose over all and continually increased. It grew louder—louder—louder! And still the men chatted pleasantly, and smiled. Was it possible they heard not? Almighty God!—no, no! They heard!—they suspected!—they *knew!*—they were making a mockery of my horror!—this I thought, and this I think. But anything was better than this agony! Anything was more tolerable than this derision! I could bear those hypocritical smiles no longer! I felt that I must scream or die!—and now—again!—hark! louder! louder! louder! *louder!*—"Villains!" I shrieked, "dissemble no more! I admit the deed!—tear up the planks!—here, here!—it is the beating of his hideous heart!"

APPENDIX 1.7

Sample Spinner for Student Participation

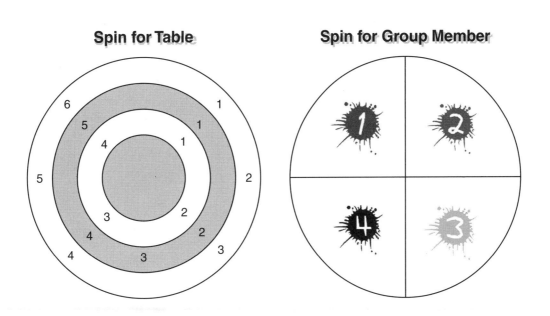

Spin for Table   Spin for Group Member

A TALE OF TWO AUTHORS

Tone and Mood

Using your knowledge of tone and mood, show the relationship between the concepts of tone, mood, author, and audience.

Author	*Audience*

Author	Audience
• The author uses words, sentence structure, images, and punctuation to create tone.	• The audience uses clues in the words, sentence structure, images, and punctuation to understand tone.
• The author tries to create a tone that will invoke his or her desired mood in the audience.	• The audience's mood and overall response to a text reflect his or her identity and the way in which this identity has impacted his or her attitude toward the subject and the message.
• The author's tone reflects his or her identity and how his or her identity has impacted his or her attitude toward the subject and message.	• When determining mood, the audience generally takes clues from a speaker with whom they feel empathetic (if the character feels hopeful, audience members often feel hopeful).
	• If the author's tone is convincing, it may change the audience's mood and overall attitude toward the subject and the message.

APPENDIX 1.9

Author Study Chart

Selection	Author	Tone of Selection	Observations: Word Choice	Observations: Punctuation	Reader's Thoughts

APPENDIX 1.10

Coded Excerpt from Seedfolks

Kim

I stood before our family altar. It was dawn. No one else in the apartment was awake. I stared at my father's photograph—his thin face stern, lips latched tight, his eyes peering permanently to the right. I was nine years old and still hoped that perhaps his eyes might move. Might notice me.

> SENTENCE FLUENCY This sentence fragment seems to be tacked on. I can imagine her voice falling off as she slips this last comment in, almost hiding it in her other thoughts.

The candles and the incense sticks, lit the day before to mark his death anniversary, had burned out. The rice and meat offered him were gone. After the evening feast, past midnight, I'd been wakened by my mother's crying. My oldest sister had joined in. My own tears had then come as well, but for a different reason.

> WORD CHOICE Kim stands out; she's different

I turned from the altar, tiptoed to the kitchen, and quietly drew a spoon from a drawer. I filled my lunch thermos with water and reached into our jar of dried lima beans. Then I walked outside to the street.

> WORD CHOICE This word makes me think of loneliness.

The sidewalk was completely empty. It was Sunday, early in April. An icy wind teetered trash cans and turned my cheeks to marble. In Vietnam we had no weather like that. Here in Cleveland people call it spring. I walked half a block, then crossed the street and reached the vacant lot.

> WORD CHOICE This word reinforces images of loneliness with a feeling of cold.

> IMAGERY The image of marble is one that is cold and doesn't show emotion

I stood tall and scouted. No one was sleeping on the old couch in the middle. I'd never entered the lot before, or wanted to. I did so now, picking my way between tires and trash bags. I nearly stepped on two rats gnawing and froze.

> SENTENCE FLUENCY This sentence is very short. It seems to signal a break. Perhaps there will be a break or shift in tone too.

> IMAGERY This image makes the setting seem scary and mysterious.

IMAGERY This image of being "hidden from view" makes Kim's actions seem mysterious and secretive.	Then I told myself that I must show my bravery. I continued further, and chose a spot far from the sidewalk and hidden from view by a rusty refrigerator. I had to
WORD CHOICE The word project sounds a little mysterious	keep my project safe.

I took out my spoon and began to dig. The snow had melted, but the ground was hard. After much work, I finished one hole, then a second, then a third. I

SENTENCE FLUENCY This sentence stands out because it is so short. The sentence really makes the idea that Kim didn't know her father as well stand out as being important.	thought about how my mother and sisters remembered my father, how they knew his face from every angle and held in their fingers the feel of his hands.
SENTENCE FLUENCY This sentence stands out because it is so similar to the previous short sentence. It really shows how disconnected Kim feels.	I had no such memories to cry over. I'd been born eight months after he'd died. Worse, he had no memories of me. When his spirit hovered over our altar, did it even know who I was?

IMAGERY The alliteration here really makes this image stand out. The image of plumping, and getting larger is a shift from all the images of being different and hidden. Kim is talking about standing out.	I dug six holes. All his life in Vietnam my father had been a farmer. Here our apartment house had no yard. But in that vacant lot he would see me. He would watch my beans break ground and spread, and would notice with pleasure their
SENTENCE FLUENCY (see comment 14)	pods growing plump. He would see my patience and my hard work. I would
SENTENCE FLUENCY This parallel sentence starter gives the sense of growing confidence and volume in the voice of the author.	show him that I could raise plants, as he had. I would show him that I was his daughter.
IMAGERY This image of covering up shifts the focus from growing larger and getting noticed back to the quiet hidden promise Kim is making.	My class had sprouted lima beans in paper cups the year before. I now placed a bean in each of the holes. I covered them up, pressing the soil down firmly with
WORD CHOICE 'vowing' to herself reinforces the quiet hidden image of the seeds being folded away from view, into the earth.	my fingertips. I opened my thermos and watered them all. And I vowed to myself that those beans would thrive.

Seedfolks excerpt retrieved from http://www.paulfleischman.net/disc.htm

APPENDIX 1.11

Gallery Walk Through Effective Voice

Directions: Today you will be visiting a gallery of great artists in the area of voice. Like most galleries, this gallery showcases the artists' work on the wall at a distance from the surrounding artists. Also, like most galleries, this gallery has a quiet air of respect and regard. As you visit the pieces, you will be considering the following question: *How do authors construct a voice that is effective for their audiences?* You should remain at one piece, reading and rereading it as you need during the allotted time. You should also keep a scholarly atmosphere, whispering only when necessary, but otherwise studying quietly. Also as you rotate, you will be recording your thoughts on this graphic organizer. You may also choose to use sticky notes to indicate observations or questions you have as you walk around.

Text One

Text: _____ *Author:* _____

Purpose: _____

Audience: _____

Tone(s): _____

Does the text's tone suit the purpose and the audience? (Circle One) **Yes**   **No**

Evidence:

Text _____

Text: _____ *Author:* _____

Purpose: _____

Audience: _____

Tone(s): _____

Does the text's tone suit the purpose and the audience? (Circle One) **Yes**   **No**

Evidence:

APPENDIX 1.12

FINAL ASSESSMENT

Voice

Now that you have studied the way that authors, artists, and musicians create mood and voice, it's your turn to create a voice that speaks to a real audience. Carefully consider what the prompt asks you to do. Are you to entertain? Persuade? Explain? Then think about the structure of your writing and its influence on your audience. How will your structure help you to communicate mood? How will the voices of various characters align in one piece to create a unified impression of your voice as a writer? What role will grammar, mechanics, and word choice have in shaping that voice?

Directions: Select one of the options from those below. Regardless of the choice, you will want to consider the ways that mechanics, grammar, and word choice blend to create voice, tone, and mood. Think also of the message and audience to be sure that the voice you craft is appropriate for its purpose. Masterfully crafted pieces will connect strongly with the audience through engaging language that reveals personality and commitment to the ideas. After completing the option of your choosing, write a reflection that responds to the following questions:

- Which had more of an impact, your message or your voice? Why?
- What did you do to create voice in your piece?
- How does what you did reflect your identity?

Option #1: Creative. Craft a scary story for an audience of your peers using your knowledge of voice, tone, and mood. Stories will be entered in a scary story contest at the local bookstore, so keep in mind the guidelines outlined in the contest rules. Turn in the various stages of writing, so that we can see the way your writing evolves.

Option #2: Analytical. Select a variety of texts from one author or from a group of authors who are contemporaries of each other. Then look for patterns in the ways that the author or authors create voice, tone, and mood. Turn in copies of annotated text and an expository essay in which you describe what you found to be the strategies that the author or authors use to create voice, tone, and mood.

Option #3: Practical. Create a graphic representation of the choices you make in your various forms of writing to create an effective voice, tone, and mood. Then apply this model to writing you do in one of your classes, in your personal life, or as part of a club or team activity. Using a copy of this writing, code the text to demonstrate your application of the model you drew to represent the choices you make in writing. Turn in your graphic representation and a copy of your coded text.

TEACHER RESOURCES

Arts Edge. (n.d.) *Haunting music.* Retrieved June 10, 2008, from http://artsedge.kennedy-center.org/content/3686/

This Web site is a resource for teachers offering a listening guide and background for *Danse Macabre.* Students may also hear part of the piece in a podcast on this Web site.

Baroque Music Organization. (n.d.) *Baroque composers and musicians: Antonio Vivaldi.* Retrieved June 10, 2008, from http://www.baroquemusic.org/bqxvivaldi.html

This resource provides biographical background about the composer and has a collection of links including those that provide lyrics to the *Four Seasons* sonnets.

Dean, N. (2000). *Voice lessons: Classroom activities to teach diction, detail, imagery, and tone.* Gainesville, FL: Maupin House.

Fleischman, P. (1985). *I am phoenix: Poems for two voices.* New York: Harper Trophy.

Fleischman, P. (1988). *Joyful noise: Poems for two voices.* New York: Harper Trophy.

Fleischman, P. (2000). *Big talk.* Cambridge, MA: Candlewick Press.

Fleischman, P. (2008). *Paul Fleischman's official website.* Retrieved June 10, 2008, from http://www.paulfleischman.net/index.htm

While visiting this Web site, readers can read articles about how books like *Seedfolks* came to be, read excerpts of books, and read about the author himself.

Giordano, P. (2008). *Tell-tale heart.* Retrieved June 20, 2008, from http://www.poestories.com/text.php?file=telltaleheart

This Web site hosts a collection of material about and by Edgar Allan Poe.

Harper Collins. (2006). *Meeting the author.* Retrieved June 10, 2008, from http://www.harperchildrens.com/hch/parents/teachingguides/fleischman.pdf

You can read Paul Fleischman's interview about the craft of writing and about writing *Seedfolks.*

Kagan Publishing and Professional Development. (2008). *Teacher tools.* Retrieved June 10, 2008, from http://www.kaganonline.com/Catalog/TeacherTools2.html

This Web site is a collection of teacher tools including spinners designed to increase student participation.

Lyon, G. E. (n.d.) *Where I'm from.* Retrieved June 20, 2008, from http://www.georgeellalyon.com/about.html

The author has included poetry, biographical information about herself, and information about her books and visits in this Web site.

Northwest Regional Educational Laboratory. (2009). Northwest Regional Educational Laboratory (NWREL) Web site. Retrieved March 31, 2009, from http://www.nwrel.org/

This Web site includes information on six-trait writing.

Project Gutenberg. (2008). *The legend of Sleepy Hollow by Washington Irving.* Retrieved June 10, 2008, from http://www.gutenberg.org/etext/41

Project Gutenberg provides a collection of free ebooks for works whose copyrights have expired.

Scieszka, J. (2008). *Guys write for guys read.* New York: Viking Juvenile.

Swartz, A. (1986). *More scary stories to tell in the dark: Collected and retold from folklore.* New York: Harper Collins.

Teenreads. (2000, March). *Author profile: Paul Fleischman.* Retrieved June 10, 2008, from http://www.teenreads.com/authors/au-fleischman-paul.asp

In this transcript of an interview, students and teachers can read biographical information about author Paul Fleischman.

The History Channel. (2008). *Great speeches.* Retrieved July 20, 2008, from http://www.history.com/media.do?action=listing&sortBy=1&sortOrder=A&topic=GREAT%20SPEECHES

This Web site holds a collection of famous speeches in audio and video format.

2

The Little Napoleon in Us All

Literary Criticism and the Battle for Power

A Middle School Unit in Language Arts, Grade 8

Lee-Ann Hayen

INTRODUCTION TO THE UNIT

Our lives are a constant shift of power, experiencing being both powerful and powerless over phenomena. When we begin to look closely at those battles of power, we notice that we are continually battling for power. While power can take on many forms, how we choose to handle that power will make or break us as humans. When our power corrupts us, we then change the balance of power for others and ourselves. This power of corruption can be a wicked cycle, as demonstrated in *Animal Farm.* The animals of Manor Farm yearn for a world of equality, free from the power of human beings. What they don't realize is that when they begin to fight for that power, someone must take charge and thus take on elements of power. Orwell is masterful as he spins the tale of a group of blind animals so driven toward their dreams of a utopian future that they do not see the dystopia taking over. Because *Animal Farm* is an allegory for the Russian Revolution, there are many layers to reading this text. This is when literary criticism becomes an essential tool to peel back the layers of meaning, allowing for a deeper understanding of the written text.

Literary criticism encourages a reader to read carefully, patiently, and critically in order to reveal the multiple layers of meaning within a text. Literary theories, in general, have a singular strength and weakness. In terms of weakness, literary theory can be limiting in how a reader views a text because specific criticisms ask students to narrow their focus to only those critical variables as defined by the theory. For example, while valid, a feminist analysis of *Animal Farm* would arguably miss much of the history and allegorical representations in the text. In terms of strength, literary theory forces the critic to read a text in a way that might reveal new meaning. To observe that Orwell does in fact negate the female character in *Animal Farm* is not something that may be noticed when focusing on the historical connections. A good critic looks beyond the storyline of a text and goes to the heart of the craft of writing.

For students to be prepared for literary criticism, they need to have plenty of opportunities to analyze literature and synthesize their findings in their writing. For that reason, this unit should be taught later on in the year after students have a solid understanding of literary analysis. I believe that the importance of this unit lies in the craft of writing and what it means to be an author, which is at the heart of the Parallel Curriculum Model (PCM). For us to appreciate literature, there must be an appreciation of the infinite care that a writer takes in drafting a novel. An allegory shows the craft of writing on several different levels and pushes the reader to deconstruct a text more closely than they might a regular novel. By deconstructing the novel as a class, students can see the real craft in writing.

All criticism is autobiographical, including literary criticism. As readers, we bring a certain amount of background knowledge, experience, and bias to a text. This background undoubtedly shapes our understanding of a text. Coupled with this is literary theory, which leverages our background to help decode a text. When this takes place, the literary critic is born. While students are strong on personal experiences, they lack formal training in literary criticism. To compensate for this deficiency, students in this unit use several lenses to analyze *Animal Farm*. Students will have the opportunity to choose between lenses such as feminism, historical criticism, Marxism, ideological criticism, and Burke's Pentad as they analyze a text. By giving students a choice, these lenses will allow for different student backgrounds and experiences.

This unit addresses the Core Curriculum parallel because it is at the heart of why we write, but also focuses especially on the parallel of the Curriculum of Connections because students are asked to make connections in several different ways. First of all, students need to make the connections of an allegory by linking the novel to the Russian Revolution. Second, students are asked yet again to make another connection with the concept of revolution or revolutionary acts over time. Students previously studied the American Revolution and should see many parallels between the American and Russian Revolutions, especially the big ideas of change and conflict that took place during these times. Students become practitioners in the Curriculum of Practice when they are asked to choose a lens (i.e., historical, feminist, Marxist, ideological, pentadic) to deconstruct the text, asking them yet again to make a connection between their own background or past experience and the novel. The Core Curriculum, the Curriculum of Connections, and the Curriculum of Practice learning experiences of this unit should help students to answer some of the great essential questions such as *Why do we write?* Students will realize that their own identity shapes who they are as writers and that criticism is autobiographical (Parallel of Identity). Students will make connections as they address questions such as *How does literary theory shape the reader?* and *How does genre shape the writer?* (Curriculum of Connections). Students will address the Core Curriculum as they identify patterns in literature and why they exist, as well as determine what makes a text a "classic."

Background for the Unit

Students have been asked to analyze literature throughout the entire year and, as a result, by now (spring) students should be able to explicate certain pieces of a text for a purpose. It is important that students have already learned to read with a purpose. Throughout the year, students have been exposed to writing prompts that have been released from previous AP tests. They have responded to these prompts many times. These questions support and accentuate the PCM because themes and big ideas are at the heart of every question. These questions may be found under the formative assessment section.

To provide students with a visual display of allegory taking place in *Animal Farm*, the entire back wall in our classroom is devoted to the project. The wall is blacked out with butcher paper and there are large cutouts of the farm animals. Rather than labeling them with their names, they have been labeled with their allegorical comparison. For example, Boxer, the large cart horse, is labeled as the "proletariat." As students read, it becomes easier for students to see the comparisons. The class records the characteristics of that character on a note card and staples it near the character. Later, students will be asked to show how these characteristics reflect their allegorical representation. The novel includes seven commandments to living. These are also painted on the wall in white paint (this is what the pigs do on the farm). As the commandments are changed subtly by the pigs, they are also changed on the wall. For example, one of the commandments states that, "All animals are equal." As the novel progresses and the pigs are corrupted by power, they change the rules in the middle of the night to "All animals are equal, but some are more equal than others."

The lessons in this unit are focused more on the writing portion of language arts. The focus is less on the novel and more on the educational implications of the novel.

CONTENT FRAMEWORK

Organizing Concepts

Macroconcepts	Discipline-Specific Concepts	Principles
M1: Identity (Why do we write? How is criticism autobiographical?)	C1: Literary Criticism	P1: History (including time, place, culture, circumstance) shapes the voices of writers as well as literature movements.
M2: Power (Does power corrupt?)	C2: Classics	P2: Who we are and what we have experienced shapes the way that we view and understand literature.
M3: Systems (Why are there patterns in literature? What is a classic? How does literary theory shape the reader? How does genre shape the writer?)	C3: Genre: Allegory	P3: The purpose of allegory is to reveal the essence of what is being portrayed. (In this case, personification in the extreme. The purpose of allegory is also to be able to write and express in a time period where this may not be allowed. For example: Orwell wrote Animal Farm, a novel that

(Continued)

(Continued)

Macroconcepts	Discipline-Specific Concepts	Principles
		is very anti-Stalin, in a time when many were pro-Stalin. Orwell was also his pen name—Eric Blair is his real name. Because his political view during this time did not agree with the consensus, he took a huge risk in his writing.)
	C4: Literary Elements	P4: A classic is considered a model of its form and reflects a turning point in history.
	C5: Character Analysis	P5: Authors are very purposeful in the crafting of a novel. (The use of literary elements is an integral part of the novel. Literary tools are especially important in the crafting of an allegory. One must have a deep understanding of concepts such as characterization, setting, plot, and poetic elements in order to symbolically represent it.)
		P6: Allegory is a form of extended metaphor in which objects, persons, and actions in a narrative are equated with meanings that lie outside of the narrative itself.
		P7: An author can communicate a message through what is said and what isn't said.
		P8: A reader of allegory searches for both literal and symbolic meaning to the story.
		P9: Literary criticism asks readers to narrow the focus of their reading of a text to pull out specific ideas to support a particular lens (e.g., feminist, ideological, pentadic). The reader must then support how that type of critic would view a particular text.

National and/or State Standards

SD1: Students read a wide range of print and nonprint texts to build an understanding of texts, of themselves, and of the cultures of the United States and the world; to acquire new information; to respond to the needs and demands of society and the workplace; and for personal fulfillment. Among these texts are fiction and nonfiction, classic and contemporary works.

SD2: Students apply a wide range of strategies to comprehend, interpret, evaluate, and appreciate texts. They draw on their prior experience, their interactions with other readers and writers, their knowledge of word meaning and of other texts, their word identification strategies, and their understanding of textual features (e.g., sound-letter correspondence, sentence structure, context, graphics).

SD3: Students participate as knowledgeable, reflective, creative, and critical members of a variety of literacy communities.

SD4: Students use spoken, written, and visual language to accomplish their own purposes (e.g., for learning, enjoyment, persuasion, and the exchange of information).

SD5: Students read and recognize literature as a record of human experience. Apply literary terminology and knowledge of literary techniques to understand text. Understand how figurative language supports meaning in a given context.

SD6: Students apply thinking skills to their reading, writing, speaking, listening, and viewing. Analyze text to make predictions and draw conclusions.

Skills

S1: Critique literature using a chosen lens.

S2: Use compare/contrast to see the minute details of an allegory.

S3: Discuss and argue who decides whether a book is a classic, what the characteristics of a classic are, and how a book becomes a part of the canon.

S4: Use reading skills/strategies to determine the patterns of literature.

- Make connections.
- Ask questions.
- Determine importance.
- Infer and predict.
- Visualize.
- Synthesize.
- Use fix-up strategies. (When they read and don't understand what they read, they use certain strategies to make sure that they understand before moving on: reread, underline, use a dictionary, read aloud, ask questions.)

S5: Analyze characters and their characteristics and compare them to the allegorical representation.

S6: Write a literary critique using quotes as support from the novel.

S7: Write a final response to the unit using a variety of modes of writing.

ASSESSMENTS

Preassessment

At the beginning of the unit, students are asked to respond to the essential questions that guide this unit of study. Students are asked to answer these questions based on their prior experience and background knowledge. On completion, students pair-share their answers and then as a class, and create a brainstorm map for each question. These brainstorms are created in the computer program Inspiration because they can easily be converted into outline format.

Formative Assessments

Periodic quizzes are given to students throughout the unit to check for student understanding. Assessments also will vary as we discuss the book as a class. Students are also assigned periodic essay reflections of the novel using several AP prompts. The prompt choices are from the College Board and are as follows:

1. In the novel that you are currently reading, the main characters struggle between their own belief systems and the acceptance of society. Write an essay in which you analyze how this struggle between self and society contributes to the meaning of the novel.

2. Critic Roland Barthes has said, "Literature is the question minus the answer." Using your novel, write an essay that explains the question that your novel is asking and what the author wants you to understand.

3. One of the strongest human drives seems to be a desire for power. Write an essay in which you discuss how a character in your novel struggles to free himself or herself from the power of others or seeks to gain power over others. Be sure to demonstrate in your essay how the author uses this power struggle to enhance the meaning of the novel.

4. The most important themes in literature are sometimes those in which a death or deaths take place. Write a well-organized essay in which you show how a specific death scene helps to understand the meaning of the whole novel.

5. Novels and plays often depict characters caught between colliding cultures (e.g., national, regional, ethnic, religious, institutional). Such collisions can call a character's sense of identity into question. Discuss your character's response to this collision and explain how it is important to the meaning of the novel as a whole.

6. "Nobody but he who has felt it, can conceive what a plaguing thing it is to have a man's mind torn asunder by two projects of equal strength, both obstinately pulling in a contrary direction." Choose a character from your novel whose mind is pulled in conflicting directions by two compelling desires, ambitions, obligations, or influences. Identify the two conflicting forces and explain how this conflict within one character gives meaning to the novel as a whole.

Postassessments

At the beginning of the school year, students took an inventory based on Sternberg's thinking/interest style inventory (Appendix 2.1). Responses from the students are analyzed to provide students with a specific learning task that relies on more of an analytical, practical, or creative use of knowledge and understanding that is acquired during this unit of study, *Animal Farm*. Three possible projects are designed to demonstrate their understanding of *Animal Farm*, but allow for their strengths. The rubric focuses on how the written piece addresses the essential questions, how well the response is written, and the degree of depth and understanding of both the novel and how it fits within the context of all the concepts that have been taught. The project options for the unit are:

- Analytical Task:

Read the novel *1984*, also by George Orwell, and write a criticism of Orwell's two novels. Use your background research on him as an author to explain why Orwell writes. How has history, his past, his background, and so on shaped who he is as a writer?

Use ideological criticism as your lens for writing. This should include a minimum of a five-paragraph essay in order to pass. You should use quotes from both novels, as well as cite at least three outside sources for research. The final essay should be typed and free of spelling errors. Your ideological criticism essay should contain the following elements: (1) Write an introduction, which contains your question and its importance of being discussed. (2) Create a description of both novels and their contexts. (3) Locate evidence of support for criticism, using several quotes from the novel. (4) Explain the significance of why Orwell wrote in this manner. And (5) Explain why the contribution of Orwell is significant and its role as being termed a "classic."

- Practical Task:

Animal Farm teaches us a cautionary lesson about government and the possible abuse of power that comes with it. We have discussed in great length types of government and how each system has both positives and negatives. Now, think about your own life and government's role. Why should you be cautious of government? Where do you see government playing a role in your life? Find examples of laws that you feel have been imposed on your life. Research the background of those laws and explain why you would have those laws changed. What are the possible ramifications of those changes? How might it help society change for the better? How might society change for the worse?

Create a case study for three laws that you believe invade your own personal freedoms. Your case study should follow the following format: (1) Write an introduction that acquaints your reader with the laws that you will be discussing, using their background and history, as well as the basis of your argument for why the laws are intrusive. (2) Identify the problems and subproblems (this is your argument section) and make an argument for why each law invades your personal freedoms and why that law should be removed. Remember to address anything that someone may argue with you about. (3) In the analysis and discussion section, discuss in great detail how you address the essential question, "Does power corrupt?" as well as how your understanding of Orwell's way of writing has shaped your thinking.

- Creative Task:

Write an allegory for a major current event in your own life. Remember the intricacies of creating an allegory. Each character is picked out very carefully to match its symbolic representation. The setting also plays a powerful role in allegory. How are you going to craft a story that honors the symbolism involved, but also follows the event in history with careful detail?

Before writing your allegory, create a list of characters and whom they symbolize, as well as a brief synopsis of the current event that you chose. Next, write an allegory that is a minimum of five paragraphs. This allegory should follow the patterns of literature, such as plot, setting, character, literary, and poetic elements. After writing your allegory, add a section that discusses the importance of allegory as a style of writing and as a form of expression. Why do writers write in allegory? What have you learned as a result of writing in allegory?

UNIT SEQUENCE, DESCRIPTION, AND TEACHER REFLECTIONS

Lesson 2.1: Preassessment/Brainstorming (Two Class Periods)

Discipline-Specific Concepts

C1: Literary Criticism
C2: Classics
C3: Genre: Allegory
C4: Literary Elements

Principles

P2: Who we are and what we have experienced shapes the way that we view and understand literature.

Standards

SD6: Students apply thinking skills to their reading, writing, speaking, listening, and viewing.

Unit Sequence	Teacher Reflections
Preassessment Learning Task	
Ask students to respond to the following questions in complete sentences. Because this is a preassessment, they are not required to have the "correct" answer (if there is even one), but rather to show thought and an attempt to make some kind of a connection with the question. If students do not understand what is being asked, I have them write a question that would promote class discussion on the topic (something beyond asking what does this mean). These are the questions posed: 1. Why do we write? 2. How is criticism autobiographical? 3. Does power corrupt? 4. Why are there patterns in literature? 5. What is a classic? 6. How does literary theory shape the reader? 7. How does genre shape the writer? After students have had enough time to respond and pair-share (about twenty minutes), ask students to come back together as a class. I open the Inspiration software (this software is excellent for brainstorming and outlining), and we	*This preassessment asks students to think about what they have read, written, heard, or saw somewhere before and fit it into the context of what is being asked. Determining a student's background knowledge is important in shaping the entire unit and how we differentiate for that knowledge base. Based on their answers and past experience with these concepts, I might vary my types of questions or the assignments that they complete.* *For example, many students did not know how to answer the following question: How is criticism autobiographical? Most struggled with the wording alone. After students have had the time to discuss what the answers may be, we begin to construct meaning for these words as a class. By using other student clues and background knowledge, as well as word recognition clues, we create class definitions for the words. The students that immediately understand these words are asked then to focus on the implications of the questions rather than the actual question.* *Becoming a practitioner in a given discipline requires practice, and in this case, students need to constantly practice the art of writing.*

Unit Sequence	Teacher Reflections
Preassessment Learning Task	

discuss the essential questions as a class. As we go through the questions, I ask students to think about their answers. For example, when I ask students, *Why do we write?* they have become almost automated in their response by this time and say: "To inform, to persuade, to entertain, to describe." They know these are the correct answers, but they don't often stop to ask themselves why. My favorite question to ask them is: *Why do we write to entertain?* It seems so simple that we read for pleasure, but we don't really stop and ask why that is so important. As they respond, I keep adding to the brainstorm webs. When we finish all the questions, I convert the maps into outline format and print out copies for the class. This becomes their skeleton notes for the unit (Appendix 2.2 and 2.3 for examples from Inspiration). The expectation is that as they gain new knowledge, they are to add to these notes, find quotes from their novels as support, and even do some research and investigating on their own. To encourage students to challenge themselves and their peers, another challenge is to also write down at least one idea that may challenge the very ideals that the class brainstormed together. They will be able to use these thoughts in their postreflections.	*This involves the entire writing process from brainstorming to drafting to revision to publication. I like to use this approach as much as possible. Therefore, I shape my preassessments as a draft. The writer brings what they know to the table. It is by no means a finished, polished draft, but rather a preview of what will be developed later on. I ask the students to answer the essential questions at the beginning of the unit by reflecting on them in complete sentences. I collect these and keep them to hand back at the end of the unit. After the final assessment, I hand back their preassessments and ask them to answer the questions again. Students write another written reflection on the questions and their grade is based on their growth and depth of understanding. If I have taught the unit well, their answers should show more depth and reflection, but also hopefully a little cognitive dissonance as well. A student who has mastered the concepts should start to challenge the traditional ideas and beliefs of the discipline.* **Concept Rationale** *The concepts chosen for this unit of study ask students to be prepared for an AP (advanced placement) course. Students in AP literature courses are asked to look at texts more deeply and to pull their own new knowledge and arguments from that text. Literary criticism is an integral part of deconstructing a text. Allegory asks students to look at a text not only for its surface meaning, but for other possible parallels, such as moral, social, political or religious meaning. In order for students to be prepared to take an AP course, they should be able to easily identify these things. Literary elements are something that students should have been exposed to for quite some time in their schooling. At this point, students should not only be able to identify literary elements, but also to explain their significance or role in a text. Finally, classics are important to discuss because a work that has been termed a classic is seen as a model of its form, and therefore worth study and scrutiny.*

(Continued)

Unit Sequence	Teacher Reflections
Preassessment Learning Task	
	Principle Rationale *If literary criticism is autobiographical, then we bring an element of ourselves to a text. These experiences we have are so varied and diverse that it is important we acknowledge them. Identity is the lens and it shapes our understanding of the world.*
Closure	
Using the 3-2-1 exit card (Appendix 2.4), students are asked to write three questions that they are interested in finding answers to for the unit, two things they have learned, and a connection to one big idea (e.g., power, change, conflict, identity, systems, communication).	*Again, to encourage students to take on the role of practitioner and really be writers, I do not let them leave my classroom without reflecting on the learning that took place. This lesson was the introduction to the unit and through the use of discussion I want students to be engaged and curious about what we are studying. The 3-2-1 exit card asks them to review what they learned, but also look forward to what is upcoming in the unit.*

Lesson 2.2: What Is Allegory? (Two Class Periods)

Macroconcepts

M1: Identity
M3: Systems

Discipline-Specific Concepts

C3: Genre: Allegory

Principles

P3: The purpose of allegory is to reveal the essence of what is being portrayed.

P6: Allegory is a form of extended metaphor, in which objects, persons, and actions in a narrative are equated with meanings that lie outside of the narrative itself.

P7: The meaning behind an allegorical story has great moral, social, religious, or political significance, and the characters are often personifications of abstract ideas (e.g., greed, innocence, superficiality).

P8: A reader of allegory searches for both literal and symbolic meaning to the story.

Skills

S4: Use reading skills/strategies to determine the patterns of literature.

- Make connections.
- Ask questions.
- Determine importance.
- Infer and predict.
- Visualize.
- Synthesize.
- Use fix-up strategies. (When they read and don't understand what they read, they use certain strategies to make sure that they understand before moving on: reread, underline, use a dictionary, read aloud, ask questions.)

S5: Analyze characters and their characteristics and compare them to the allegorical representation.

Standards

SD6: Students apply thinking skills to their reading, writing, speaking, listening, and viewing. Analyze text to make predictions and draw conclusions.

Guiding Questions

- How does genre shape the writer?
- Why do we write?

Unit Sequence—Core Curriculum	Teacher Reflections
Introduction	
The Structure of Allegory Begin class with a journal entry that asks students to respond to the following questions: (1) What are some examples of books, movies, art, sayings, and so on that have double meanings? (2) Why do you think they have double meanings? Have students discuss their answers at their tables of four, which have been previously organized by their readiness or ability levels. Each group needs to pick their best example to discuss with the class. Give students about five minutes to respond in their journals and then two minutes to share at their tables. Class discussion for sharing the examples will last about ten minutes. During this	*The purpose of this Core Curriculum lesson is to introduce students to the anatomy of allegory prior to the reading of* Animal Farm *so that students can then transfer the meaning of the concept of allegory as they read this classic.* *During this lesson, students are asked to think both literally and symbolically, two very different hats to try on. By reminding students that what one sees is not always what one gets, students can begin to see the true mastery behind the writing in the genre of allegory.* *Asking students to produce a written response to a prompt encourages them to*

(Continued)

Unit Sequence—Core Curriculum	Teacher Reflections
Introduction	
discussion, groups will share their best examples and the class will talk about whether they have seen or heard a similar example and why these examples tend to repeat and hold meaning over time, place, culture, or circumstance.	*practice the craft of writing, something they should be accustomed to as they walk into a language arts classroom, and take on the role of a professional writer.* *I value the importance of students discussing ideas within their own groups. I think that discussion asks students to think critically about their own thoughts and evaluate their place within a discussion. But I also value group discussion because it frees me to float about the groups and pose further questions. Because the students are grouped by readiness, I focus my more-advanced students on questions that promote more cognitive dissonance or really try to play devil's advocate. For students who are less ready for the content, I get them to the same place, but scaffold their questions in a way that helps them feel more successful. I tend to use more examples as I talk to them.*
Teaching Strategies and Learning Experiences	
Following this discussion, place the following words on the board and ask students to complete a KWL (Appendix 2.5) chart. The words are as follows: (1) *Allegory* (discuss the idea that the Greek derivation *allegoria* stands for "speaking otherwise"); (2) *Parable* (a short allegorical story designed to illustrate or teach some truth, religious principle, or moral lesson); (3) *Fable* (a short tale to teach a moral lesson, often with animals or inanimate objects as characters; "The Fable of the Tortoise and the Hare," *Aesop's Fables*); and (4) *Myth* (a traditional or legendary story, usually concerning some being or hero or event, with or without a determinable basis of fact or a natural explanation, especially one that is concerned with deities or demigods and explains some practice, rite, or phenomenon of nature). To encourage students to use their thinking skills, they are asked to use at least two	*During this lesson, the use of graphic organizers is helpful in understanding an otherwise abstract idea. Helping students to consolidate information in a meaningful way will not only help them as they begin to write a response on a given piece, but also help them to see the many layers that it takes to craft a novel or short story. These characteristics will come in handy later on as they begin to craft their own work. They can look back to the characteristics that originally defined the work and use them in their own writing.*

Unit Sequence—Core Curriculum	Teacher Reflections
Teaching Strategies and Learning Experiences	

resources to find the meaning of these words. These range from the use of a partner to a dictionary to a thesaurus, and so on. Next, students complete a Venn diagram to compare/contrast all four types of writing (Appendix 2.6). Based on the information recorded on the Venn diagram, students should see that allegory is a story that has both a literal as well as symbolic representation, and that there are very subtle variations to all four types, but their purpose is to explain our lives or the human condition through a different perspective, paralleling ourselves as humans to other connections that we have made and begun to understand within our world.	
Students are then asked to practice with the concept of allegory by reading an excerpt from Plato's *Allegory of the Cave*. In pairs, students are asked to try to figure out what the dual meanings are for the text. Using Appendix 2.7 students will read the excerpt, draw a picture of what they see in their heads as they read, and fill in a graphic organizer that has literal items in the left-hand column and educated guesses with rationales as to what their symbolic meanings may be in the right-hand column.	*Plato's* Allegory of the Cave *is an ideal excerpt to use for several reasons. First, it is pretty easy to find excerpts online if you struggle with resources. One of the biggest reasons I discuss this reading selection with students is the age of the text. Plato was discussing these ideas long before we ever came to be, and if Orwell chose to use allegory, then there must be some importance behind the idea. The next reason for choosing the excerpt is because, for me, it is very visual. It is easy to draw a picture of the conversation taking place. Because it is an easy visual, it is a great place to begin teaching allegory. The last reason is simply to get them excited about what they have accomplished. I tell them that I did not study Plato's allegory until I was in college and that they should be proud of their interpretations. This also sets up the argument that they are capable of interpreting any text I give them as long as they use the tools they have learned.*
Homework	*Later on in the unit, students will be learning about literary criticism, but this lesson is also a great introduction to that idea. By asking the students to acknowledge the author's background and life and how that shapes his writing, students will be looking at the heart of one of the next big essential questions: How is criticism autobiographical?*
Ask students to research and locate a brief biography of Plato and the period in which he lived. Students must answer the following questions: Based on what you know about Plato as an author and what he wrote about in the *Allegory of the Cave*, what do you think is the moral, social, religious, or political significance of the piece? What is the message that Plato wants preserved for all eternity? How does this genre shape the writer? Why do you think people write?	

(Continued)

Unit Sequence—Core Curriculum	Teacher Reflections
Teaching Strategies and Learning Experiences	
	For those students who may need some assistance or scaffolding, remind them again that a big idea or theme is something that we can understand no matter what time period or place that we find ourselves in and ask them why "some dead guy's" words are still so important that we learn them today. *Remind students to use the reading skills and strategies that they have acquired to determine the patterns of literature, which include making connections, asking questions, determining importance, inferring and predicting, visualizing, and synthesizing.* *Additionally they can use fix-up strategies when they read and don't understand what they have read, such as rereading passages, underlining text, using a dictionary, and reading aloud.*
Closure	
When students return with their homework, discuss with students how allegory is used in the text, *Allegory of the Cave.* Have students reveal how they identified the symbolic meaning of the text that appeared literal and what moral, social, religious, and political significance did the piece represent. This same analysis will be required from students as they record and organize information in an allegory diary of *Animal Farm* as they read (Appendix 2.8).	*This reiterates the importance of graphic organizers. By keeping an allegorical diary, students will be able to come back and reference important symbols, but also place them within the entire context of the novel to give meaning as a whole. The next day in class, I will model how to continue with the allegory diary as we read out loud from* Animal Farm. Animal Farm *is a great way to introduce allegory because it really is written in personification. All animals are personified to equal a real historical person. It is easier to see their characteristics this way. Orwell is a distinguished writer of allegory and every last object, action, and symbol contained some metaphorical comparison.* *Orwell wrote* Animal Farm, *an anti-Stalin piece, in a very pro-Stalin time period. Because this was a time of great political upheaval, it was not necessarily safe to be outright with one's thoughts and beliefs (as evidenced in* Animal Farm *as well). While this provides some anonymity as an author, it also gives Orwell credit to his craft. He wrote a story with great political significance, one that transcends time, place, culture, or circumstance. Although his story is about the Russian Revolution, his cautionary message about government transcends time and place.*

Lesson 2.3: Diary of an Author (One Class Period)

Macroconcepts

M1: Identity
M3: Systems

Discipline-Specific Concepts

C3: Genre: Allegory

Principles

P2: Who we are and what we have experienced shapes the way that we view and understand literature.
P5: Authors are very purposeful in the crafting of a novel.

Skills

S4: Use reading skills/strategies to determine the patterns of literature.

- Make connections.
- Ask questions.
- Determine importance.
- Infer and predict.
- Visualize.
- Synthesize.
- Use fix-up strategies. (When they read and don't understand what they read, they use certain strategies to make sure that they understand before moving on: reread, underline, use a dictionary, read aloud, ask questions.)

Guiding Questions

- Why do we write?
- How does genre shape the writer?

Unit Sequence—Core Curriculum	Teacher Reflections
Introduction, Teaching Strategies, and Learning Experiences	
Thinking Like a Writer Begin class with a journal entry asking students to reflect on the following questions: • What do you think authors consider as they write a novel? • What things constantly circulate through their minds as they go through the writing process?	*We ask students to write all the time and we ask them to go through the writing process, but I don't believe we tell our students enough about why we go through this process. I don't think we ask students to reflect on their thinking enough. We give them the assignment, we model the revision process, and we grade. While this superficially asks them to go through the motions of a writer, it does not really ask them to think like a writer. Thinking*

(Continued)

(Continued)

Unit Sequence—Core Curriculum	Teacher Reflections
Introduction, Teaching Strategies, and Learning Experiences	

When students have had enough time to think and reflect, brainstorm these ideas by placing them on the board. I tell my students that the class with the most quality ideas will win a prize (this encourages them to keep thinking). At their tables of four (still based on readiness levels), students need to take the brainstormed list of terms/ideas and organize them into groups or categories that make sense to them. As a group, students will title their clusters of words and define the items/words/concepts that fit under that group. Each group needs to come up with a rationale for their grouping preferences. Once students have completed this task, place their groupings on another board. Once all groups have presented their ideas, we decide as a class the best groupings. There will undoubtedly be a lot of overlap, but some of the more creative ideas will be worth discussing when thinking about the craft of the writer. The groups that the students all finally agree on will guide their future journal writing.	*like a writer does not just mean knowing that one needs to draft and revise multiple times. Thinking like a writer means being aware of so much more. Writers need to be aware of genre, voice, style, structure, human relationships, theme, audience, purpose/intent, syntax, literary elements/devices, perspective, conflict, development, support, and so on. This list really can be endless. All of these concepts and ideas are things that we often teach in isolation and expect students to remember them. By eighth grade, most of these topics and concepts have already been taught several times. Asking students to now take that base knowledge and then consider it as they write takes these concepts to a much deeper level.*
	This lesson falls under the Core Curriculum because students are being asked to take on the role of a writer, but more than that, to think about what they are bringing to a text through their thought processes. This lesson asks students to take their knowledge of the discipline, their own background and experiences, create a piece that reflects who they are, and then most importantly, reflect on that experience.
	I tell the students that a writer does not just sit down and write. A writer has to think of many things while writing. Students will receive a writing assignment the next day. I would like them to think of themselves as writers and journal their thoughts and experiences as they complete their writing assignment. As they journal, students need to be mindful of the groups and the ideas that fall under each group. This will not only help them to take on the role of the writer, but will encourage them to think explicitly about improving their writing on their own as they craft, rather than me editing their work and giving them suggestions.
	Students need to acknowledge their voice and style as writers in order to be effective. The experiences that we go through shape both that voice and that style.
	Students must be conscious of what it takes to craft a writing piece of any kind. It is more than simply taking an idea and expanding on it. There really is no limit to what a writer can think about when crafting a writing piece. Even the way that a writer punctuates a piece can and should be taken into consideration.

Unit Sequence—Core Curriculum	Teacher Reflections
Closure	
Close the sessions with students by asking them to discuss whether they agree or disagree with the following ideas: 1. Who we are and what we have experienced shapes the way that we view and understand literature. 2. Authors are very purposeful in the crafting of a novel. The use of literary elements is an integral part of the novel. Literary tools are especially important in the crafting of an allegory. One must have a deep understanding of concepts such as characterization, setting, plot, and poetic elements in order to symbolically represent it.	*Throughout the unit, students will write in their diary every time they work on their allegory from brainstorming through revision to the publication stage. Students will be asked to acknowledge certain aspects of writing (i.e., their responses to these closure questions), and also to think creatively.* *I would like students to acknowledge the things they have learned in language arts, such as literary elements, poetic elements, grammar, mechanics, genre, and so on.*

Lesson 2.4: Write a Personal Allegory (Five Class Periods)

Macroconcepts

M1: Identity
M3: Systems

Discipline-Specific Concepts

C3: Genre: Allegory

Principles

P3: The purpose of allegory is to reveal the essence of what is being portrayed.
P6: Allegory is a form of extended metaphor, in which objects, persons, and actions in a narrative are equated with meanings that lie outside of the narrative itself.
P7: The meaning behind an allegorical story has great moral, social, religious, or political significance, and the characters are often personifications of abstract ideas (i.e., greed, innocence, superficiality).
P8: A reader of allegory searches for both literal and symbolic meaning to the story.

Skills

S2: Use compare/contrast to see the minute details of an allegory.
S5: Analyze characters and their characteristics and compare them to the allegorical representation.

Standards

SD4: Students use spoken, written, and visual language to accomplish their own purposes (e.g., for learning, enjoyment, persuasion, and the exchange of information).
SD6: Students apply thinking skills to their reading, writing, speaking, listening, and viewing. Analyze text to make predictions and draw conclusions.

Guiding Questions

- Why do we write?
- How does genre shape the writer?

Unit Sequence—Core Curriculum	Teacher Reflections
Introduction, Teaching Strategies, and Learning Experiences	

Personal Allegory
 	
Begin the class with a journal entry asking them to think about three major events in their lives that have shaped who they have become. For each event, they should respond to the following questions: (1) Who was involved? (2) Where did the event take place? (3) Why is or was this event so significant? (4) What does this event symbolize for you (remember that a symbol is something representing or recalling something else, especially an idea or quality)?
 	
   These responses become the basis for students writing their personal allegories. Using the symbol they create, students then choose appropriate characters and settings to tell the story of their life using allegory.
	I break this assignment into parts before students look at the whole process of writing a personal allegory. The first question asks them to look at characterization. I hand them a graphic organizer (Appendix 2.9) and have them complete the organizer about themselves. When they have completed this organizer, students complete answers to a set of questions (Appendix 2.10) to jump start their allegory. They will then develop their symbols or metaphors before they begin writing. After this groundwork is completed, students may begin the drafting process.
	
	   I want to give students plenty of time to write and reflect on this process so I give them about twenty minutes to complete this activity. This time can be adjusted if I sense that they are growing restless. When students have finished writing, I ask if anyone would be willing to volunteer to share their ideas. If so, I use these as my examples and if not, I use one of my own. I do all of the assignments with my students because (1) it gives me great samples to use, (2) it helps me to find the snags and flaws in my assignments, and (3) the students are more encouraged to complete the assignments themselves. As I list the event on the board, I show students where my focus for an allegory is coming from. Question 1 is asking students to give me a character list. Question 2 is asking students to consider the setting. Question 3 asks students to address the purpose of the essential question, Why do we write? Finally, Question 4 asks students to get at the heart of allegory, which is symbolism.

Closure	
Students will have various checkpoints to meet throughout the week of drafting.	*I give students the entire checklist and rubric (Appendix 2.11 and 2.12) at the beginning of the assignment so that students can work at their own pace. This allows me more time for individualized instruction.*

Lesson 2.5: Character Analysis Part I (Two Class Periods)

Macroconcepts

M1: Identity
M3: Systems

Discipline-Specific Concepts

C3: Genre: Allegory
C4: Literary Elements

Principles

P5: Authors are very purposeful in the crafting of a novel.
P6: Allegory is a form of extended metaphor, in which objects, persons, and actions in a narrative are equated with meanings that lie outside of the narrative itself.
P8: A reader of allegory searches for both literal and symbolic meaning to the story.

Skills

S5: Analyze characters and their characteristics and compare them to the allegorical representation.

Standards

SD5: Students read and recognize literature as a record of human experience. Apply literary terminology and knowledge of literary techniques to understand text.
SD6: Students apply thinking skills to their reading, writing, speaking, listening, and viewing. Analyze text to make predictions and draw conclusions.

Guiding Questions

- Why are there patterns in literature?
- Why do we write?

Unit Sequence—Core Curriculum	Teacher Reflection
Introduction, Teaching Strategies, and Learning Activities	
Character Analysis Begin the class with a few questions to get them thinking about the importance of characterization in a novel. Students responded to the following questions in their journals: (1) How does an author create a character? (2) What makes a character strong or weak? (3) How do all characters come together to create meaning? And	*This lesson assumes that the class has begun to read* Animal Farm. *Most of the reading for this novel will be completed aloud or in partners during class to ensure student understanding. I usually read at least one novel aloud as a class a year because it helps me to assess my students' fluency and comprehension. Because there are so many*

(Continued)

(Continued)

Unit Sequence—Core Curriculum	Teacher Reflection
Introduction, Teaching Strategies, and Learning Activities	

<table>
<tr>
<td>

(4) what is the central issue affecting all characters in *Animal Farm*? I give them approximately ten minutes to respond and then we discuss our reflections as a class. This is a great introduction to begin talking specifically about the characters in *Animal Farm*. Using the topical questions that they answered at the beginning of class, students will create a set of notes on the characters of *Animal Farm*.

As soon as most major characters are introduced, students are given an assignment called Character Analysis Map Part I (Appendix 2.13). In this assignment, students need to complete an analysis chart for every character in the book. In each box, they draw a picture of the character or create a symbolic representation. This will help visual learners to connect with the text. Additionally, they will complete the following tasks: (1) label the character, (2) come up with three characteristics from the novel used to describe each character, (3) write a prediction for the character based on what you have read thus far, and (4) connect to another character from another book you have read and explain why.

</td>
<td>

intricacies and levels to this book, I believe this is the most valuable to read aloud.

This format asks students to organize information into a graphic organizer, as well as to create a tool that will come in handy later on. The second part of this map will give students a list of actual people in the Russian Revolution. As they research these people, they will see that the characteristics of the people will match the characteristics of the animals from Animal Farm. *This also asks students to stop and think about what they are reading*

As we read, students are asked to use their reading skills/strategies and to keep a dialectical journal of the readings. In their journals, students are asked to use the following strategies:

- Make connections. (C)
- Ask questions. (?)
- Determine importance. (!)
- Infer and predict. (P)
- Visualize. (V)
- Synthesize. (S)
- Use fix-up strategies. (When they read and don't understand what they read, they use certain strategies to make sure that they understand before moving on: reread, underline, use a dictionary, read aloud, ask questions.) (F)

As they keep their journals, they are to use the "codes" above in parentheses. They use the code, write the quote and page number from the book, and respond with their thoughts and reflections. Students understand by this time of the year that the more effort that they put into these dialectical journals, the better resource they have when responding to writing prompts.

After discussing the role of characters in Animal Farm, *students should begin to see just how deep and purposeful Orwell is in his characterization. Characterization goes beyond just basic description. Because* Animal Farm *is an allegory, the use of literary elements plays an integral role in characterization. Personification and metaphor play a large role in characterization of an allegory.*

</td>
</tr>
</table>

Unit Sequence—Core Curriculum	Teacher Reflection
Closure	
For homework, choose the character you believe holds the most power and connect him or her to another leader that you have learned or read about already, demonstrating, in particular, a shift in power and the consequences, both positive and negative.	*The unit that students studied before* Animal Farm *was about genocide. Students studied the history of genocide in various countries. This unit really addressed the big idea of power and the corruption that can take place. Students focused a lot of their research on the leaders of genocide and should be able to make some great connections between these leaders and the animals holding power in* Animal Farm. We will begin class the next day by sharing several examples that students generated, and as we read from *Animal Farm* that day, students identify power characteristics and quotes that match with their leaders.

Lesson 2.6: Orwell's Responsibility (Two Class Periods)

Macroconcepts

M1: Identity
M3: Systems

Discipline-Specific Concepts

C1: Literary Criticism
C3: Genre: Allegory

Principles

P1: History (including time, place, culture, circumstance) shapes the voices of writers as well as literature movements.
P2: Who we are and what we have experienced shapes the way that we view and understand literature.

Skills

S4: Use reading skills/strategies to determine the patterns of literature.

- Make connections.
- Ask questions.
- Determine importance.
- Infer and predict.
- Visualize.
- Synthesize.
- Use fix-up strategies. (When they read and don't understand what they read, they use certain strategies to make sure that they understand before moving on: reread, underline, use a dictionary, read aloud, ask questions.)

(Continued)

(Continued)

Standards

SD1: Students read a wide range of print and nonprint texts to build an understanding of texts, of themselves, and of the cultures of the United States and the world; to acquire new information; to respond to the needs and demands of society and the workplace; and for personal fulfillment. Among these texts are fiction and nonfiction, classic and contemporary works.

SD2: Students apply a wide range of strategies to comprehend, interpret, evaluate, and appreciate texts. They draw on their prior experience, their interactions with other readers and writers, their knowledge of word meaning and of other texts, their word identification strategies, and their understanding of textual features (e.g., sound-letter correspondence, sentence structure, context, graphics).

SD6: Students apply thinking skills to their reading, writing, speaking, listening, and viewing. Analyze text to make predictions and draw conclusions.

Guiding Questions

- Why do we write?
- How is criticism autobiographical?

Unit Sequence—Core Curriculum	Teacher Reflections
Introduction, Teaching Strategies, Learning Activities	
A Writer's Responsibility Students begin class with a journal entry. Today's prompt is: *What are your responsibilities as a writer? What might you have to sacrifice for success?* As a class, discuss the responses. Next, hand out some biographical information about Orwell, as well as his rules for writing (Appendix 2.14). I ask students to read and "code the text," as well as answer the questions on a separate sheet of paper. When students finish reading the text, students are asked to respond to the same journal prompt, but from the perspective of George Orwell. Students should see that government and politics shaped much of Orwell's beliefs as a writer. Orwell's life experiences taught him to be cautious of government and he believed it was his moral responsibility to share that with the public. As a class, we discuss why this was so important to Orwell and how we are influenced as writers.	*This lesson focuses on helping students to understand that a writer thinks carefully about a topic or theme before beginning to write, and that much of the focus on that topic or theme is a result of the writer's experiences in life. We feel more comfortable writing about what we know, and what we know most often results from our experiences.* *It is also important for students to realize that writers feel responsible for the information or thoughts that they are passing on. Orwell felt a responsibility to warn and to inform readers about why they should be cautious of government. This was a result of his observations during the Spanish Civil War. However, there were certain risks for writing an antigovernment piece during a time when that government was in power. Orwell felt his responsibility outweighed that risk, but had to choose a way to make his point. This is where* Animal Farm *came from. Both* Animal Farm *and* 1984 *were written in a way that allowed Orwell to speak his message, but do so in a safe way. It is an interesting discussion to compare his rules for writing to what he actually wrote. Did he sacrifice his rules for writing in order to send his message or were his rules for writing a satire in itself?*

Unit Sequence—Core Curriculum	Teacher Reflection
Closure	
After students have completed the reflection, I ask them to reflect on their own learning. Students respond to the following questions: • What did you learn about today? • How do Orwell's beliefs differ from your own? • How are Orwell's beliefs similar to your own? • What new burning question has been raised as a result of discussing the responsibilities of a writer?	*Students have learned throughout the year that when I ask them to "code the text," they are to employ the various reading strategies I taught at the beginning of the year (see previous lesson).*

Lesson 2.7: Literary Criticism (Two Class Periods)

Macroconcepts

M1: Identity
M3: Systems

Discipline-Specific Concepts

C1: Literary Criticism

Principles

P1: History (including time, place, culture, circumstance) shapes the voices of writers as well as literature movements.
P2: Who we are and what we have experienced shapes the way that we view and understand literature.

Skills

S1: Critique literature using a chosen lens.
S6: Write a literary critique using quotes as support from the novel.

Guiding Questions

• How is criticism autobiographical?
• How does literary theory shape the reader?

Unit Sequence—Core Curriculum	Teacher Reflections
Introduction, Teaching Strategies, and Learning Activities	
Looking Through the Lens Students begin class by journaling again. They respond to the following question for five to	*By beginning class with what students remember from fairy tales before rereading them, we can really discuss how our experiences shape our understanding.*

(Continued)

(Continued)

Unit Sequence—Core Curriculum	Teacher Reflections
Introduction, Teaching Strategies, and Learning Activities	

ten minutes: *What do you remember most about your favorite childhood fairy tales?* (List the ones being used today so they can narrow their focus.) Students will share responses as a class.

Next, hand out the giant sunglasses that have the criticism and questions (see right-hand column for this description) to groups of students who have been organized into teams of seven. These groups have been arranged based on their interest in a particular fairy tale. Each group is given a different fairy tale (*The Princess and the Pea, Jack and the Beanstalk,* and *Goldilocks and the Three Bears*) to read aloud. After students read their assigned tale, each student within the group is assigned a different literary lens to respond to the questions using the form found in Appendix 2.15.

When students finish reading, they need to (1) report on their interpretation of the story using each of their lenses; (2) identify the differences among the lenses and discuss why those lenses were "invented" and what time periods may have shaped those lenses; and (3) reflect in their groups on the essential question: *How does literary theory shape the reader?*

When all groups have finished reading and discussing in their group, chart each lens and story on the board in an organized manner. As a class, we discuss the patterns that we see and how they are different from what we remember as children about those same stories. When students begin to grapple with these ideas, it is opportunistic to bring back the essential question: *How is criticism autobiographical?*

This lesson introduces literary criticism in the Core parallel, and will serve as a model for future lessons in the Curriculum of Connections. This lesson simply introduces the varying types of literary criticisms and their foci.

Literary criticism is a tough subject to both teach and learn. I have worked to make this process easier for students to understand and make it interesting. I went to a local party supply store and bought huge plastic sunglasses. On the frames of those sunglasses, I labeled the type of lens and the questions that lens would ask of a text. This is a good demonstration that when we use a lens of literary criticism, we narrow our focus to those particular questions. I used seven different modes of criticism and placed students in groups of seven.

- Mode 1: Pentadic. Where is there freedom of choice, purpose or will, and action? Identify (1) Act (Who?), (2) Agent (What?), (3) Scene (When, where?), (4) Agency (How or means?), and (5) Purpose (Why?).
- Mode 2: Ideological. What is the dominant group being addressed? Why discuss this group? What key phrases or terms give evidence of the group being discussed?
- Mode 3: Structuralist. What is the structure of the piece? What are the relationships/connections? What patterns exist? Why do all writers discuss these same things?
- Mode 4: Feminist. What genders are represented and why? Are women negated? Does the text present a patriarchal view? What are women's roles? What about the time period helps to explain this?
- Mode 5: Economist. Is there struggle tied to economy? Is there a lower class rising above? How does the literary work display economy? How does the literary work reflect a time period?

(Continued)

Unit Sequence—Core Curriculum	Teacher Reflections
Introduction, Teaching Strategies, and Learning Activities	
	• Mode 6: Moral. What is the lesson or message? Why stress this moral or lesson? How will this help your life or improve your understanding of the world? • Mode 7: Historical. What is the historical time period? What were the circumstances that influenced this period? Why should this piece of history be remembered? *Because all criticism is difficult for an eight grader to conceptualize, distribute the more difficult criticisms to the more advanced students and the easier criticisms to the students with less readiness. I ask the students to look through the lens they have been assigned and to respond to the questions that the sunglasses are asking the student to focus on.*
Closure	
For homework, students will write one-sentence criticism statements for *Animal Farm* using all seven of the lenses.	*This assignment serves as a bridge to the next day's activity in which students share their responses to generate conclusions. We discuss how these could become the thesis statements of a literary critique*

Lesson 2.8: Write a Literary Critique of *Animal Farm* (Five Class Periods)

Macroconcepts

M1: Identity

Discipline-Specific Concepts

C1: Literary Criticism

Principles

P1: History (including time, place, culture, circumstance) shapes the voices of writers as well as literature movements.

P2: Who we are and what we have experienced shapes the way that we view and understand literature.

(Continued)

(Continued)

P9: Literary criticism asks the reader to narrow the focus of their reading of a text to pull out specific ideas to support a particular lens (e.g., feminist, ideological, pentadic). The reader must then support how that type of critic would view a particular text.

Skills

S6: Write a literary critique using quotes as support from the novel.

Standards

SD2: Students apply a wide range of strategies to comprehend, interpret, evaluate, and appreciate texts. They draw on their prior experience, their interactions with other readers and writers, their knowledge of word meaning and of other texts, their word identification strategies, and their understanding of textual features (e.g., sound-letter correspondence, sentence structure, context, graphics).

SD3: Students participate as knowledgeable, reflective, creative, and critical members of a variety of literacy communities.

SD4: Students use spoken, written, and visual language to accomplish their own purposes (e.g., for learning, enjoyment, persuasion, and the exchange of information).

SD6: Students apply thinking skills to their reading, writing, speaking, listening, and viewing. Analyze text to make predictions and draw conclusions.

Guiding Questions

- Why do we write?
- How is criticism autobiographical?

Unit Sequence—Curriculum of Practice	Teacher Reflections
Introductions, Teaching Strategies, and Learning Activities	
The Literary Critique Students begin class by journaling to the following prompt: Choose a critique statement from last night's homework assignment that you are either most proud of or the statement to which you are most drawn. Write a well-developed paragraph rationale as to why it may be worth writing an essay on *Animal Farm* using this particular lens. If you were absent or did not do the assignment, pick a lens and write a statement that ties in with *Animal Farm*. Give students about ten minutes to write and then ask for volunteers to post their statements on the board. After several volunteers have posted theirs, select one as a class to analyze and develop. Ask students to pull out their quote	*In this lesson, students are to take on the role of a literary critic. Using the lenses that they learned about yesterday, I want them to assume the personality and identity of that critic. (They have to train themselves to be in that particular mind-set.) It might be helpful to read a piece of literary criticism by a practicing professional, to show how the writer critiqued a piece of literature using one of these lenses. Orwell has written a variety of essays and many critique other pieces of literature. These would work well and may be a little more accessible to students as opposed to other more difficult critiques.* *I allow students to choose their own lenses for this assignment because all are difficult and have their own unique styles. If I think*

Unit Sequence—Core Curriculum	Teacher Reflections

Introduction, Teaching Strategies, and Learning Activities

packets and novels and see if they can find at least one quote from the novel that may help to support the statement being made. We then talk about thesis statements and how to find supporting evidence.	*that my more advanced students are picking an easier lens, I usually request that they pick something a little more challenging.*
After we discuss this process, explain the assignment that students will work on for the remainder of the week. For this assignment, students are to write a literary criticism of *Animal Farm* using a lens of their choice. To scaffold this activity, provide them with a brainstorming graphic organizer (Appendix 2.16). Once they have filled in their graphic organizer, they can begin working on their essay. I tend to give them time in class to work and a list of tasks to complete so that students can work at their own pace, and I can meet with students individually. In this case, I have found that breaking the essay into single paragraphs works really well. If students see that they only have to write one really well-developed paragraph at a time and there is a checklist of things to cross off for that paragraph, they tend to work more willingly toward that goal (Appendix 2.16). This also allows me to check their writing periodically along the way rather than awaiting a final product that could be a potential disaster. This also makes grading very easy because by the time they have finished, I have read most of their essays. This really puts an emphasis on the writing process and the craft of writing as opposed to a final grade.	*For example, a student who chooses the feminist lens will make some kind of statement that demonstrates how the role of women is minimized in some way or another. An example of a good feminist statement would be: George Orwell negates the role of women in his novel by only giving minor roles to women or by portraying them in a negative manner. This is an effective statement because the student is going to have to discuss a variety of characters. This statement will allow them to develop two main arguments: (1) the minimal roles of characters such as Clover, Muriel, and Bluebell; and (2) the very negative role of Mollie.* *This is a great opportunity to bring in the reminder about writing strong thesis statements. We begin the year by making thesis statements very formulaic so that students can see the parts. By now, students who are ready to experiment a little can move on, but all are still reminded of the basic tenets of creating a strong thesis statement. Since we are analyzing literature, students know to follow the following formula: author + verb + topic + opinion = thesis statement. If we bring that feminist statement from above down, students should see how it fits. By putting it on the board, we underline the pieces so that they can check to see if the formula works.* George Orwell *(author)* negates *(verb)* the role of women in his novel *(topic)* by only giving minor roles to women or by portraying them in a negative manner *(opinion).*

Closure

Throughout the week of working on the project, the closure questions will address anything that I see that pops up as we work through the essay, whether that relates to purpose, choosing quotes or topic sentences, and so on.	*Make sure at this point that students address the guiding questions.*

Lesson 2.9: Character Analysis Map, Part II (Two Class Periods)

Macroconcepts

M1: Identity
M3: Systems

Discipline-Specific Concepts

C5: Character Analysis

Principles

P5: Authors are very purposeful in the crafting of a novel.

Skills:

S5: Analyze characters and their characteristics and compare them to the allegorical representation.

Standards

SD5: Students read and recognize literature as a record of human experience. Apply literary terminology and knowledge of literary techniques to understand text.
SD6: Students apply thinking skills to their reading, writing, speaking, listening, and viewing. Analyze text to make predictions and draw conclusions.

Guiding Questions

- Why are there patterns in literature?
- Why do we write?

Unit Sequence—Core Curriculum	Teacher Reflections
Introduction, Teaching Strategies, and Learning Experiences	
Character Analysis II To complete this task, students need to work in the library as much as possible, so no journal entry is assigned. Distribute the Character Analysis (Part II) worksheet (Appendix 2.17). Tell students that today they will be researching the characters' allegorical representations from *Animal Farm*. They will receive a list of people involved in the Russian Revolution. Their job is to (1) label the person, (2) label three strong characteristics of that person, and (3) write a brief synopsis of that person's role in the Russian Revolution. Since this is the second part to the character analysis project, students are asked to complete the task individually again.	*Students have already completed the character map for all of the characters in* Animal Farm. *This time, they will receive a list of historical figures from the Russian Revolution. Students will use the library and computers to research each of these people who played a role in the Russian Revolution. Once they complete this character map, they should be able to connect the people with the character from the novel based on the common characteristics, as well as their role in the Russian Revolution. By the end of this lesson, students should really be able to see just how in-depth an allegory is created.* *Extended metaphor and personification are best represented in the allegory of* Animal Farm. Orwell *demonstrates this using a strong*

Unit Sequence—Core Curriculum	Teacher Reflections
Introduction, Teaching Strategies, and Learning Experiences	
	knowledge of other literary elements such as characterization, plot, and setting. An extended metaphor is a metaphor carried out frequently throughout a work. Students are already aware of metaphor, but what I want them to see here is that this metaphor is not something to be acknowledged and then move on, but that students need to see these deep connections throughout the novel and that even the most subtle words are chosen carefully to reference those metaphors.
Closure	
Cut out and connect the historical people of the Russian Revolution with whom you believe is their symbolic representation. Use the characteristics as your guide. Students should see a strong resemblance when they compare the characteristics. If they are struggling with characteristics, they are encouraged to go back and do more research. They should see a correlation between their characters' actions and the actions of the person involved in the Russian Revolution.	*Cutting out and matching the characters serves a specific purpose, especially for those visual learners. This activity clearly shows the mastery of allegory and the great extent that an author goes through to create a novel of extended metaphor.*

Lesson 2.10: What Is a Classic? (Two Class Periods)

Macroconcepts

M1: Identity

Discipline-Specific Concepts

C2: Classics

Principles

P4: A classic is considered a model of its form and reflects a turning point in history.

Skills

S3: Discuss and argue who decides whether a book is a classic, what the characteristics of a classic are, and how a book becomes a part of the canon.

(Continued)

Continued)

Standards

SD5: Students read and recognize literature as a record of human experience. Apply literary terminology and knowledge of literary techniques to understand text. Understand how figurative language supports meaning in a given context.

SD6: Students apply thinking skills to their reading, writing, speaking, listening, and viewing. Analyze text to make predictions and draw conclusions.

Guiding Questions

- What is a classic?
- Why do we write?

Unit Sequence—Core Curriculum	Teacher Reflections
Introductions, Teaching Strategies, and Learning Experiences	
What Is Meant by *Classic*? Start out class with a PowerPoint presentation of slides showing various items that have been deemed "classics," from cars to movies to books. The journal entry will ask students what these all have in common. Based on the criteria that they give as we brainstorm these ideas, we will develop a working definition for what is a classic. Next, break the class into groups of genres (mystery, science fiction, horror, romance, fantasy, western, and narrative). Each group of four or so students will then have to discuss and decide what criteria writers use when writing in that genre, and how they could go about making a novel in that genre become a classic (something revolutionary in that form). Once they have had time to have this discussion, record students' responses on the board	*There really is no right or wrong answer when it comes to this lesson because of the subjectivity behind the idea of a "classic." Is a classic so named because others have said so and who are we to argue? Is something a classic simply because it is old? What makes a classic "classic"? These are all questions that should come up during the lesson. Students' first responses to the question "What is a classic?" are that it is something old. My question to them is then: How will anything created in their lifetime become a classic? And what is your responsibility to the literary world then if nothing you write will be significant until much later on? Some authors/artists/inventors only became famous posthumously, but others became famous long before their death. If time and age are taken out of the equation, what really then is the definition of a classic? When we take the time out of the answer, we can begin to see what makes the work truly unique and outstanding.*
Closure	
Discuss and argue who decides whether a book is a classic, what the characteristics of a classic are, and how a book becomes a part of the canon.	
Homework	
Discuss and argue with a parent or grandparent (someone from an older generation) who gets to decide what will be considered a classic and what a classic will look like in the future. Write a	*I think this is a great conversation piece with parents because while addressing the idea of a classic, it also addresses the autobiography that we bring to a text. Generations have*

Unit Sequence—Core Curriculum	Teacher Reflections
Homework	
half-page reflection about your beliefs verses those of the older generation. What are similar and what are different?	*experienced different things and different events have shaped their identities, beliefs, and philosophies. A person of the Great Depression is going to view* The Grapes of Wrath *much differently than an adolescent today because they lived in a time when so many suffered. When my students read Steinbeck's work, they cannot understand why wealthy landowners would destroy the crops rather than giving it away to the thousands of hungry people. The same goes for* Animal Farm. *Students cannot fathom why the animals would not rebel. We live in a democratic and capitalist society, very different from the land and time of* Animal Farm. *Therefore, our understanding and what we bring to that text is so very different.*

Lesson 2.11: Survivor: The Isms (Two Class Periods)

Macroconcepts

M1: Identity
M2: Power

Discipline-Specific Concepts

C3: Genre: Allegory

Principles

P1: History (including time, place, culture, circumstance) shapes the voices of writers as well as literature movements.
P2: Who we are and what we have experienced shapes the way that we view and understand literature.

Skills

S2: Use compare/contrast to see the minute details of an allegory.

Standards

SD4: Students use spoken, written, and visual language to accomplish their own purposes (e.g., for learning, enjoyment, persuasion, and the exchange of information).

Guiding Questions

- Does power corrupt?
- How does genre shape the writer?

Unit Sequence—Curriculum of Connections	Teacher Reflections
Introductions, Teaching Strategies, and Learning Experiences	

Isms Task Students will be placed in three main groups, representing capitalism, communism, and totalitarianism. Students are given a brief informational guide to each of these "isms" (Appendix 2.18). We will discuss the "isms" as a class and go over some examples of what each looks like and some countries that are demonstrative of each "ism." Based on the characteristics of an "ism," students need to complete tasks on the task cards. In their three groups, students will build a bridge using only some popsicle sticks and tape. The contest is to see who will complete the bridge that will hold the most weight. In the communist group, place the students together and place the materials in the center of the table (no one gets their own supplies). The rules for them are that they cannot leave anyone out and there cannot be a leader. Everyone must do exactly the same amount of work. In the totalitarian group, give all of the supplies to one person and tell that person that they must be in charge of the entire project and they can make their group members do whatever they want, even beyond building the bridge (like getting them a glass of water or taking their school supplies). In the capitalist group, divide the supplies evenly among all group members and tell them to do whatever they like (I have instructed some beforehand to say that they wanted to build their own bridge). They have ten minutes to build their bridge, and the bridge that holds the most weight is the winner. After completing the contest, students start to analyze each of the "isms." First, students will analyze what the positives are of being a member of each society. Next, students will analyze what the possible downfalls are. We will also discuss as a class our natural behaviors and how they might be predetermined by memberships in societies.	*The purpose of this Curriculum of Connections task is to get students to see that the events that take place in the novel are not a serendipitous result of plot development, but rather that the entire novel was developed from the idea of government and its role with the people. It is also important that students can see beyond disciplines and that many contexts influence how we read, write, speak, and listen.* *I will group students ahead of time. Some of the tasks in the group require some acting and some strong personality traits. This is a great opportunity to group them based on their traits. Those students that typically don't work well with others will go into the capitalism group so they can feed off of the opportunity to complete the task on their own and in their own manner. The students that struggle to make decisions and wait for strong leaders to take control will be placed into the communism group. Every class typically has a strong leader. I will pick them beforehand and talk to them about how I want them to act. Based on my decisions, I will give them one of three colors as they enter class.*

Closure	

Students are assigned to look back at their novels and identify what "isms" are present. Students need to identify what the positive and negative consequences of the systems are.	*Students should see that Old Major's (the boar at the beginning of the novel) dream for the farm was reflective of a communist society. They should also see that this dream was not sustainable and that ultimately communism turns to totalitarianism.*

Lesson 2.12: Final Assessment (Two Weeks)

Macroconcepts

M3: Systems

Principles

P2: Who we are and what we have experienced shapes the way that we view and understand literature.
P5: Authors are very purposeful in the crafting of a novel.
P8: A reader of allegory searches for both literal and symbolic meaning to the story.

Skills

S7: Write a final response to the unit using a variety of modes of writing.

Standards

SD2: Students apply a wide range of strategies to comprehend, interpret, evaluate, and appreciate texts. They draw on their prior experience, their interactions with other readers and writers, their knowledge of word meaning and of other texts, their word identification strategies, and their understanding of textual features (e.g., sound-letter correspondence, sentence structure, context, graphics).
SD3: Students participate as knowledgeable, reflective, creative, and critical members of a variety of literacy communities.
SD4: Students use spoken, written, and visual language to accomplish their own purposes (e.g., for learning, enjoyment, persuasion, and the exchange of information).
SD6: Students apply thinking skills to their reading, writing, speaking, listening, and viewing. Analyze text to make predictions and draw conclusions.

Guiding Questions

- Why do we write?
- How is criticism autobiographical?
- Does power corrupt?
- Why are there patterns in literature?
- What is a classic?
- How does literary theory shape the reader?
- How does genre shape the writer?

Unit Sequence—Curriculum of Identity	Teacher Reflections
Introductions, Teaching Strategies, Learning Experiences	
Final Assessment Task At the beginning of the school year, students took an inventory based on Sternberg's thinking/interest style inventory (Appendix 2.1). Responses from the students were analyzed to	*This final assessment fits in the Curriculum of Identity, which asks students to understand and apply the lessons allegory reveal more fully by connecting them to their lives and experiences and to think about themselves as readers and writers.*

(Continued)

(Continued)

Unit Sequence—*Curriculum of Identity*	*Teacher Reflections*
Introductions, Teaching Strategies, and Learning Experiences	

provide students with a specific learning task that relied on more of an analytical, practical, or creative use of knowledge and understanding that they had acquired during this unit of study, *Animal Farm.* Three possible projects are designed to demonstrate their understanding of *Animal Farm,* but allow for their strengths to be used. The rubric focuses on the how the written piece addresses the essential questions, how well the response is written, and the degree of depth and understanding of both the novel and how it fits within the context of all the concepts that have been taught (Appendix 2.19).

The project options for the final assessment include:

- Analytical Task
    1. Read the novel *1984,* also by George Orwell, and write a criticism of Orwell's two novels. Use your background research on him as an author to explain why Orwell writes. How has history, past, background, and so on shaped who he is as a writer?
    2. Use ideological criticism as your lens for writing. This should be a *minimum* of a five-paragraph essay in order to pass. You should use quotes from both novels, as well as cite *at least* three outside sources for research. The final essay should be typed and free of spelling errors. Your ideological criticism essay should contain the following elements: (a) an introduction, which contains your question and its importance of being discussed; (b) a description of both novels and their contexts; (c) evidence of support for criticism, using several quotes from the novel; (d) explain the significance of why Orwell wrote in this manner; and (e) explain why the contribution of Orwell is significant and its role as being termed a "classic."

- Practical Task
    1. *Animal Farm* teaches us a cautionary lesson about government and the possible abuse of power that comes with it.

This Curriculum of Identity lesson asks students to draw from previous lessons they have experienced as a catalyst for self-definition and self-understanding, with the belief that by looking outward to the discipline, students can find a means of looking inward.

Students have approximately two weeks to complete the assignment. Throughout this time, students will be going through the writing process. As we go through this process as a class, I identify skill areas that the class as a whole are struggling with and teach them as mini-lessons. One of our "6 Big Ideas" at our school is "Systems." I like to teach grammar and the writing process under the "Systems" idea. Our essential understandings for systems are as follows:

1. *Systems consist of internal and external interaction.*
2. *Systems are structures with varying degrees of organization.*
3. *Systems are synergistic.*

These understandings fit so well with grammar, sentence structure, mechanics, and the like.

This analytical task will help students to look at George Orwell in greater detail. By reading another novel by him, students should see an even deeper meaning when it comes to the essential questions: Why do we write? Why are there patterns in literature? How does genre shape the writer? The task also asks students to look at themselves as writers again as they address the question: How is criticism autobiographical?

This practical task will help students to look at contexts. They are asked to pull out the major idea that government can help and harm people and apply it to their own lives.

This creative task will help students to apply the skills of writing and more specifically writing allegory, in order to judge not only their understanding of writing within a genre,

Unit Sequence—Curriculum of Identity	*Teacher Reflections*
Introductions, Teaching Strategies, Learning Experiences	

We have discussed in great length types of government and how each system has both positives and negatives. Now, think about your own life and government's role. Why should you be cautious of government? Where do you see government playing a role in your life? Find examples of laws that you feel have imposed on your life. Research the background of those laws and explain why you would have those laws changed. What are the possible ramifications of those changes? How might it help society change for the better? How might society change for the worse?

2. Create a case study for *three* laws that you believe invade your own personal freedoms. Your case study should follow the following format: (a) An *introduction* that gets the reader acquainted with the laws that you will be discussing using their background and history, as well as the basis of your argument for why the laws are intrusive. (b) A listing of *problems and subproblems*. This is your argument section where you make an argument for why each law invades your personal freedoms and why that law should be removed. Remember to address anything that someone may argue with you about. (c) An *analysis and discussion* section where you discuss in great detail how you address the essential question, "Does power corrupt?" as well as how your understanding of Orwell's way of writing has shaped your thinking.

- Creative Task
1. Write an allegory for a major current event in history. Remember the intricacies of creating an allegory. Each character is picked out very carefully to match its symbolic representation. The setting also plays a powerful role in allegory. How are you going to craft a story that honors the symbolism involved, but also follows the event in history with careful detail?

but a true understanding of satire and metaphorical thinking. Many students choose this project because they believe that it sounds the easiest, but as they create their work, they find it difficult to align characters and setting in a fashion that not only makes sense, but aligns itself with the historical context. Many find that their choice for metaphorical comparison does not fit and they have to make a new choice that is more appropriate to the story.

(Continued)

(Continued)

Unit Sequence—Curriculum of Identity	Teacher Reflections
Introductions, Teaching Strategies, Learning Experiences	
2. Before your allegory, I would like a list of characters and who they symbolize, as well as a brief synopsis of the current event that you chose. Next, write an allegory that is a *minimum* of five paragraphs. This allegory should follow the patterns of literature we have discussed this year, such as plot, setting, character, and literary and poetic elements. After your allegory, you need to add a section that discusses the importance of allegory as a style of writing and as a form of expression. Why do writers write in allegory? What have you learned as a result of writing in allegory?	
Closure	
Once students have turned in their projects, I give them back their original preassessments, along with a green pen. They answer the exact same questions that were posed in the preassessment.	*I like to do this with all of my units because it gets students to look back and see how far they have come. All students show some kind of growth through this process and are proud of what they have learned.*

APPENDIX 2.1

Sternberg's Inventory

Mark each sentence *T* if you like to do the activity and *F* if you do not like to do the activity.

1. Analyzing characters when I'm reading or listening to a story	
2. Designing new things	
3. Taking things apart and fixing them	
4. Comparing and contrasting points of view	
5. Coming up with ideas	
6. Learning through hands-on activities	
7. Criticizing my own and other kids' work	
8. Using my imagination	
9. Putting into practice things I learned	
10. Thinking clearly and analytically	
11. Thinking of alternative solutions	
12. Working with people in teams or groups	
13. Solving logical problems	
14. Noticing things others often ignore	
15. Resolving conflicts	
16. Evaluating my own and other's points of view	
17. Thinking in pictures and images	
18. Advising friends on their problems	
19. Explaining difficult ideas or problems to others	
20. Supposing things were different	
21. Convincing someone to do something	
22. Making inferences and deriving conclusions	
23. Drawing	
24. Learning by interacting with others	
25. Sorting and classifying	
26. Inventing new words, games, approaches	
27. Applying my knowledge	
28. Using graphic organizers or images to organize your thoughts	
29. Composing	
30. Adapting to new situations	

(Continued)

(Continued)

Transfer your answers from the survey to the key. The column with the most *T* responses is your dominant intelligence.

Analytical	Creative	Practical
1. ___	2. ___	3. ___
4. ___	5. ___	6. ___
7. ___	8. ___	9. ___
10. ___	11. ___	12. ___
13. ___	14. ___	15. ___
16. ___	17. ___	18. ___
19. ___	20. ___	21. ___
22. ___	23. ___	24. ___
25. ___	26. ___	27. ___
28. ___	29. ___	30. ___

Total Number of *T*:

Analytical ____   Creative _____   Practical _____

Source: Sternberg, Robert J. & Gregorenko, Elena L. (2007). *Teaching for Successful Intelligence: To Increase Student Learning and Achievement.* Thousand Oaks, CA: Corwin

APPENDIX 2.2

Use the Inspiration Program

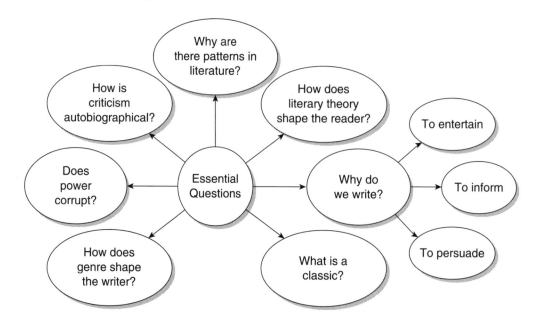

APPENDIX 2.3

Inspiration Converts to Skeleton Notes

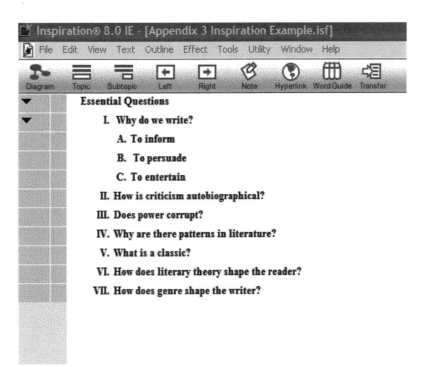

APPENDIX 2.4

3-2-1 Exit Card

Ticket Out

3 Questions I have about this unit/topic:

2 Things I learned today:

1 Big Idea that I connected with today:

APPENDIX 2.5

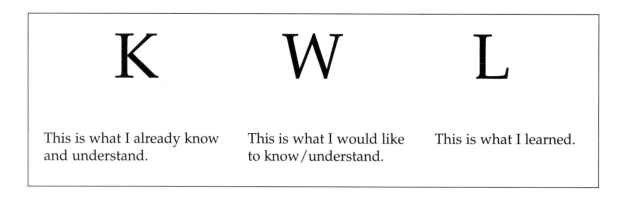

K	W	L
This is what I already know and understand.	This is what I would like to know/understand.	This is what I learned.

APPENDIX 2.6

Venn Diagram

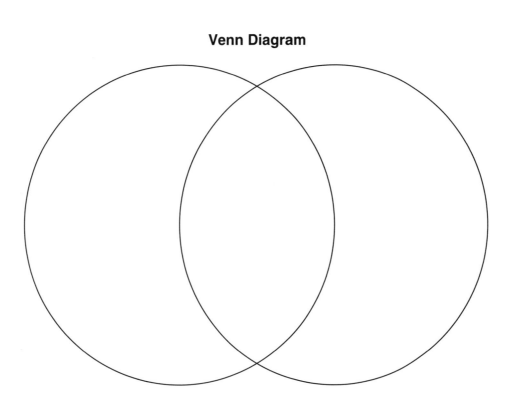

APPENDIX 2.7

Excerpt from Plato's Allegory of the Cave

Draw a picture on this page, or a separate piece of paper, of what you see as you are reading. When you are done, go back over the passage and fill out the following graphic organizer.

[**Socrates**]   And now, I said, let me show in a figure how far our nature is enlightened or unenlightened:—Behold! human beings living in a underground cave, which has a mouth open towards the light and reaching all along the cave; here they have been from their childhood, and have their legs and necks chained so that they cannot move, and can only see before them, being prevented by the chains from turning round their heads. Above and behind them a fire is blazing at a distance, and between the fire and the prisoners there is a raised way; and you will see, if you look, a low wall built along the way, like the screen which marionette players have in front of them, over which they show the puppets.

(Continued)

(Continued)

[Glaucon]	I see.
[Socrates]	And do you see, I said, men passing along the wall carrying all sorts of vessels, and statues and figures of animals made of wood and stone and various materials, which appear over the wall? Some of them are talking, others silent.
[Glaucon]	You have shown me a strange image, and they are strange prisoners.
[Socrates]	Like ourselves, I replied; and they see only their own shadows, or the shadows of one another, which the fire throws on the opposite wall of the cave?
[Glaucon]	True, he said; how could they see anything but the shadows if they were never allowed to move their heads?
[Socrates]	And of the objects which are being carried in like manner they would only see the shadows?
[Glaucon]	Yes, he said.
[Socrates]	And if they were able to converse with one another, would they not suppose that they were naming what was actually before them?
[Glaucon]	Very true.
[Socrates]	And suppose further that the prison had an echo which came from the other side, would they not be sure to fancy when one of the passers-by spoke that the voice which they heard came from the passing shadow?
[Glaucon]	No question, he replied.
[Socrates]	To them, I said, the truth would be literally nothing but the shadows of the images.

Literal Meaning	Symbolic Meaning

APPENDIX 2.8

Allegorical Diary

Have you ever heard the saying that you don't know where you're going until you know where you have been? In this unit, you will be asked to keep several kinds of diaries for that exact reason. These diaries will help you to see where you are going once you are on your own.

We are studying allegory for this unit. An allegory is a form of extended metaphor, in which objects, persons, and actions in a narrative are equated with meanings that lie outside of the narrative itself. I would like you to identify these extended metaphors. Every time you see something that may hold a deeper or double meaning, I would like you to write it down here.

Page #	Literal Object, Person, or Action	Symbolic Meaning (Hypothesize)

APPENDIX 2.9

Characterization Template

Items found around your home/ dwelling.	Items that are hidden/kept secret.	Items found in your neighborhood.
Names of other characters in your life.	**Names of dishes and food at family gatherings.**	**Names of places that hold memories.**
Sayings. . .		

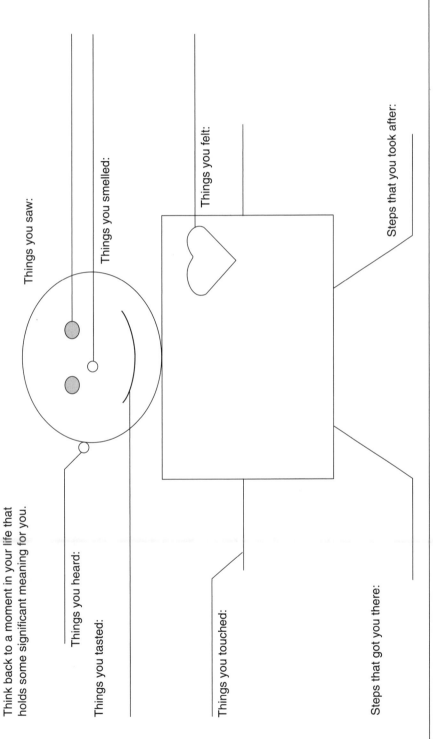

Think back to a moment in your life that holds some significant meaning for you.

Things you saw:

Things you smelled:

Things you heard:

Things you tasted:

Things you felt:

Things you touched:

Steps that you took after:

Steps that got you there:

APPENDIX 2.10

Developing Setting

Time: Consider the following things: day or night; past, present, or future; season; mood.

Place: Describe the immediate feeling in this place. Now base your description on this feeling or vice versa. It is okay to exaggerate here.

Culture: Are there objects in this setting that help to describe a culture, philosophy/belief system? What sets this setting apart in your mind from other memories?

Circumstance: Describe things that may have led up to this time and place. Could it have been different? How did setting shape this story?

APPENDIX 2.11

Checkpoints for Personal Allegory

Task   *Teacher Signature*

1. Answer the four questions based on one final chosen event.   _____

(1) Who was involved? (2) Where did the event take place?
(3) Why is or was this event so significant? (4) What does this
event symbolize for you (remember that a symbol is something
representing or recalling something else, especially an idea or quality)?

2. Fill out the two characterization templates for your story.   _____

3. Complete the setting template.   _____

4. Rough draft turned in and edited by a peer.   _____

5. Evidence of revision in story based on edit.   _____

6. Final draft submitted!   _____

APPENDIX 2.12

Personal Allegory Rubric

	Expert	*Practitioner*	*Apprentice*	*Novice*
Character Page (5 pts.)	Student included a character page that lists characters and who they represent. The characters align well and fit within the context of the story. It is obvious a lot of time and thought was put into allegorical connections.	Student included a character page that lists characters and who they represent. The characters align well and fit within the context of the story.	Student included a character page that lists characters and who they represent. Most characters align well and fit within the context of the story.	Student fails to include a character page or it does not connect with the allegory.
Allegory (40 pts.)	The student has written a unique, well thought out allegory. The student has obviously spent much time developing the story line and connecting it to the actual event. It is easy to see the real events lying behind their symbolic representations. It is creative and flows well.	The student has written a well thought out allegory. The student has spent time developing the story line and connecting it to the actual event. Most events connect clearly and the story is creative overall.	The student has written an allegory. The allegory sometimes strays from the actual event. The story is sometimes unclear or lacks creativity.	Student fails to include an allegory or the story is not an allegory.
Grammar and Mechanics (10 pts.)	Spelling, punctuation, and writing mechanics are nearly perfect.	Few spelling and punctuation errors; writing mechanics generally correct.	Several spelling errors, incorrect punctuation, and/or awkward phrasing disrupts reading; draft form.	Numerous spelling, punctuation, and mechanical errors; no careful editing; rough draft turned in.
Checkpoints (5 pts.)	The student met all checkpoints before the assignment was due. It is obvious that a lot of time and effort were put into the creation of this final piece.	The student met all checkpoints before the assignment was due. It is obvious that time and effort were put into the creation of this final piece, but a few errors detract from its overall meaning.	The student met most of the checkpoints before the assignment was due. Some time and effort were put into the creation of this final piece, but errors or missing pieces detract from its overall meaning.	Student failed to meet the checkpoints or failed to turn in the assignment.

TOTAL: _____ /60 Points

Comments:

APPENDIX 2.13

Animal Farm: *Character Analysis*

Worth 50 points!

You have been provided with a grid. Your mission for today is to begin to create a character analysis grid. I would like you to create a character map for each character, beginning with the major ones. For every box, please do the following:

1. Label, diagram, or draw the character.

2. Find *at least* three characteristics from your novel to support who your character is. Try not to be superficial (blonde hair, blue eyes). Dig deeper (motherly and nurturing).

3. Write one prediction that you have for this character based on his or her characteristics and what you have read thus far.

4. Pick another character from another book and describe how the characters are alike (you may not use the same character more than once).

You probably will not finish this if you are spending time thinking about the details. However, if you do, I would like you to pick the character that you think is most like you. In a well-developed paragraph, tell me why you think that character is similar to you and why you are drawn to that character.

Label/diagram/draw:	Label/diagram/draw:
Three novel-based characteristics:	Three novel-based characteristics:

(Continued)

(Continued)

Prediction:	Prediction:
Other character:	Other character:
Label/diagram/draw:	Label/diagram/draw:
Three novel-based characteristics:	Three novel-based characteristics:
Prediction:	Prediction:
Other character:	Other character:

APPENDIX 2.14

George Orwell

Pen Name: Eric Arthur Blair *(What stands out to you here? What could be the significance?)*

Born: June 25, 1902

Died: January 21, 1950

George Orwell took on many roles as an author. He was a known novelist and critic as well as political and cultural commentator. Orwell lived in what he described as a "lower-upper-middle class" background and did well in school. Because of his successful education, he earned a scholarship to Eton, where he received mixed grades. It was reported that some of his teachers disliked him because they believed he disrespected their authority. *(What do his teachers' opinions tell us about him as a person? How might this shape him as a writer?)*

One of the major things that influenced Orwell as a writer was his political views. He took mainly a left point of view and always opposed totalitarianism. His experience in the Spanish Civil War strengthened his view and caused him to be strongly anti-Stalinist. *(How do his political views shape him as a writer?)*

Orwell supported himself financially as a book reviewer/critic. One of his essays stated, "When one reads any strongly individual piece of writing, one has the impression of seeing a face somewhere behind the page. It is not necessarily the actual face of the writer. . . What one sees is the face that the writer ought to have . . . In the case of Dickens, it is the face of a man who is always fighting against something, but who fights in the open and is not frightened, the face of a man who is generously angry—in other words, of a nineteenth century liberal, a free intelligence, a type hated with equal hatred by all the smelly little orthodoxies which are now contending for our souls." This quote not only describes his critique of Dickens, but also very much his style of writing. *(What does this quote mean? What does this say about Orwell's personality?)*

One of Orwell's essays titled "Politics and the English Language" sets up six rules for writers to follow. They are:

1. Never use a metaphor, simile, or other figure of speech you are used to seeing in print.
2. Never use a long word where a short one will do.
3. If it is possible to cut a word out, always cut it out.
4. Never use the passive word where you can use the active.
5. Never use a foreign phrase, a scientific word, or jargon word if you can think of an everyday English equivalent.
6. Break any of these rules sooner than say anything outright barbarous.

(Do you see Orwell breaking any of these rules in Animal Farm? *Do you think he does so purposely or accidentally? What is the significance of the last rule? What does this say about his writing?)*

Orwell died at the age of 46 from tuberculosis. His gravestone mentions only his real name and has no reference to his pen name.

Source: Paraphrased from Wikipedia.

APPENDIX 2.15

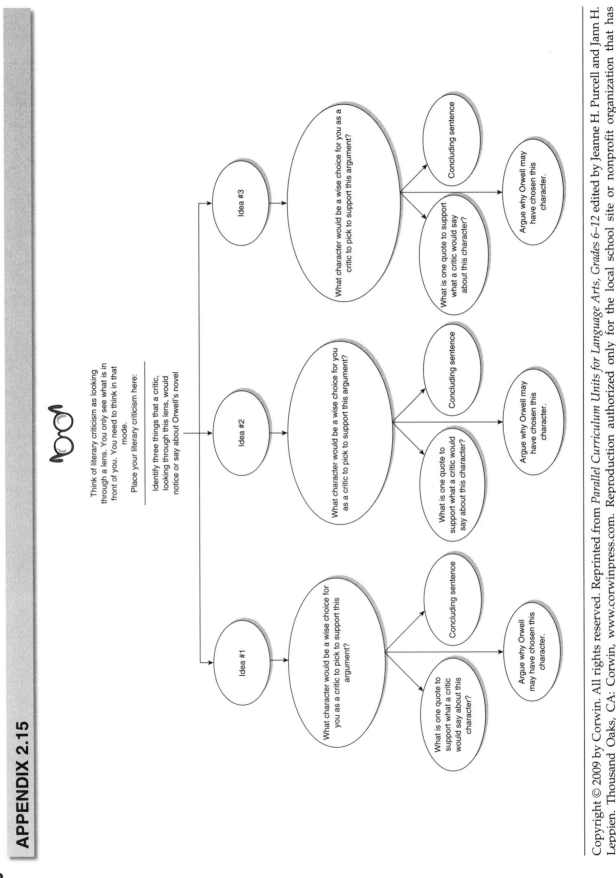

Think of literary criticism as looking through a lens. You only see what is in front of you. You need to think in that mode.

Place your literary criticism here:

Identify three things that a critic, looking through this lens, would notice or say about Orwell's novel

Idea #1

What character would be a wise choice for you as a critic to pick to support this argument?

What is one quote to support what a critic would say about this character?

Concluding sentence

Argue why Orwell may have chosen this character.

Idea #2

What character would be a wise choice for you as a critic to pick to support this argument?

What is one quote to support what a critic would say about this character?

Concluding sentence

Argue why Orwell may have chosen this character.

Idea #3

What character would be a wise choice for you as a critic to pick to support this argument?

What is one quote to support what a critic would say about this character?

Concluding sentence

Argue why Orwell may have chosen this character.

APPENDIX 2.16

Literary Criticism Essay Checklist

As you work through your essay, use the following checklist as a guide. As you finish a section, have someone else sign off that they have read the paragraph. You may not use the same student more than once. You are encouraged to ask parents or teachers to sign off as well.

Introductory Paragraph: Does the paragraph contain a strong thesis statement that fits the formula: author + verb + topic + opinion? Is the thesis statement clear and arguable? Does the paragraph contain some kind of hook?

Peer Edit Signature _____

Write one suggestion to help the writer with the introductory paragraph:

_____

_____

Body Paragraph #1: Does the paragraph contain a strong topic sentence that supports the original thesis statement? Is the topic sentence clear and arguable? Is there a quote from the novel that supports the topic sentence? Is the quote inserted seamlessly and explained clearly?

Peer Edit Signature _____

Write one suggestion to help the writer with Body Paragraph #1:

_____

_____

Body Paragraph #2: Does the paragraph contain a strong topic sentence that supports the original thesis statement? Is the topic sentence clear and arguable? Is there a quote from the novel that supports the topic sentence? Is the quote inserted seamlessly and explained clearly?

Peer Edit Signature _____

Write one suggestion to help the writer with Body Paragraph #2:

_____

_____

_____

(Continued)

(Continued)

Body Paragraph #3: Does the paragraph contain a strong topic sentence that supports the original thesis statement? Is the topic sentence clear and arguable? Is there a quote from the novel that supports the topic sentence? Is the quote inserted seamlessly and explained clearly?

Peer Edit Signature _____

Write one suggestion to help the writer with Body Paragraph #3:

_____

_____

Conclusion Paragraph: Does the paragraph restate that strong thesis statement that fits the formula: author + verb + topic + opinion? Does it truly wrap up the arguments of the essay?

Peer Edit Signature _____

Write one suggestion to help the writer with the conclusion paragraph:

_____

_____

A Reminder of Purpose: Remember that this is a literary critique. Your argument for the lens that you picked needs to be very strong, clear, and one sided. This is not an essay for the writer to sit on the fence. Look at the essay as a whole and look back at the guide questions for the literary lens that they chose. Are they clearly answered throughout the essay and do they present a clear opinion?

Peer Edit Signature _____

Write one suggestion to help the writer improve on the literary critique as a whole:

_____

_____

APPENDIX 2.17

Animal Farm: *Character Analysis (Part II)*

Worth 50 points!

You have been provided with a grid. Your mission for today is to begin to extend your thinking. You now need to figure out who your character symbolizes. You have been provided with a list. Based on your previous research, you need to match up your animals with their allegorical representation. The left-hand column is for the picture of the person or thing in history. The right-hand column is for your written information. You may have to cut the grids to match them up. For every box, please do the following:

1. Label the person or thing in history.

2. Label three characteristics of that person or thing based on your previous research.

3. Write one prediction that you have for this person based on the corresponding character in the novel and what you have read thus far.

4. Write one *strong* adjective that you believe describes this person or thing.

5. Which animal does this character most likely resemble? Cut out the square and match it with the character from the novel.

List of people in history to match:

Lenin   KGB/Secret Police
Trotsky   Mass followers
Stalin   Cynics/Skeptics
Propaganda Department/Pravda   Bourgeoisie
Russian Orthodox Church   Gypsies, con men, circus folk
Proletariat   Leader of England
Communist Manifesto   Hitler
Czar Nicholas II   Literate, but voiceless older generation

Label/diagram/draw person/event in history:	Label/diagram/draw person/event in history:

(Continued)

(Continued)

Three characteristics:	Three characteristics:
Prediction:	Prediction:
A strong adjective you infer:	A strong adjective you infer:
Label/diagram/draw:	Label/diagram/draw:
Three novel-based characteristics:	Three novel-based characteristics:
Prediction:	Prediction:
A strong adjective you infer:	A strong adjective you infer:

APPENDIX 2.18

The "Isms"

- Socialism: A system based on public ownership of the means of production and distribution of wealth. An economic, social, and political doctrine that expresses the struggle for the equal distribution of wealth by eliminating private property and the exploitative ruling class. In practice, such a distribution of wealth is achieved by social ownership of the means of production, exchange, and diffusion.

- Communism: An economic theory that stresses that the control of the means of producing economic goods in a society should reside in the hands of those who invest their labor for production. In its ideal form, social classes cease to exist, there is no coercive governmental structures, and everyone lives in abundance without supervision from a ruling class. Karl Marx and Friedrich Engels popularized this theory in their 1848 *Communist Manifesto.*

- Marxism: This is an economic principle and is the essence of what is taking place in the novel. The working class (the proletariat) is working so hard and not getting anything in return while the rich (the bourgeoisie) are the ones benefiting from the hard work. In the beginning of the novel, the proletariat are the animals and the bourgeoisie are the humans, but this will shift yet again as the novel progresses. Boxer becomes the proletariat and Mollie is the bourgeoisie.

- Capitalism: Under capitalism, the capitalists own the means of production, the proletariat own only their capacity to work. Landlords rule the land, and the peasants are less significant than workers and are trapped in the idiocy of rural life. The proletariat definitely includes those who produce objects in factories with their hands, but Marxists dither about whether it includes people who work with their minds but are employees and live by their salaries.

- Totalitarianism: This term is employed by some political scientists, especially those in the field of comparative politics, to describe modern regimes in which the state regulates nearly every aspect of public and private behavior.

- Fascism: An authoritarian political ideology and mass movement that seeks to establish a society in which individual interests would be subdued to the good of the nation. Various scholars attribute different characteristics to fascism, but the following elements are usually seen as its integral parts: nationalism, authoritarianism, militarism, corporatism, collectivism, totalitarianism, anticommunism, and opposition to economic and political liberalism. Although a number of fascist movements expressed racist beliefs, racism is not a constitutive element of fascism.

Homework: Research and identify a country that has had an example of each type of "ism." Look into the background of each country. What classes of people were there? What was the economy like? What are the positives of this type of rule? What are the negatives? Prepare a three-paragraph summary of your findings.

APPENDIX 2.19

Animal Farm *Rubric*

	Expert	*Practitioner*	*Novice*
The Heart (100)	The writer has obviously done everything possible to understand the format of the writing and it is evident in the writing piece. It is well-crafted, flows well, and contains all key elements. The writer has gone beyond the bare minimum requirements and focused on quality over quantity.	The writer shows an understanding of the format and it is evident in the writing piece. It is well-crafted, flows, and contains all key elements. The writer meets the minimum requirements and focused on quality over quantity.	The writer fails to show an understanding of the format. The writing piece is not structured, lacks flow, and/or is missing key elements. The writer failed to meet the minimum requirements of the assignment.
The Bones (50)	The structure is organized and clear. Each section has headings and the guidelines are followed. The writing piece is typed, spell- and grammar-checked, proofread, and contains no errors. It is obvious that the student has undergone the revision process.	The structure is organized and clear. Each section has headings and the guidelines are followed. The writing piece is typed, spell- and grammar-checked, proofread, and contains few errors that detract from meaning. It is obvious that the student has undergone the revision process.	The structure lacks organization. The writer fails to place headings within the paper, adding to confusion. The writing piece is typed, but the spelling and grammar errors detract from meaning. It is obvious that the writer did not go through the revision process.
The Brains (50)	The student has addressed at least two essential questions seamlessly within the writing piece. The thought to the questions shows depth and understanding. The student moves beyond expectations to address one or more extension questions.	The student has addressed two essential questions within the writing piece. The thought to the questions shows depth and understanding.	The student fails to address two essential questions within the writing piece.
The Eyes	Student has met and addressed the standards set for the unit.	Student has attempted to meet and address the standards set for the unit.	Student has failed to meet and address the standards set for the unit.

3

Reacting to a Literary Model

Writing Original Pieces

Grades 9–10

Judy Walsh

INTRODUCTION TO THE UNIT

Background Information

The unit focuses on responding to a quality novel, analyzing particular elements in the novel, prewriting sentences and paragraphs that model an author's techniques, and then revising, expanding, and editing the paragraphs into finished pieces. The unit is a Core Parallel unit, as it promotes student understanding about authors' writing techniques and how to model them. All concepts and skills are those required in the National Council of Teachers of English standards and are reflected in many state curriculum framework documents. By using prewriting activities that focus on one story element at a time, the unit makes learning easier and more efficient. The novel used in this unit is *To Kill a Mockingbird*. Other novels could be substituted (*Of Mice and Men* or *The Adventures of Huckleberry Finn* come to mind), but the story chosen should be one that addresses prejudice as a major conflict in the story.

Students will carefully examine the way that an author creates a believable setting, an appropriate mood, characters that become real to the reader, important conflicts, and universal themes that touch the reader. After analyzing the ways that an author develops these key components in the novel, students will model writing techniques in prewriting exercises; then, they will revise and synthesize the techniques they have learned and create a longer, finished piece.

Overview of the Lessons

Students will begin with the creation of a believable setting by using figures of speech and sensory words. Prewriting exercises will take them from sentences to a paragraph to several paragraphs. Then students will find words that convey mood and revise their setting paragraphs to convey the mood that they intend. Next, students will examine the important characters in the novel and the different ways in which they are developed. They will engage in a series of prewriting activities that culminate in a character sketch of three to four paragraphs. Finally, students will take a careful look at prejudice in the novel and assess the conflicts it creates with different characters. Prewriting activities will take them from describing how a character in the novel dealt with prejudice to writing a paragraph about how they or someone in their world dealt with prejudice. With this knowledge they will revise and expand their paragraphs to include the understanding of life that the incident revealed. At this point in the unit, an extension activity will be offered in the Identity Parallel. Students will have the opportunity to explore the life of a writer of fiction and compare his or her life style, values and work ethics to the expectations they hold for their own aspirations and future plans.

The unit consists of eight lessons, including a preassessment lesson and a postassessment lesson. It could easily be taught in several weeks, or it could be combined with a literature unit, which would give students even more models and techniques to analyze and then apply to their writing.

Several national standards are covered in the unit as students read, interpret, evaluate, and appreciate a particular text, as well as excerpts from other books. The knowledge they will glean from these interpretations and evaluations will translate into writing strategies that they can apply to various writing tasks. The unit also emphasizes their proficiency in writing, which reflects knowledge of language conventions. Each lesson specifically lists the national standards that are covered in the lesson. In addition to meeting several national standards, the unit also stresses skills that are tested in many state assessments.

The unit should be appropriate for all levels of students in ninth or tenth grade. There are suggestions in the reflections column for making the material more accessible for students who may be struggling. There are also some extension and Ascending Intellectual Development (AID) activities for advanced students who need more challenge and those students who work well independently, as well as those with high interest in the subject.

The ideal time to begin this unit is immediately after students have finished reading the novel you are using. It is essential to have one common text that all students can relate to as a model. I believe that *To Kill a Mockingbird* by Harper Lee is an ideal choice, especially for freshmen and sophomores, but if you want a book that is more accessible, *Of Mice and Men* by John Steinbeck will also work well.

The resources I gathered as I prepared to teach the course were varied. In addition to my main text, *To Kill a Mockingbird,* I also collected short stories and nonfiction pieces that had excerpts that provided good examples of story components, as well as suitable stories for the preassessment and postassessment.

CONTENT FRAMEWORK

Organizing Concepts

Macroconcepts	Discipline-Specific Concepts	Principles
M1: Reacting to Literature/Writing	C1: Setting	P1: Great literature can serve as a model for writing.
	C2: Mood	P2: Setting can be important in creating the mood of a story.
	C3: Tone	P3: Different points of view provide more or less knowledge of characters' thoughts.
	C4: Characterization	P4: Creating a realistic character is achieved by using a variety of methods, including dialogue and a character's actions.
	C5: Point of View	P5: Well-developed characters in quality literature are good models for characters in original stories.
	C6: Conflict	P6: Prejudice can exist on many levels.
	C7: Prejudice	P7: An understanding of life can evolve from a conflict.
	C8: Theme	P8: Universal themes transcend a particular story and teach us about life.
	C9: Sensory Words	P9: Students employ a wide range of strategies as they write and use different writing elements.
	C10: Personification	
	C11: Simile	
	C12: Allusion	
	C13: Dialogue	
	C14: Internal Conflict	
	C15: External Conflict	
	C16: Resolution	
	C17: Universal Theme	

National Standards

SD1: Students apply a wide range of strategies to comprehend, interpret, evaluate, and appreciate texts. They draw on their prior experience, their interactions with other readers and writers, their knowledge of word meaning and of other texts, their word identification strategies, and their understanding of textual features.

SD2: Students employ a wide range of strategies as they write and use different writing process elements appropriately for a variety of purposes.

SD3: Students use spoken, written, and visual language to accomplish their own purposes (e.g., for learning, enjoyment, persuasion, and the exchange of information).

SD4: Students apply knowledge of language structure, language conventions, media techniques, figurative language, and genre to create, critique, and discuss print and nonprint texts.

Skills

S1: Respond with understanding to a piece of literature.

S2: Understand and evaluate mood.

S3: Interpret personality traits in a fictional character.

S4: Judge the major characters in a work of fiction as being prejudiced or fair-minded.

S5: Distinguish a conflict and classify it as internal or external.

S6: Analyze a message an author intended from a particular conflict.

S7: Recognize and categorize theme as to its universality.

S8: Apply the rules of standard English, using correct grammar, spelling, and punctuation.

S9: Recognize figures of speech and sensory words in a description.

S10: Incorporate figures of speech and sensory words when writing a description.

S11: Integrate words that convey mood when writing a description of a place.

S12: Point out passages in a work of fiction that develop a particular character.

S13: Create a character sketch using dialogue and a character's actions.

S14: Individualize the concept of prejudice by giving an example from one's personal world.

ASSESSMENTS

The unit incorporates a variety of formative assessment opportunities throughout, and a preassessment and postassessment for the unit overall.

Preassessment

The preassessment is designed to evaluate how well students can read a short story and react to it. Specifically, it assesses students' understanding of specific literary elements such as setting, mood, and characterization. Further, student work on the preassessment will illuminate how well students can weave together story elements to arrive at a theme or universal message. Of course, the written aspect of this preassessment will give the teacher a deeper understanding of students' writing skills.

For students who struggle with reading and writing, an abbreviated version of the preassessment may be given to provide information without placing impossible demands on the student. Also, the preassessment can be given orally to students who would struggle extensively with the written word.

Formative Assessments

Three formative assessments are included, and all require written responses. The first writing assignment, aligned with Lessons 3.2 and 3.3, invites students to explore how sensory words and figurative language can create mood. The second formative assessment aligns with Lessons 3.4 and 3.5 and invites students to create a character sketch. Lessons 3.6 and 3.7 also have a written assignment that can provide formative feedback to the teacher about students' knowledge of conflict and theme. All three formative assessments include a trait rubric that teachers can use to not only assess student work, but also determine students' strengths and weaknesses. Once students' strengths and weaknesses are pinpointed, teachers can modify their instruction accordingly.

Postassessment

The postassessment invites students to consider the short story, "The Scarlet Ibis," a story that is more complex than "All Summer in a Day," used in the preassessment. Students are asked to share their reflections in a series of questions that parallel the ones in the preassessment. A trait rubric is included to assess student progress and it mirrors the rubric provided for the preassessment, thereby enabling teachers to measure true gains for students.

UNIT SEQUENCE, DESCRIPTION, AND TEACHER REFLECTIONS

Lesson 3.1: Preassessment (Forty-Six Minutes)

Discipline-Specific Concepts

C1: Setting
C2: Mood
C3: Tone
C4: Characterization
C5: Point of View
C6: Conflict
C7: Prejudice
C8: Theme

Principles

P2: Setting can be important in creating the mood of a story.
P3: Different points of view provide more or less knowledge of characters' thoughts.
P4: Creating a realistic character is achieved by using a variety of methods, including dialogue and a character's actions.
P6: Prejudice can exist on many levels.
P7: An understanding of life can evolve from a conflict.
P8: Universal themes transcend a particular story and teach us about life.
P9: Students employ a wide range of strategies as they write and use different writing elements.

(Continued)

(Continued)

Skills

S2: Understand and evaluate mood.

S3: Interpret personality traits in a fictional character.

S4: Judge the major characters in a work of fiction as being prejudiced or fair-minded.

S5: Distinguish a conflict and classify it as internal or external.

S6: Analyze the message an author intended from a particular conflict.

S7: Recognize and categorize a theme as to its universality.

S8: Apply the rules of standard English, using correct grammar, spelling and punctuation when writing.

Standards

SD1: Students apply a wide range of strategies to comprehend, interpret, evaluate, and appreciate texts. They draw on their prior experience, their interactions with other readers and writers, their knowledge of word meaning and of other texts, their word identification strategies, and their understanding of textual features.

SD2: Students employ a wide range of strategies as they write and use different writing process elements appropriately for a variety of purposes.

SD3: Students use spoken, written, and visual language to accomplish their own purposes (e.g., for learning, enjoyment, persuasion, and the exchange of information).

Guiding Questions

- How does an author synthesize the different elements in a story, such as setting, mood, character, and conflict, to create a universal theme?
- How is prejudice an important part of the story?
- How does the story enhance your understanding of life?

Unit Sequence	Teacher Reflections
Introduction (Two Minutes)	
<ul><li>Begin by telling students that they will read a short story and then answer some questions about the story.</li><li>Tell them to answer each question in a well-developed paragraph or two and to do the best job that they can.</li></ul> Reassure them that this is not a test, but a preassessment. The purpose of such a preassessment is so that the teacher can find out what students know and do not know. With that information, the teacher can structure the activities and instructions for the unit in a way that will best fit students' learning needs.	*The preassessment evaluates how well students can read a short story and react to it by understanding the different elements, such as setting, mood, and characterization. Going further, it also tests whether students can perceive how these different story elements work together to create a theme or universal message. The preassessment also gives a teacher a good idea of students' writing skills. Finally, the preassessment—along with the postassessment at the end of the unit— provides a measurement of the learning that took place during the unit.*

Unit Sequence	Teacher Reflections
Teaching Strategies and Learning Experience (Forty-Two Minutes)	
<ul><li>Give each student a copy of the short story, "All Summer in a Day," by Ray Bradbury and a copy of the questions for the preassessment.</li><li>Distribute a couple of sheets of lined paper for students to write their answers.</li><li>Circulate occasionally while students are working to answer any questions about procedures, but not about the content of the preassessment. Encourage students to do their best.</li></ul>	*The short story, "All Summer in a Day," by Ray Bradbury can be found in many short story collections, including* Characters in Conflict, *edited by Evler Mescal (1996). It can also be found online at http://www.westbury friends.org/online/ela/giver/all%20summer% 20reading.pdf.* *The questions for the preassessment and a scoring rubric can be found at the end of this lesson.*
Closure (Two Minutes)	
<ul><li>Collect the stories and students papers.</li></ul>For homework, ask students to write a journal entry describing a town where they have lived or spent some time.	*I used the preassessment results to adjust the lessons. I could see, for example, that my students needed a lot of work on understanding theme.* *In assessing their writing skills, I saw that my students needed some help with transitions, subject/verb agreement, and unity. You can add lessons in using standard English and writing skills in between lessons or as an add-on to a lesson.* *The journal assignment will lead the class into the next lesson, which deals with creating a vivid setting, including a mood that fits the intended story.*

Preassessment Questions for "All Summer in a Day"

Directions: After reading "All Summer in a Day," answer each the following questions in a couple of well-developed paragraphs on the lined paper that has been provided to you.

1. What is the setting and why is it important in the story? Tell how it helps establish the tone and mood.

2. What is the point of view in the story and how does it lend itself to the development of the theme?

3. How is Margot's character developed?

4. What is the main conflict and how does it involve a form of prejudice?

5. Explain fully the theme or message the story develops?

6. How does the story enhance your understanding of life?

Preassessment Rubric

Criteria	1	2	3	4	Your Score
Content Importance of setting and mood, and their connection	Importance of setting is not noted and little or no mention is made of mood.	Importance of setting is mentioned, but no real connection is made between setting and mood.	Good perception of importance of setting is evident and some connection between it and mood.	Excellent awareness of the importance of setting is present, as well as how setting and mood can work together.	1 2 3 4
Content Point of view and its role in development of theme	Point of view is not mentioned or is identified incorrectly. Theme is not mentioned.	Some awareness of point of view is evident but no connection is made to theme.	Good perception of point of view and some mention of its role in theme development are seen.	Insightful analysis of point of view is seen, as well as its role in theme development.	1 2 3 4
Content Characterization— means of development	Means of character development is not mentioned or is incorrect.	There are some points about character development, but it is limited.	There is awareness of the author's character development.	Excellent perception of methods of character development is evident.	1 2 3 4
Content Main conflict and how it involves prejudice	The main conflict is not identified or is incorrect. There is no mention of the prejudice involved.	The main conflict is identified but only a minor reference is made to the prejudice or it is incorrect.	There is an accurate awareness of the main conflict and the prejudice involved.	There is an excellent perception of the main conflict and the prejudice it involves.	1 2 3 4
Content Theme or universal truth that story develops	The theme is not mentioned or is incorrect. There is no connection to the student.	The theme is mentioned but it is incorrect or is unexplained, and there is no connection to student's life.	There is some good perception of the theme, but it is not fully explained. Some connection is made to the student's life.	The theme is insightfully perceived, fully explained, and connected to the student's life.	1 2 3 4
Writing Skills Proficient organization, proper mechanics, usage and spelling	Writing is disordered. Mechanical, grammar, and spelling errors are numerous.	Writing is adequate in organization, mechanics, usage, and spelling, but errors are evident.	Writing is organized and there are few errors in mechanics, usage, and spelling.	Writing has excellent organization and is free of almost any mechanical, usage, or spelling errors.	1 2 3 4

Lessons 3.2 and 3.3: Setting and Mood (Ninety Minutes)

Discipline-Specific Concepts

C1: Setting
C2: Mood
C9: Sensory Words
C10: Personification
C11: Simile
C12: Allusion

Principles

P1: Great literature can serve as a model for writing.
P2: Setting can be important in creating the mood of a story.
P9: Students employ a wide range of strategies as they write and use different writing elements.

Skills

S2: Understand and evaluate mood.
S8: Apply the rules of standard English, using correct grammar, spelling, and punctuation.
S9: Recognize figures of speech and sensory words in a description.
S10: Incorporate figures of speech and sensory words when writing a description.
S11: Integrate words that convey mood when writing a description of a place.

Standards

SD1: Students apply a wide range of strategies to comprehend, interpret, evaluate, and appreciate texts. They draw on their prior experience, their interactions with other readers and writers, their knowledge of word meaning and of other texts, their word identification strategies, and their understanding of textual features.
SD2: Students employ a wide range of strategies as they write and use different writing process elements appropriately for a variety of purposes.
SD3: Students use spoken, written, and visual language to accomplish their own purposes (e.g., for learning, enjoyment, persuasion, and the exchange of information).

Guiding Questions

- How does the setting of a story help to create the mood?
- What writing techniques create a mood and make a setting vivid for a reader?

Introduction (Ten Minutes)
<ul><li>Begin by telling students that today we will be reading some short excerpts that describe particular settings. Then we will look at the techniques the different authors used to produce the effects they created in these descriptions.</li><li>Distribute handout 3.2/3.3A.</li><li>Ask students to make notes about any words, phrases, or writing techniques that they find especially effective.</li></ul>

Unit Sequence	Teacher Reflections
Teaching Strategies and Learning Experiences (Seventy Minutes)	
<ul><li>Invite students to share an observation they have seen in the passages. If they just mention a word or phrase, guide them to name the particular technique that describes the use of the word or phrase.</li><li>Scaffold if necessary to elicit these points you want to emphasize:<ul><li>Use of specific sensory words</li><li>The use of figurative language: personification, simile, metaphor, and allusion</li></ul></li><li>Have students list the specific sensory words in each passage.</li><li>Invite students to share their findings. Ask other students to add to the list. Guide if necessary to make sure that students see that sensory words can be nouns and verbs as well as adjectives and adverbs.</li><li>If students do not notice it, point out that the sensory words in these passages not only give details that allow the reader to see the scene but also convey a temperature.</li><li>Now invite students to write four original sentences describing a scene. In each, they are to include a mention of color as well as words or phrases that indicate a temperature.</li><li>Remind students that sensory words can convey sounds, smells, and tastes, and they can also add words to indicate these senses.</li><li>Now, have students look once more at the story excerpts for examples of figures of speech: simile, metaphor, personification, and allusion.</li><li>Instruct students to add at least one example of a metaphor, personification, or simile to the two best sensory scene descriptions that they have created. Differentiation—Have students add an allusion to the description that conveys a time period.</li></ul>	*If students seem at all confused, review the terms* personification, simile, metaphor, *and* allusion. *Put the definitions on the board, along with an example of each.* *Let student responses dictate the order of the points you wish to emphasize. I have started with sensory words and ended with the use of figurative language, but the order is not important. It is more important to have students be as much a part of the lesson as possible.* *For students who are struggling, it would be a good idea to put students' findings on the board so they can refer to them.* *For students who are struggling, you may have to do some guiding. These students need the structure of listing some examples of sensory words on the board.* *You may have to help with the allusion that is found in the excerpt from* To Kill a Mockingbird. *"Maycomb County had recently been told that it had nothing to fear but fear itself." is a reference to the famous quote by FDR. This allusion gives a general time period to the reader.* *These more challenging learning activities are appropriate for students who have a high interest in creative writing, and/or for students who need an extra challenge.* *The mood of the excerpt from* To Kill a Mockingbird *is sultry, muggy, languorous,*

(Continued)

(Continued)

Unit Sequence	Teacher Reflections
Teaching Strategies and Learning Experiences (Seventy Minutes)	
<ul><li>Ask students to define a mood. Scaffold if necessary. Pair students and then ask partners to describe the mood of each excerpt and to underline the words that led them to choose that mood.</li><li>Distribute Handout 3.2/3.3B. In pairs, have students come up with as many words as they can that create the moods that are listed. Encourage them to be creative.</li><li>Have partners share lists with class.</li><li>Now ask students to look at the two sensory descriptions that they have expanded with figurative language. Have them choose the piece they like best. They can also ask their partner's opinion.</li><li>After choosing, they should expand that particular piece by adding words to establish the mood they wish to convey. Tell them to also eliminate words or phrases that do not fit with that mood.</li><li>Tell students to exchange papers with their partners and make suggestions for each other's work.</li><li>Finally, tell students to get out the journal entry they wrote for homework. With their partner's input, if desired, they should choose the piece of writing they like best, the sensory piece they just wrote in class or the journal entry.</li><li>The writing assignment is to revise and expand the piece they choose into three well-developed paragraphs. These paragraphs should create a vivid setting that uses sensory words, figurative language, and words and phrases that create a unified mood.</li><li>Differentiation—For students requiring more challenge: they may notice that both excerpts seem to be written from a child's point of view, but looking closely, we can see that they are not. In actuality, they are from a child's point of view, but were created by the author—an older person looking back at a childhood memory. For your assignment, choose a vivid childhood memory and describe it as you are now, looking back at that memory. Be sure to include the figurative language, sensory words, and a unified mood as well.</li></ul>	*or slow moving, while the mood of the excerpt from "Circus at Dawn" is excited and energetic.* *Other answers could also be correct; accept any that are reasonable.* *Pairing students here provides a needed change of pace. This is also an activity that is more fun with a partner because students can move at a snappier pace.* *Sharing is a good way of acknowledging student's work and originality. It can also jump start students who may be struggling.* *Some students will rely on their partner more than others. For students who are struggling, the partner may provide help. Other students who are more independent may wish to work alone at this point. Let them choose whichever method works best. Some students may also want your opinion.* *Be sure to review the rubric with students. It reinforces the assignment and prevents misunderstandings.* *Suggest this assignment for students who especially like creative writing, as well as those students who need a challenge.*

Unit Sequence	Teacher Reflections
Teaching Strategies and Learning Experiences (Seventy Minutes)	
• Review the grading rubric with students so that they understand what is expected of them and how they will be graded. • Remind students to carefully proofread their final draft before its submission.	
Closure (Ten Minutes)	
• Invite students to explain one writing technique that makes a setting vivid to the reader. Ask for an example. • Ask a student how setting can create a mood. • Have students state the ways a writer can use words in a description to create a particular mood.	*Repeat the question until you have elicited both techniques you focused on today: sensory language and figurative language.* *Give students a chance to ask any questions for clarification they need to complete the assignment.*

HANDOUT 3.2/3.3A

Excerpt from To Kill a Mockingbird *by Harper Lee*

Macomb was an old town, but it was a tired old town when I first knew it. In rainy weather the streets turned to red slop; grass grew on the sidewalks, the courthouse sagged in the square. Somehow, it was hotter then: a black dog suffered on a summer's day; bony mules hitched to Hoover cars flicked flies in the sweltering shade of the live oaks on the square. Men's stiff collars wilted by nine in the morning. Ladies bathed before noon, after their three o'clock naps, and by nightfall were like soft teacakes with frostings of sweat and sweet talcum.

People moved slowly then. They ambled across the square, shuffled in and out of the stores around it, took their time about everything. A day was twenty-four hours long but seemed longer. There was no hurry, for there was nowhere to go, nothing to buy and no money to buy it with, nothing to see outside the boundaries of Maycomb County. But it was a time of vague optimism for some of the people: Maycomb County had recently been told that it had nothing to fear but fear itself. (Lee, pp. 5–6)

Notes:

Excerpt from "Circus at Dawn" by Thomas Wolfe

There were times in early autumn—in September—when the greater circuses would come to town—the Ringling Brothers, Robinson's, and Barnum and Bailey shows, and when I was a route-boy on the morning paper, on those mornings when the circus would be coming in, I would rush madly through my route in the cool and thrilling darkness that comes just before break of day, and then I would go back home and get my brother out of bed. Talking in low excited voices we would walk rapidly back toward town under the rustle of September leaves, in cool streets just grayed now with that still, that unearthly and magical first light of day which seems suddenly to rediscover the great earth out of darkness, so that the earth emerges with an awful glorious sculptural stillness, and one looks out with a feeling of joy and disbelief, as the first men on this earth must have done, for to see this happen is one of the things that men will remember out of life forever and think of as they die. (Wolfe, p. 779)

Notes:

HANDOUT 3.2/3.3B

For each mood, list at many words as you can that suggest that mood.

Happiness:
Peace:
Fear:
Excitement:
Wealth:
Despair:

SETTING/MOOD RUBRIC

Criteria	1	2	3	4	Your Score
Content Setting is described vividly, using sensory language.	Limited or unrealistic use of sensory language in description of setting.	Some sensory language in description of setting, but it could be more vivid.	Good use of sensory language in description of setting. Setting seems real.	Excellent use of sensory language. The creative rendering establishes a vivid picture in the reader's mind.	1 2 3 4
Content Setting contains at least one figure of speech that enhances the description.	No figure of speech is used in the description or one is used incorrectly or ineffectively.	One figure of speech is used but it is awkward or does not fit well in the overall setting description.	Two or more figures of speech are used that enhance the picture of the setting.	Creative use of figurative language pushes the boundaries of the assignment.	1 2 3 4
Content Mood is created using numerous words and phrases that convey an atmosphere.	There is no visible attempt to convey a unified mood.	Some words convey a mood but other words and phrases contradict it, or the description does not clearly convey a definite mood.	Good use of words and phrases to create a unified mood in description.	Clear, unified mood that is clearly and creatively conveyed in the setting description.	1 2 3 4
Length Paper is three well-developed paragraphs.	Paper is not the appropriate length. It is either not three paragraphs or none of the paragraphs are fully developed.	Paper does not contain three paragraphs or if it does, only one is fully developed.	Paper is three developed paragraphs, but they are not fully unified.	Paper is the appropriate length, three well-developed paragraphs that are unified in creating a particular scene.	1 2 3 4
Writing Skills Paper reflects proficient organization and proper mechanics, usage, and spelling.	Writing is disordered. Mechanical, grammar, and spelling errors are numerous.	Writing is adequate in organization, mechanics, usage, and spelling, but errors are evident.	Writing is organized and there are few errors in mechanics, usage, and spelling.	Writing has excellent organization and is almost free of mechanical, usage, or spelling errors.	1 2 3 4
Differentiation Point of view is consistent with someone looking back at a childhood memory.	There is no attempt to create the assigned point of view.	The point of view is not consistent and is confusing.	There is an attempt to use the assigned point of view, but it lacks consistency.	Point of view is consistent with a teenager looking back at a childhood memory. It is well crafted.	1 2 3 4

Lessons 3.4 and 3.5: Creating Realistic Characters (Ninety Minutes)

Discipline-Specific Concepts

C4: Characterization
C5: Point of View
C13: Dialogue

Principles

P3: Different points of view provide more or less knowledge of characters' thoughts.
P4: Creating a realistic character is achieved by using a variety of methods, including dialogue and a character's actions.
P5: Well-developed characters in quality literature are good models for characters in original stories.
P9: Students employ a wide variety of strategies as they write and use different writing elements.

Skills

S3: Interpret personality traits in a fictional character.
S8: Apply the rules of standard English, using correct grammar, spelling, and punctuation.
S12: Point out passages in a work of fiction that develop a particular character.
S13: Create a character sketch using dialogue and a character's actions.

Standards

SD1: Students apply a wide range of strategies to comprehend, interpret, evaluate, and appreciate texts. They draw on their prior experience, their interactions with other readers and writers, their knowledge of word meaning and of other texts, their word identification strategies, and their understanding of textual features.
SD2: Students employ a wide range of strategies as they write and use different writing process elements appropriately for a variety of purposes.
SD3: Students use spoken, written, and visual language to accomplish their own purposes (e.g., for learning, enjoyment, persuasion, and the exchange of information).

Guiding Questions

- What techniques does an author use to reveal a fictional character's personality?
- How can I create a sketch of a realistic character?

Unit Sequence	Teacher Reflections
Introduction (Ten Minutes)	
<ul><li>Begin by collecting the setting/mood papers.</li><li>Tell students that Harper Lee not only provided good models in her descriptions of places, but she also portrayed realistic characters.</li><li>Inform students that we will pinpoint the personality traits of some of the main characters in *To Kill a Mockingbird*.</li></ul>	*The entire Introduction is a whole class activity. You need to give students a certain amount of information before they can work more independently in groups.* *In the paperback edition of* To Kill a Mockingbird, *the section introducing Dill begins in the next to last paragraph at the bottom of page 6, beginning, "That was the*

Unit Sequence	Teacher Reflections
Introduction (Ten Minutes)	

• Now with the class as a whole, turn to the character of Dill. Scout first recalls meeting Dill the summer she was six. She describes him and recalls the first conversation she and Jem had with him.
• Read the pertinent text in Chapter 1 of *To Kill a Mockingbird*. Then ask students what important aspects to Dill's personality are revealed in these passages of description and dialogue. Further, ask them to defend the observations they have made with specific support from the text.
• As you begin to examine the character of Dill, ask students how they made their decisions about his personality traits.
 	
   o Scaffold if necessary to come up with a list:
   o Character's description
   o Character's actions, including dialogue
	summer Dill came to us." Read all of the next page and end in the middle of page 8 with the sentence, "Dill blushed and Jem told me to hush, a sure sign that Dill had been studied and found acceptable."
	
	   List the descriptive words and the justification for them on the board. They will make a good frame of reference when students start writing.

Teaching Strategies and Learning Experiences (Seventy Minutes)	

• Now, tell students that they will be grouped with two other students and the three of them will be assigned a particular character. They will have fifteen minutes to determine three discerning words (adjectives or nouns) that best reflect their character's personality, as well as choosing a perceptive passage (at least a paragraph but no more than a page) from the novel that shows something important about their character's personality. Each group should be prepared to defend their choices when they present their findings to the class.
• Assign characters: Scout, Jem, Atticus, Calpurnia, Tom Robinson, Mayella Ewell, Bob Ewell, Mrs. Dubose, Arthur "Boo" Bradley, and Aunt Alexandra. Circulate while students work so that you can guide those who are struggling and remind those who choose too quickly that the three words should be insightful and the passage should reflect the personality traits they choose.
	Give students a chance to ask questions about the assignment but emphasize that they may not choose their character.
	   Groups for this assignment provide support for those who need it as well as quickening the pace.
	
	   For best results, assign the easier characters to those students who may be below grade level readers. You might also want to choose the partners for these students
	   Adjust time as needed.
	   If necessary, step in to guide away from incorrect or weak choices of the words or the text selection. Pose questions such as, "What does this particular section of text reveal about the character?" "Does this passage reveal the most critical aspects of your character?" "What criteria did you use to select your passage?" "Does this adjective (or noun) represent a strong trait in your character?" If students have trouble coming up with three words to

(Continued)

(Continued)

Unit Sequence	Teacher Reflections
Teaching Strategies and Learning Experiences (Seventy Minutes)	

	describe a person, ask them, "What three words would you use to describe yourself?"
	
	If students are struggling with point of view, ask them how the story would be different if it were told from the point of view of Aunt Alexandra or Bob Ewell. You might also give a mini-lesson on point of view for those students.
	
	Add to the list: "information supplied by other characters"
	
	While it is easier to write about a real character, emphasize that students are not to write about another student in the class (or school). If students are not comfortable basing a character on someone real, they can either use a fictional character or create one from their imagination.
	
	As they write, stress the fact that they can begin with the idea of a real person and then exaggerate characteristics or change that character as they write.
	
	Have them reflect on the fact that if the actions do not fit the personality traits, maybe they need to change the traits, not the actions.
	
	Put the list of ways of developing a character on the board:
	
	   – *Description of the character (usually by author unless it represents what others say about character)*
	
	   – *Character's actions, including dialogue*
	
	   – *Character's thoughts*
	
	   – *What others say about the character*
	
	Remind students that they will only be able to reveal the character's thoughts if the character or some omniscient narrator is telling the story.
	
	It is likely that above-grade level students will need more challenging learning activities. These students will be those who grasp the ideas quickly, respond with insightful answers, and move quickly and creatively through the assignment. They can also be the students who obviously enjoy creative writing.

- Begin with the group that was assigned the character of Scout. Ask the group if they used any information other than her description and her actions to make their choices? Scaffold if necessary to add "character's thoughts" to the earlier list.
- If they did not see if before, they should now see that since Scout tells the story, we can't know any character's thoughts except hers.
- Next, look at the group who was assigned the character of Arthur "Boo" Radley. Ask this group if they used any information other than his description and his actions to reach their conclusions? Guide students, if necessary, to see that characters are also defined by what others say about them.
- If that is the case, ask them how do we resolve the dilemma about conflicting information from different characters in the story? Remind them of the rumors of Boo peeking into windows and eating raw squirrels. Whose voice can the reader trust?
- Ask them if Scout's opinion of Boo changes as the book evolves? When does her voice give us an honest assessment of Boo?
- Query students about whose voice Scout represents? Scaffold if necessary to help students see that she is the author's voice. The author's voice is also the one that supplies the first description of Dill.
- Finish other groups and other characters. In each case, invite the class to question or add to a group's analysis of a character once they have finished their presentation.
- When all groups have finished, review the ways a character is developed before moving on to the writing task.
- Now have students return to their own seats. Remind them that Harper Lee based *To Kill a Mockingbird* on her own life experiences and many of the characters are modeled after actual people she knew.

Unit Sequence	Teacher Reflections
Teaching Strategies and Learning Experiences (Seventy Minutes)	
• Ask them to think of an interesting person they have known and to jot down three adjectives that describe that person. • Now ask them to write down several actions of that person. Remind them that the actions should be consistent with the personality traits they have assigned. • Next, ask them to have the character engage in a conversation that reveals something important about the character. • Now have them to put their thoughts together in a character sketch of two pages. They can add information about the character's thoughts, knowledge about the character supplied by other characters, or a description by the author. Since the sketch is only two pages, it is unlikely that all of these techniques will be used (or should be used), but the sketch should develop the character using at least one of these methods in addition to the character's actions and conversation. • Differentiation—One of the interesting actions of Arthur Radley was his putting surprises as well as some of his treasures in the tree hollow for Scout and Jem. As part of your character sketch, reveal a collection of a few treasures that your character would keep. • Review the grading rubric with students so that they understand what is expected of them and how they will be graded. • Remind students to carefully proofread their character sketch before submission.	
Closure (Ten Minutes)	
• Invite students to explain one technique for developing a realistic character. • Ask students to name their favorite character in *To Kill a Mockingbird* and explain what makes the character seem real. • Have a student explain why the first person point of view is effective in *To Kill a Mockingbird*.	*Invite various students to answer this question so that you can revisit the different techniques.* *Give students a chance to ask any questions for clarification they need to complete the assignment.*

CHARACTER SETCH RUBRIC

Criteria	1	2	3	4	Your Score
Content Character engages in a conversation that reveals something important about him or her.	There is no attempt at a dialogue or conversation by character, or if there is, it does not reveal anything significant about the character.	Some effective dialogue or conversation is used, but it does not reveal much about character's personality.	Dialogue or conversation reveals some personality traits of character.	Dialogue or conversation insightfully reveals important personality traits of character.	1 2 3 4
Content Character's actions show something significant about his or her personality.	Sketch fails to use any actions to reveal character's personality or actions are used ineffectively.	Some attempt to depict actions that reveal character's personality.	There is a good attempt at revealing personality traits by character's actions.	Excellent use of actions by character in revealing important personality traits.	1 2 3 4
Content Character's personality is further developed by one or more of the following: character's thoughts, character's description by the author, or information about the character supplied by another character (s).	No visible attempt is made to further develop character sketch by using the character's thoughts, description, or information about the character supplied by another character.	There is an attempt to add to character description by using character's thoughts, description, or information about the character from another character, but it is not consistent or it adds little.	Use of thoughts, description, or information from another character adds to character sketch.	Character's personality is given clarity and further dimension by use of thoughts, description, or information from another character.	1 2 3 4
Length Character sketch is two cohesive pages.	Paper is not the appropriate length, and the different sections do not work together to present a unified sketch.	Paper is either too long or two short, or it lacks cohesion.	Paper is the appropriate length, and the different techniques work together to give one overall sketch of a character.	Paper is the appropriate length, and it presents an insightful and unified character sketch.	1 2 3 4
Differentiation Character is further developed by revealing his or her collection of treasured items.	There is no attempt to integrate the collection of treasures, or it is not mentioned at all.	The collection of treasures is not smoothly combined with the rest of the character sketch.	The collection of treasures reveals a personality consistent with the one already developed.	Another facet of the character's personality is revealed by his or her collection of treasures.	1 2 3 4

Lessons 3.6 and 3.7: Prejudice, Conflict, and Theme (Ninety Minutes)

Discipline-Specific Concepts

C7: Prejudice
C14: Internal Conflict
C15: External Conflict
C16: Resolution
C17: Universal Theme

Principles

P6: Prejudice can exist on many levels.
P8: Universal themes transcend a particular story and teach us about life.
P9: Students employ a wide range of strategies as they write and use different writing elements.

Skills

S4: Judge the major characters in a work of fiction as being prejudiced or fair-minded.
S5: Distinguish a conflict and classify it as internal or external.
S6: Analyze the message an author intended from a particular conflict.
S7: Recognize and categorize theme as to its universality.
S8: Apply the rules of standard English, using correct grammar, spelling, and punctuation.
S14: Individualize the concept of prejudice by giving an example from one's personal world.

Standards

SD1: Students apply a wide range of strategies to comprehend, interpret, evaluate, and appreciate texts. They draw on their prior experience, their interactions with other readers and writers, their knowledge of word meaning and of other texts, their word identification strategies, and their understanding of textual features.
SD2: Students employ a wide range of strategies as they write and use different writing process elements appropriately for a variety of purposes.
SD3: Students use spoken, written, and visual language to accomplish their own purposes (e.g., for learning, enjoyment, persuasion, and the exchange of information).
SD4: Students apply knowledge of language structure, language conventions, media techniques, figurative language, and genre to create, critique, and discuss print and nonprint texts.

Guiding Questions

- What is prejudice and what effect does it have on people?
- What effect has prejudice had in my world?
- What makes a theme universal?

Unit Sequence	Teacher Reflections
Introduction (Ten Minutes)	
• Begin by collecting the character sketches. • Tell students that today we will be doing another writing task and it will implement the skills that they have developed from the two previous writing assignments. • Remind students that they created a realistic setting with sensory words, figurative language, as well as specific words that created an atmosphere or mood for that setting. In addition, in the last lesson they crafted a character, using dialogue and action to make that character realistic. • Ask students if a particular setting or environment would be more likely to encourage some type of prejudice. • Going further, ask students if the setting and mood present in *To Kill a Mockingbird* encouraged some types of prejudice? • Now query students about the types of characters in *To Kill a Mockingbird* who held one or more types of prejudice? Were there certain characteristics common to people that held prejudice?	*The introduction should be done as a whole class. This lesson is the one that will take the writing skills that students developed in earlier lessons. They will use the skills to enhance a new writing task that will focus on a personal incident of prejudice that created a conflict and an understanding of life that resulted from that conflict.*
Teaching Strategies and Learning Experiences (Seventy Minutes)	
• Start by stating that we all use the word *prejudice*, but what exactly does it mean? Ask students to define the word. • After different students define the word, read the dictionary definition at the right. • Invite students to give examples of prejudice in the history of the United States. • Which of these examples is present in *To Kill a Mockingbird*? • Tell students that we will be looking at the kinds of prejudice in the book, as well as the kinds of prejudice that exist in our own community. Start the lesson by reviewing the different types of prejudice that are found in *To Kill a Mockingbird*. • Place students in groups of three. • Give each group a copy of handout 3.6/3.7A and assign them two characters from the novel to assess in terms of prejudice. In each case, the group must decide if the person holds some type of prejudice and/or is a victim of prejudice, and then describe in writing how their character dealt with the prejudice.	*Keep the class together for the beginning part of the lesson, so that all students are focused on understanding the task before they break into groups.* **Prejudice (noun)** 1. an unfavorable opinion or feeling formed beforehand or without knowledge, thought, or reason. 2. any preconceived opinion or feeling, either favorable or unfavorable 3. unreasonable feelings, opinions, or attitudes, esp. of a hostile nature, regarding a racial, religious, or national group 4. such attitudes considered collectively (Dictionary.com) *Write the different types on the board. Make sure that racial, religious, gender, class, and age prejudice are included. Add any others that are*

Unit Sequence	Teacher Reflections

Teaching Strategies and Learning Experiences (Seventy Minutes)

- Give groups time to discuss their characters, reach conclusions, and find supporting examples.
- Circulate to help those students who need scaffolding.
- After an appropriate amount of time, have groups share their conclusions and examples with the class.
- After groups complete their judgments and examples, give other students a chance to add their opinions. In some cases, you may have to guide the class toward the best judgment.
- Now examine two main characters who were not on the worksheet: Tom Robinson and Arthur Radley. Ask students how prejudice created a conflict for these two men. Ask further if these conflicts were external or internal or both.
- Then tell students to describe how these two men dealt with prejudice.
- Have a volunteer explain how Tom Robinson dealt with prejudice. Ask another to describe how Arthur Radley dealt with the prejudice in his life.
- What themes or messages do each of these conflicts and their resolutions reveal?
- Discuss these conflicts and resulting themes thoroughly and write the characters, conflicts, resolutions, and themes on the board as models.
- Ask students what makes a theme universal.
- Can the themes from *To Kill a Mockingbird* be applied to other situations and other people?
- Have students return to their regular seats and get out their journals. Ask them to think of an incident of prejudice in their lives that that has created a conflict for them and describe it in a couple of sentences. This conflict could be external, internal, or both.
- Explain further that this incident of prejudice could be something that happened to them personally or to someone in their world, their family, or friends.

pertinent to the book that students may suggest.

Be on the lookout for students who seem confused or who lack focus. Place these students in groups with at least one other stronger student.

Groups work well with this activity, as they quicken the pace as well as give support to each other.

As characters are discussed, add their names to the headings of different types of prejudice on the board (racial, religious, gender, class, and age)

Review internal and external conflict and give an example of each.

- *Internal*
  - o *Character versus self*
- *External*
  - o *Character versus character*
  - o *Character versus society*
  - o *Character versus nature*

You might want to outline these characters and their conflicts on the board as examples.

Tom Robinson has internal and external conflicts. He has an internal conflict (character versus self) with Mayella, as he feels sorry for her but at the same time he does not want to get involved with her sexually. His external conflict (character versus character) is with her father, Bob Ewell, who falsely accuses him of raping and beating his daughter. This external conflict becomes one of character versus society when Tom is arrested and then found guilty, despite the overwhelming evidence in his favor. He becomes disheartened following the unjust verdict and does not believe he will ever be vindicated. He tries to escape and is shot and dies (character versus society). Themes that can be drawn from Tom's conflicts are: social prejudice, end of innocence, and responsibility for one's fellow person. (The class may come up with slightly different themes, as well as additional ones. Use the ones that they discover, as long as they have validity. Resist just telling them the themes.)

(Continued)

(Continued)

Unit Sequence	Teacher Reflections
Teaching Strategies and Learning Experiences (Seventy Minutes)	
• Now, tell them to explain in a couple of sentences what kind of conflict was involved and how it was resolved. If it has not been resolved, tell them to clarify it by explaining that it is an ongoing conflict. • Give students the opportunity to exchange journals with a partner if they wish. Also give them the alternative of having you read over what they have written. • After reading over the description of the incident, the kind of conflict it created, and how the conflict was resolved, tell students to decide on a message or theme that can be drawn from it. Write this theme in a sentence or two. Again, if students wish, they can consult a partner for a second opinion. • Now instruct students to turn their sentences into a narrative by adding details and descriptions for both the setting and the people involved. Remind them that a particular setting and mood can contribute to a conflict. Tell them to use the descriptive skills they used in their setting/mood paper. • Remind them that for their incident to be powerful, the characters involved must be believable. Invite a student to explain what details will make the characters seem realistic in the story. • Give them this outline to follow: First, explain the incident, the people involved, and the setting in a well-developed paragraph. Transition to the second paragraph and define the type of conflict(s) (external, internal, or both), again adding details where appropriate. In the third paragraph, describe how the conflict was resolved (or that it is ongoing), again adding descriptive details for both the setting and the characters. Finally, in the fourth and final paragraph, reveal a message(s) or theme that could be drawn from the incident. Justify this theme as being universal. If you can't extract a universal theme from the situation, then explain the message as being specific to a particular situation. • Review the grading rubric so students fully understand how they will be graded and what is expected of them.	*Arthur Radley has internal and external conflicts as a result of parental punishments that left him isolated and friendless. He originally had an external conflict (character versus society) when he and some friends are charged with disorderly conduct, disturbing the peace, and assault and battery. Arthur is released into the care of his father who punishes him more than the town ever would (character versus character). Fifteen years later, he has become a recluse, lonely and friendless, and undoubtedly he has internal conflicts (character versus self) caused by low esteem. He's been neglected and treated as someone with no worth. He resolves his conflict enough to be able to look out for Jem and Scout, and in a move that must have taken tremendous courage, he kills Bob Ewell (character versus character) when Ewell attacks Jem and Scout. After the rescue, he again seeks refuge in his house, unable to be a hero and reenter society. Themes that can be drawn from his conflicts are: social prejudice, end of innocence, responsibility for one's fellow person, and goodness that overcomes evil. Again, use the themes that the class comes up with as long as they are appropriate.* *Ask students not to write about a fellow student.* *If students resist revealing an incident that is too personal or painful, tell them to change some of the facts or characters.* *If students have trouble getting started, give examples of prejudice that could result from age or gender. You can also provide an example from your own life.* *Since this incident of prejudice might be quite personal, give students the right to privacy if they so choose.* *The point here is that readers learn something about life along with Scout when they read* To Kill a Mockingbird. *What message about life is revealed in the student's personal account of prejudice?* *Go over any questions that students have about the assignment so that they are clear about the expectations.*

Unit Sequence	Teacher Reflections
Teaching Strategies and Learning Experiences (Seventy Minutes)	
• Remind students to read over their papers to ensure that the paragraphs work together to present a unified account. They should also check for errors in grammar, spelling, and punctuation.	*The differentiation activities are for students who are interested in creative writing, students who work well independently, and those who need more challenge.* *Stephen King has written a book,* On Writing: A Memoir of the Craft, *that interested students might find helpful for this assignment.*

(Continued)

(Continued)

Unit Sequence	Teacher Reflections
Teaching Strategies and Learning Experiences (Seventy Minutes)	
• Differentiation—Write a chapter that follows the end of the story in which you tell what happens to Scout, Jem, Atticus, and Boo Radley. • Differentiation—Invite a local writer to visit the class and talk to students about his or her work. Give students the chance to interview the writer. • Differentiation/Identity—Harper Lee published the Pulitzer Prize–winning novel *To Kill a Mockingbird* in 1960. Research her life or the life of another writer you admire. Look especially at their educational backgrounds and their life styles before they became established writers. Often writers have supported themselves with other jobs while getting established in writing. How did they approach their craft before they were successful? As an established writer, how do they keep creative ideas flowing? Working independently, how do they keep motivated to meet deadlines? Then ask yourself if these insights and answers are compatible with your way of approaching life and work? Write a personal essay about making your dream of becoming a published writer a reality, citing ideas and insights from at least one writer you admire.	
Closure (Ten Minutes)	
• Ask students what the effect of prejudice had on the people of Maycomb? Were there any changes after Tom Robinson and Bob Ewell were killed? • If a similar trial were held today, what do you think would be the outcome? • What changes have occurred in prejudice in our world today? • Explain how one of the themes from *To Kill a Mockingbird* is universal and still applies to our lives today. • Ask students how the examples from *To Kill a Mockingbird* were good models for the writing tasks.	*As you pose these questions, encourage students to share honestly their thoughts. Their feedback will be another means of assessing how much they learned in the unit. If they don't express their thoughts specifically, you can coach them about some of the main principles in the unit.* *Using a literary model is a good way to learn techniques for original writing.* *Writing strategies for one task can be used for another writing task.* *Examining the setting, the characters, the conflicts, and the themes in detail gave an insight into how all of those components work together to create a meaningful story.*

HANDOUT 3.6/3.7A

Analysis of Prejudice in To Kill a Mockingbird

Many types of prejudice exist in the novel *To Kill a Mockingbird.* On a separate piece of paper, describe each character you have been assigned as prejudiced or fair-minded, and then explain how the character dealt with the prejudice. If you denote the character as prejudiced, specify what kind(s) of prejudice the person holds, using an example from the book. In some cases, a person may hold prejudice toward a particular group or person as well as also being a victim of prejudice from others. If this is the case, cite an example of the prejudice toward the person as well.

1. Mrs. Dubose

   Nathan Radley

2. Miss Maudie Atkinson

   Mr. Cunningham

3. Miss Stephanie Crawford

   Calpurnia

4. Atticus Finch

   Mr. Gilmer

5. Mayella Ewell

   Aunt Alexandra

6. Rev. Sykes

   Scout

7. Arthur "Boo" Radley

   Mr. Underwood

8. Cecil Jacobs

   Dill

9. Heck Tate

   Cousin Francis

10. Dolphus Raymond

    Jem

RUBRIC FOR INCIDENT OF PREJUDICE PAPER

Criteria	1	2	3	4	Your Score
Content Incident of prejudice is described fully, with specific details of the setting and the characters.	The incident of prejudice has little description; it is confusing and lacking in detail.	The incident of prejudice is described, but it lacks specific details for the setting and the characters.	The incident of prejudice is fully described. Description of the setting and the characters is clear.	The incident of prejudice is fully, clearly, and vividly described. The setting has a mood that is appropriate to the incident, and the characters involved are realistic.	1 2 3 4
Content Type of conflict is described well.	The type of conflict is not described with any clarity, or it is not described at all.	There is some attempt at an explanation of the type of conflict.	Explanation of the type of conflict is good.	Insight in the explanation of the type of conflict is excellent.	1 2 3 4
Content Conflict's resolution is fully explained, or the fact that it is ongoing is clarified.	Little or no explanation about the conflict's resolution, or the fact that it is ongoing, is made.	There is an attempt to explain the conflict's resolution or the fact that it is ongoing, but it is confusing.	Conflict's resolution, or the fact that it is ongoing, is explained.	Conflict's resolution, or the fact that it is ongoing, is fully and insightfully explained.	1 2 3 4
Content Universal message or theme is applied to the situation.	No theme or an incorrect theme is drawn from the incident of prejudice.	A theme is suggested from the incident of prejudice, but it is limited and weak.	A suitable universal theme is drawn from the incident of prejudice.	A most insightful and fitting universal theme is drawn from the incident of prejudice.	1 2 3 4
Length Account of an incident of prejudice is four well-developed and unified paragraphs.	Paper is not the appropriate length and lacks unity.	Paper is either too long or two short and generally lacks unity.	Paper is the appropriate length and unified to present an account of an incident of prejudice.	Paper is the appropriate length, four well-developed paragraphs that present an insightful, unified account of an incident of prejudice.	1 2 3 4
Writing Skills Paper reflects proficient organization and proper mechanics, usage, and spelling.	Writing is disordered. Mechanical, grammar, and spelling errors are numerous.	Writing is adequate in organization, mechanics, usage, and spelling, but errors are evident.	Writing is organized and there are few errors in mechanics, usage, and spelling.	Writing has excellent organization and is almost free of mechanical, usage, or spelling errors.	1 2 3 4

134

Lesson 3.8: Postassessment (Forty-Five Minutes)

Discipline-Specific Concepts

C1: Setting
C2: Mood
C3: Tone
C4: Characterization
C5: Point of View
C6: Conflict
C7: Prejudice
C8: Theme

Principles

P2: Setting can be important in creating the mood and tone of a story.
P3: Different points of view provide more or less knowledge of characters' thoughts.
P4: Creating a realistic character is achieved by using a variety of methods, including dialogue and description.
P6: Prejudice can exist on many levels.
P7: An understanding of life can evolve from a conflict.
P8: Universal themes transcend a particular story and teach us about life.
P9: Students employ a wide range of strategies as they write and use different writing elements.

Skills

S2: Understand and evaluate mood.
S3: Interpret personality traits in a fictional character.
S4: Judge the major characters in a work of fiction as being prejudiced or fair-minded.
S5: Distinguish a conflict and classify it as internal or external.
S6: Analyze the message an author intended from a particular conflict.
S7: Recognize and categorize a theme as to its universality.
S8: Apply the rules of standard English, using correct grammar, spelling, and punctuation when writing.

Standards

SD1: Students apply a wide range of strategies to comprehend, interpret, evaluate, and appreciate texts. They draw on their prior experience, their interactions with other readers and writers, their knowledge of word meaning and of other texts, their word identification strategies, and their understanding of textual features.
SD2: Students employ a wide range of strategies as they write and use different writing process elements appropriately for a variety of purposes.
SD3: Students use spoken, written, and visual language to accomplish their own purposes (e.g., for learning, enjoyment, persuasion, and the exchange of information).

Guiding Questions

- How does an author synthesize the different elements in a story, such as setting, mood, character, and conflict, to create a universal theme?
- How is prejudice an important part of the story?
- How does the story enhance your understanding of life?

Unit Sequence	Teacher Reflections
Introduction (One Minute)	
• Begin by telling students that they will read a short story and then answer some questions about the story. • Tell them to answer each question in a well-developed paragraph or two and to do their very best work. • Explain to them that this is a postassessment to measure what they have learned in the unit. It is similar to the preassessment that they took at the beginning of the unit, but they should be more comfortable with this test.	*The postassessment tests how well students can read a short story and react to it by understanding the different elements, such as setting, mood, and characterization. Going further, it also tests whether students can perceive how these different story elements work together to create a theme or universal message. This postassessment, when compared to the preassessment that was given at the beginning of the unit, should give the teacher a good idea of how much students learned during the unit.*
Teaching Strategies and Learning Experiences (Forty-Three Minutes)	
• Give each student a copy of the short story, "The Scarlet Ibis," by James Hurst and a copy of the questions for the postassessment. • Distribute a couple of sheets of lined paper on which students can write their answers. • Circulate occasionally while students work to answer any questions about procedures, but not the content of the postassessment. Encourage them to do their best.	*The short story, "The Scarlet Ibis," used for the postassessment is a longer and more challenging story than the preassessment story, "All Summer in a Day." "The Scarlet Ibis," by James Hurst can be found in many short story collections, including Characters in Conflict by Evler Mescal (1996). It can also be found online at http://www.dixon.troyhigh.com/ibis.pdf.* *The questions for the postassessment and a scoring rubric are at the end of this lesson.*
Closure (One Minute)	

• Collect the stories and students papers.	*I used the postassessment results to measure the learning that took place in the unit.*
	    All students should reflect a greater understanding of how the different parts of a story work together to form a powerful whole in quality literature.
	    All students should show some improvement in writing. That improvement should be noticeable in a student's ability to get started with a writing task, add details that are meaningful, and incorporate ideas and skills from earlier lessons.
	    My findings were as follows:
	    Above-grade level students relished the opportunity for creative writing that the unit gave them. Many chose to do the differentiation activities and in some cases, they completed writing pieces that went beyond the bounds of the assignment. The unit seemed to give them a greater appreciation for the skills of professional writers.
	    On-grade level students did well with the writing tasks and seemed especially responsive to the step-by-step approach that made the tasks more accessible. The rubrics gave structure and specificity to the expectations for the writing tasks, and as a result their writing showed improvement in organization as well as detail and creativity. While most of these students were familiar with the concept of theme, they showed a greater understanding of it after the unit's completion.
	    Below-grade level students showed a marked improvement in writing skills. Many were students who had always had trouble getting started with a writing assignment. By taking the writing tasks one step at a time, they were much more receptive and successful in completing them. They also showed an improvement in adding appropriate details. Many of these students were confused by the concept of theme at the start of the unit, but by responding to particular conflicts and their resulting themes in the model, To Kill a Mockingbird and deciding on a theme in their own prejudice writing piece, they gained a greater understanding.

Postassessment Questions for "The Scarlet Ibis"

Directions: After reading "The Scarlet Ibis," answer each the following questions in a couple of well-developed paragraphs on the lined paper that has been provided to you.

1. What is the setting and why is it important in the story? Tell how it helps establish the tone and mood.

2. What is the point of view in the story and how does it lend itself to the development of the theme?

3. How is Doodle's character developed? How is his older brother developed?

4. What is the main conflict and how does it involve a form of prejudice?

5. Explain fully the theme or message the story develops?

6. How does the story enhance your understanding of life?

Postassessment Rubric: Unit 3

Criteria	1	2	3	4	Your Score
Content Importance of setting, mood and their connection	Importance of setting is not noted and little or no mention made of mood.	Importance of setting is mentioned, but no real connection is made with setting and mood.	Good perception of importance of setting is evident and some connection between it and mood.	Excellent awareness of the importance of setting is present as well as how setting and mood can work together.	1 2 3 4
Content Point of view and its role in development of theme	Point of view is not mentioned or is identified incorrectly. The theme is not mentioned.	Some awareness of point of view but no connection made to theme.	Good perception of point of view and some mention of its role in theme development are seen.	Insightful analysis of point of view is seen as well as its role in theme development.	1 2 3 4
Content Characterization—means of development	Means of character development is not mentioned or is not correct.	There are some points about character development but it is limited.	There is good awareness of the author's character development.	Excellent perception of means of character development is evident.	1 2 3 4
Content Main conflict and how it involves prejudice	The main conflict is not identified or is incorrect. The prejudice involved is not mentioned.	The main conflict is identified but only a minor reference is made to the prejudice or it is incorrect.	There is an accurate awareness of the main conflict and the prejudice involved.	There is an excellent perception of the main conflict and the prejudice it involves.	1 2 3 4
Content Theme or universal truth that story develops	The theme is not mentioned or is incorrect. There is no connection to student's life.	There is mention of the theme but it is not correct or is not explained, and there is no connection to student's life.	There is some good perception of the theme, but it is not fully explained. There is some connection to the student's life.	The theme is insightfully perceived, fully explained, and connected to the student's life.	1 2 3 4
Writing Skills Proficient organization, proper mechanics, usage, and spelling	Writing is disordered. There are numerous mechanical, grammar, and spelling errors.	Writing is adequate in organization, mechanics, usage, and spelling but there are errors evident.	Writing is organized and there are few errors in mechanics, usage, and spelling.	Writing has excellent organization and is free of almost any mechanical, usage, or spelling errors.	1 2 3 4

REFERENCES

King, S. (2002). *On writing: A memoir of the craft.* New York: Pocket Books.

Lee, H. (1982). *To kill a mockingbird.* New York: Warner Books.

Mescal, E. (Ed.). (1996). *Characters in conflict.* New York: Harcourt School.

Prejudice. (n.d.) Dictionary.com Unabridged (v. 1.1). Retrieved March 03, 2008, from http://dictionary.reference.com/browse/prejudice

Wolfe, T. (1980). Circus at dawn. In K. Silverman (Eds.), *Adventures in American literature* (p. 779). New York: Harcourt Brace Jovanovich.

4

You Be the Critic

Understanding, Using, and Writing Literary Criticism

Grades 11–12

Judy Walsh

INTRODUCTION TO THE UNIT

Background Information

The unit on literary criticism is an important one for high school students. It pulls together the genres of fiction, nonfiction, and media. It fits the Core Parallel as it is a course that provides access for all students, not just advanced students, to understand, use, and write literary criticism. Too many students are unfamiliar with literary criticism or are awed by a lofty sounding critical analysis. Since many students do not fully understand literary criticism, they are not sure how to use it, and certainly do not think that they could write it. The unit's purpose is to demystify literary criticism/literary analysis with lessons that build on each other as students study the components of literary analysis of fiction and nonfiction, their techniques, and their purposes. Each skill, once mastered, builds confidence and ability for the next level of student understanding.

The unit begins by honing skills that students already possess: analyzing characters, setting, and theme in a fictional passage. Building on these skills, students will then learn how to detect tone and style. By learning to closely examine a fictional passage for all of these qualities, they will more accurately interpret the author's intent, as well as how the author uses his or her literary tools to lead the reader to his or her purpose. Next, students will use these same analytical skills to evaluate nonfiction. They will study the genre of a speech and learn about rhetorical devices, what they are, and why they are important persuasive tools. Students will also understand how a writer's viewpoint affects purpose. They will see that a particular topic can be seen in vastly different ways depending on the writer's viewpoint. Students will closely examine persuasive essays and have the opportunity to write one about an issue important to them (Parallel of Identity). The Identity Parallel is important here, as students not only get the opportunity to explore the career of journalism, but they will look inward at their own values when they choose an issue of importance to them and then write a persuasive essay from their personal viewpoint. In the culminating project, students will learn to use literary criticism to support a literary analysis of a novel. They will explore various technological and print sources for pertinent literary criticism, as well as determine how to authenticate these sources for their validity.

Although the unit could be taught in three to four weeks as a stand-alone, it is actually most effective if it is taught in conjunction with a course in American literature, English literature, or world literature. In this context, students use the skills they are developing in the literary criticism unit to examine the literature they are studying. The merger of the literary criticism course with a course in literature also prepares students to take state assessments, more-rigorous college courses, as well as the AP English exams.

The unit covers several national standards as it takes students from reading movie and book reviews to writing a literary analysis. As students analyze different pieces of fiction and nonfiction, do some writing to effect a tone and style, and then write an extended literary analysis, national standards are addressed. Students will read a wide range of selections that have been chosen for the unit with care so that they represent fiction, nonfiction, classic, and contemporary works. Students will apply their knowledge of language structure, figurative language, and genre to create, critique, and discuss these texts. They will also use a variety of informational sources to communicate their ideas and purposes to an audience. Each lesson specifically lists the national standards that are covered in the lesson.

While the unit should be appropriate for advanced and above-average students, there are suggestions in the reflections column for more accessible text selections and activities that should accommodate the average students as well as those who may be reading below grade level.

It is a good idea to begin this unit the first week of school so that students can begin using the analytical skills and start to think of them as routine for discussing a piece of fiction or nonfiction. As our school had mandatory summer reading, I had several novels I could use immediately for examples in the beginning lessons. That background was helpful, as it takes a couple of weeks before students have completed a new novel, and for the first four lessons you will need a work of fiction that all students have read. If you don't have a common summer reading book, perhaps you can use excerpts from a novel that all students read last year.

The resources I gathered as I prepared to teach the course were varied: some were current editorials, book reviews, and film reviews. These can be found in a quality newspaper or magazine (e.g., *The New York Times*, *Newsweek*, *Time*). I also found a number of pieces online, and in pertinent lessons I have given the Web site addresses. I also had on hand the summer reading novels of my students and other pieces of fiction and nonfiction that I felt had good examples for some of the specific lessons. Certainly other works can be substituted.

CONTENT FRAMEWORK

Organizing Concepts

Macroconcepts	Discipline-Specific Concepts		Principles
M1: Point of View / Perspective	C1: Book Review	C18: Abstract	P1: Literary criticism is a written interpretation, analysis, and judgment of a work of fiction or nonfiction.
	C2: Film Review		P2: Analyzing the content of a passage of prose imparts information about one or more of the following: characterization, conflict, setting, and theme.
	C3: Point of View/Viewpoint	C19: Concrete	P3: Close scrutiny of a passage of prose reveals hints of the author's purpose in the work as a whole.
	C4: Literary Criticism	C20: Syntax	P4: Understanding an author's tone and use of irony reveals much of his or her true purpose and meaning in a given work.
	C5: Literary Analysis	C21: Paradox	P5: An author's style provides a key to interpreting and evaluating a given work.
	C6: Characterization	C22: Rhetoric	P6: Authors use a variety of tools to effect a purpose.
	C7: Setting (Artificial and Natural)	C23: Rhetorical Devices	P7: By recognizing and understanding literary devices, we can enhance our understanding of fiction and nonfiction.
	C8: Theme	C24: Rhetorical Questions	P8: Readers and writers are influenced by personal, political, historical, social, racial, sexual, and religious circumstances.
	C9: Symbol	C25: Allusion	P9: We can understand a work more fully by exploring multiple responses to it.
	C10: Tone	C26: Repetition	P10: Sources of literary criticism need to be evaluated to authenticate their validity.
	C11: Verbal Irony	C27: Parallel Structure	
	C12: Situational Irony	C28: Metaphor	
	C13: Dramatic Irony	C29: Hyperbole	
	C14: Style	C30: Charged Words	
	C15: Diction	C31: Persuasive Essay	
	C16: Connotation	C32: Editorial	
	C17: Denotation	C33: Thesis/ Argument	

National Standards

SD1: Students read a wide range of print and nonprint texts to build an understanding of texts, of themselves, and of the cultures of the United States and the world; to acquire new information; to respond to the needs and demands of society, and the workplace; and for personal fulfillment. Among these texts are fiction and nonfiction, classic and contemporary works.

SD2: Students employ a wide range of strategies as they write and use different writing process elements appropriately to communicate with different audiences for a variety of purposes.

SD3: Students apply knowledge of language structure, language conventions, media techniques, figurative language, and genre to create, critique, and discuss print and nonprint texts.

SD4: Students conduct research on issues and interests by generating ideas and questions, and by posing problems. They gather, evaluate, and synthesize data from a variety of sources (e.g., print and nonprint texts, artifacts, people) to communicate their discoveries in ways that suit their purpose and audience.

Skills

S1: Determine, use, and analyze text structures.
S2: Draw conclusions.
S3: Compare and contrast.
S4: Articulate tone.
S5: Appraise style.
S6: Interpret author's purpose.
S7: Make and justify inferences from explicit or implicit information.
S8: Decide and justify underlying themes.
S9: Make, support, and defend judgments.
S10: Evaluate sources to authenticate validity.
S11: Write with appropriate strategies to suit a purpose.
S12: Research a variety of technological and information sources.
S13: Gather appropriate critical sources for a specific purpose.
S14: Determine point of view.

ASSESSMENTS

This unit contains a large number of formal and informal assessments. All of the assessments can be used as formative or diagnostic assessments, including the final summative assessment included with Lessons 4.14 and 4.15. Reflection on a summative assessment can be used to modify teaching when the unit or lessons are taught again.

Preassessment

The preassessment invites students to analyze a passage from *The Scarlet Letter*. It has been purposefully designed to assess how well students can analyze and respond—in writing—to an author's use of literary elements: the placement of passages by an author, tone, diction, and point of view. A scoring rubric is provided. Of course, the written aspect of this preassessment will give the teacher a deeper understanding of students' writing skills. For students who struggle with reading and writing, an abbreviated version of the preassessment may be given.

Formative Assessments

Formative assessments abound in this lesson for high school juniors and seniors. Lessons 4.3, 4.4, and 4.5 culminate in a group project on characterization. Lesson 4.10 invites students to develop a short description for a particular scene. Lessons 4.12 and 4.13 provide an opportunity for students to compose a persuasive piece that is assessed on the following traits: content, structure, and expression. A culminating project is contained in Lesson 4.15 and requires students to complete a thoughtful literary analysis. It is assessed on the following traits: the thesis; content; structure, coherence and continuity; style; and format and appearance. All of these formative assessments contain a trait rubric that teachers can use to assess students' strengths and weaknesses and modify instruction accordingly.

Many other opportunities for "student watching" are noted and embedded throughout all the lessons. Reflection notes, based on these opportunities for student watching, provide teachers with suggestions for modifying instruction based on what was observed.

Postassessment

The postassessment invites students to consider a different passage from *The Scarlet Letter*. Students respond to the same questions as were provided in the preassessment. The rubric, identical to the one used in the preassessment, will help teachers gauge the achievement gains of students.

UNIT SEQUENCE, DESCRIPTION, AND TEACHER REFLECTIONS

Preassessment—Administer Before Lesson 4.1

(Please note that although the unit appears to begin with "Lesson 4.1: Introduction to Literary Criticism," this preassessment is actually the first lesson.) Tell students to do their best even if they may not know some or many of the answers. This assessment, along with the postassessment administered after the unit concludes, will be one yardstick by which you measure their learning in the unit. The preassessment also gives the teacher an idea of how well students can organize their thoughts and write a coherent essay.

Carefully read the following passage from *The Scarlet Letter*. Then in a well-constructed essay, analyze the paragraph and explain how the author, Nathaniel Hawthorne, uses each of the elements below to develop his purpose.

1. The placement of the passage in the novel and its implications

2. The function of the passage in the development of action, character, setting, or a theme in the novel

3. The author's tone

4. The author's style

5. The author's diction

6. The author's viewpoint

7. The author's use of any other rhetorical devices to convey his purpose and viewpoint

> The door of the jail being flung open from within, there appeared in the first place, like a black shadow emerging into sunshine, the grim and grisly presence of the town-beadle, with a sword by his side, and his staff of office in his hand. This personage prefigured and represented in his aspect the whole dismal severity of the Puritanic code of law, which it was his business to administer in its final and closest application to the offender. Stretching forth the official staff in his left hand, he laid his right upon the shoulder of a young woman, whom he thus drew forward; until, on the threshold of the prison-door, she repelled him, by an action marked with natural dignity and force of character, and stepped into the open air, as if by her own of free will. She bore in her arms, a child, a baby of some three months old, who winked and turned aside its little face from the too vivid light of day, because its existence heretofore, had brought it acquainted only with the gray twilight of a dungeon, or other darksome apartment of the prison. (Hawthorne, 2003, p. 45)

Description of Preassessment

The preassessment gives the teacher a good idea of how well students can assess a fictional passage as to the writer's viewpoint and purpose, and by what techniques this purpose and viewpoint can be discerned. The preassessment also gives the teacher an impression of how well students can organize their thoughts and write an organized essay.

Macroconcept

M1: Point of View/Perspective

Discipline-Specific Concepts

C3: Point of View/Viewpoint
C6: Characterization
C8: Theme
C10: Tone
C14: Style
C15: Diction
C23: Rhetorical Devices

Students will probably be confused by the concept of placement of passage and its implications in the preassessment. Tell them not to worry about it; they will learn what it means and its importance in the lessons to come. (See Lesson 4.2 for an explanation of placement of passage.)

Principles

P1: Literary criticism is a written interpretation, analysis, and judgment of a work of fiction or nonfiction.

P2: Analyzing the content of a passage of prose imparts information about one or more of the following: characterization, conflict, setting, and theme.

P3: Close scrutiny of a passage of prose reveals hints of the author's purpose in the work as a whole.

P4: Understanding an author's tone and use of irony reveals much of his or her true purpose and meaning in a given work.

P5: An author's style provides a key to interpreting and evaluating a given work.

P6: Authors use a variety of tools to effect a purpose.

P7: By recognizing and understanding literary devices, we can enhance our understanding of fiction and nonfiction.

P8: Readers and authors are influenced by personal, political, historical, social, sexual, cultural, and religious circumstances.

Skills

S1: Determine, use, and analyze text structures.

S2: Draw conclusions.

S4: Articulate tone.

S5: Appraise style.

S6: Interpret author's purpose.

S7: Make and justify inferences from explicit or implicit information.

S8: Decide and justify underlying themes.

S9: Make, support, and defend judgments.

Preassessment Rubric

Criteria	1	2	3	4	Your Score
Content Placement and function of passage	Placement and function of passage are perceived incorrectly or are not mentioned.	Placement and function of passage are mentioned but not fully developed.	Insight as to placement and function of passage is good.	Excellent awareness of placement and function of passage that shows original thinking.	1 2 3 4
Content Elements of tone, diction, and style to convey author's purpose	Not all elements are mentioned in analyzing the passage and/or some are perceived incorrectly.	All required elements are mentioned but their function in the passage as a whole is limited.	All required elements are mentioned as to their function in conveying the author's purpose.	All required elements are insightfully analyzed as to their role in conveying the author's purpose in the passage.	1 2 3 4
Content Author's viewpoint	The author's viewpoint is incorrect or is not mentioned.	Perception of author's viewpoint is correct but limited.	There is good perception of author's viewpoint with support from passage.	There is excellent discernment into author's viewpoint with support from passage.	1 2 3 4
Content Other strategies author uses to convey purpose	No additional strategies are mentioned.	Only one other strategy is mentioned or additional strategies mentioned add little to author's purpose.	Some additional strategies are mentioned that support author's purpose.	Strategies are mentioned that add insight and push boundaries of the assignment	1 2 3 4
Writing Skills	Writing is disordered. Mechanical errors are numerous.	Writing is adequate in organization and mechanics.	Writing is organized and relatively free of mechanical errors.	Writing has excellent organization, is coherent, and is free of mechanical errors.	1 2 3 4

Lesson 4.1: Introduction to Literary Criticism (Forty-Five Minutes)

Discipline-Specific Concepts

C1: Book Review
C2: Film Review
C4: Literary Criticism
C5: Literary Analysis

Principles

P1: Literary criticism is a written interpretation, analysis, and judgment of a work of fiction or nonfiction.
P9: We can understand a work more fully by exploring multiple responses to it.

Skills

S2: Draw conclusions.
S3: Compare and contrast.
S6: Interpret author's purpose.

Standards

SD1: Students apply knowledge of language structure, language conventions, media techniques, figurative language, and genre to create, critique, and discuss print and nonprint texts.

Guiding Questions

- What is literary criticism?
- How can there be so many different interpretations of a particular work?
- How can literary criticism enrich my life?

Unit Sequence	Teacher Reflections
Introduction (Five Minutes)	
Be sure you have administered the preassessment located at the beginning of this unit before starting Lesson 4.1.	
<ul><li>Begin by asking students to name the last movie they saw.</li><li>Next, provide a couple of minutes for students to write down why they chose that particular film.</li><li>Invite them to share their reasons.</li><li>Write down the different responses on the board.</li><li>Include *film review* if that response is not given.</li></ul>	*Most teenagers love movies, and if they realize that reading reviews of films will lead to better choices and fewer disappointments, it will spark their interest. By starting the unit with film reviews, you will build on a topic that they know and enjoy.* *For the film review exercise, choose a current PG or PG-13 film that is of high interest to students. (Many schools have restrictions on R-rated films.) I chose* Harry Potter and the Order of the Phoenix *and could find some interesting different views from* The Christian Science Monitor *(http://www.csmonitor.com/),* The New York Times *(http://moviesnytimes*

Unit Sequence	Teacher Reflections
Introduction (Five Minutes)	
	.com/), and The Catholic Sun *(http://www .catholicsun.org/). Another site (http://www .rottentomatoes.com/) features short excerpts (with the full review available) from differing reviews, so you can quickly pick out some reviews with opposing views. Choose reviews with quality writing, but shorter ones are better for students who may have difficulty with lengthy reviews. Your local newspaper may be a good source for succinct reviews.*
Teaching Strategies and Learning Experiences (Thirty-Five Minutes)	
• Start the lesson by asking students what the word *criticism* means. • Ask a volunteer to look up the word in a dictionary and share it with the class. • Emphasize the fact that the first meaning of the word is judging something as to its merits. Read all of the meanings for the word and be sure to emphasize the third meaning that pertains to literary or artistic criticism. • Write the definitions that pertain to literary criticism on the board. • Tell students to keep the definitions in mind as they think about film reviews and their uses. • Inform students that you will give them two different reviews of the same film and ask them to compare and contrast the two. • Instruct them to read carefully the reviews and then decide as a group on the main intentions of the reviews, as well as their similarities and their differences. (A Venn diagram may help them with the comparing and contrasting.) • Break them into groups of two or three and distribute the reviews. Depending on the length of the reviews, give groups ten to twenty minutes to read and discuss them and decide on the main purposes or intents of the writers. • Bring the groups back together and share the responses as a class. • Jot down the responses on the board.	*Many students think of criticism as a negative judgment, which, of course, is not always the case.* **Criticism (noun)** 1. the act of passing judgment as to the merits of anything 2. the act of passing severe judgment: censure, faultfinding 3. the act or art of analyzing and evaluating or judging the quality of a literary or artistic work, musical performance, art exhibit, dramatic production, etc. 4. a critical comment, article, or essay; critique 5. any of various methods of studying texts or documents for the purpose of dating them or reconstructing them, evaluating their authenticity, analyzing their content or style, etc. (Dictionary.com) *By putting students into groups and using graphic organizers, you encourage them to discover the important comparisons and contrasts between the two reviews and, more importantly, the ways the reviews are alike. In groups, they will gain from the ideas of others.* *Coming together as a class at the end of the group work provides a venue for students to share what they have discovered, as well as gaining ideas from other groups (and the teacher if they forget to mention an important*

(Continued)

(Continued)

Unit Sequence	Teacher Reflections
Teaching Strategies and Learning Experiences (Thirty-Five Minutes)	
• Guide the discussion, if necessary, to include the general functions of a review: informing, aiding in understanding, interpreting, expressing an opinion, and presenting a particular viewpoint. • Following the discussion, inform students that they will repeat the procedure they followed for the film review for a book review. Explain that an in-depth review of a book is often called a *literary analysis.* Tell them that at the end of this unit, they will each write a literary analysis. • Distribute two copies of the book reviews and Venn diagrams and direct students to complete the assignment for tomorrow.	*purpose). Students may find that even if they do not agree with either of the reviews, reading another viewpoint will help to formulate their own viewpoint.* *You can download a Venn diagram at http:// teacher.scholastic.com/.* *After successfully evaluating two film reviews with one or two partners and then sharing findings with the class, students should be prepared to evaluate the book reviews independently.* *Choose a current book that would be appropriate for this age group. I chose* Pretty Birds *by Scott Simon. Interesting opposing views on the book were found at the World Socialist Website (http://www.wsws.org/) and The* Christian Science Monitor *site (http:// www.csmonitor.com/). As with the film reviews, shorter, more accessible reviews may be found in local newspapers.* *An interesting choice might be to do a film review first that is an adaptation of a book and then examine a book review of that text. For example,* The Golden Compass *by Philip Pullman has recently been made into a film.*
Closure (Five Minutes)	
• Ask students the purpose of a film review or a book review, both forms of literary criticism. • Encourage them to share their experiences if they consulted a review before and/or after viewing the last movie they saw. If they did, how did the review(s) change their perception? If they did not read a review, how would consulting one have made a difference? • Have students describe some of the important attributes one must have to write film reviews or book reviews, both forms of literary criticism.	*Asking these questions and encouraging students to share their experiences will reveal students' understanding of the concepts and principles in the lesson.*

Lesson 4.2: Analyzing a Fictional Passage for Content (Forty-Five Minutes)

Discipline-Specific Concepts

C5: Literary Analysis
C6: Characterization
C7: Setting (Artificial and Natural)
C8: Theme

Principles

P2: Analyzing the content of a passage of prose imparts information about one or more of the following: characterization, conflict, setting, and theme.

P3: Close scrutiny of a passage of prose reveals hints about the author's purpose in the work as a whole.

Skills

S1: Determine, use, and analyze text structures.
S2: Draw conclusions.
S6: Interpret author's purpose.

Standards

SD3: Students apply knowledge of language structure, language conventions, media techniques, figurative language, and genre to create, critique, and discuss print and nonprint texts.

Guiding Questions

- How can analyzing an important passage from a novel help you to understand the novel as a whole?
- What fictional elements (e.g., setting, conflict, characterization, theme) shed light on understanding the passage?

Unit Sequence	Teacher Reflections
Introduction (Ten to Twenty Minutes)	
<ul><li>Begin by asking students about the book reviews they read and compared for homework.</li><li>Next have students share the ways in which the two book reviews were similar. Focus on the same elements used for the film reviews: informing, aiding in understanding, interpreting, expressing an opinion, and presenting a particular viewpoint.</li><li>Review with students the term *literary analysis* and then tell them that they have already done literary analysis when they have carefully examined the setting, a character, or a conflict in story. Using these skills, they will carefully examine a particular passage from a novel.</li><li>Explain that literary analysis is also what a critic does when he or she writes a book review or movie review. By being able to analyze an important passage from a book, one can use the tools an author employs in writing literary criticism. By learning the skills yourself, you will better understand literary criticism that you read, be able to use it to support an idea that you have about a book, and be able to write literary criticism yourself.</li></ul>	*If students seem to readily grasp the main purposes of the book reviews, you can cover the homework quickly. However, if students are struggling, take the time to draw a Venn diagram on the board and lead them to the main purposes of the book review.* *I chose a meaningful passage from a summer reading book. If your school does not have mandatory summer reading, choose a book students all read last year or this year.*

(Continued)

Unit Sequence	Teacher Reflections
Teaching Strategies and Learning Experiences (Thirty Minutes)	
• Start the class by handing out a passage from the *Joy Luck Club* (Handout 4.2A). Ask students to read the passage and jot down any insights the excerpt provides regarding characterization, setting, action, and theme. They should also note the placement of the passage in the novel and its implications. • Explain that there are two aspects to analyzing a passage of prose. The first aspect deals with the content of the passage and its relationship to the entire work. The second aspect deals with style and tone. Tell students that today you will deal with just the content of the passage—a close examination of the characters, the setting, the action, and the themes. • Use Socratic questioning and query the students first about the characters and what the scene reveals about them. How is June developed in the scene? What do her words and actions reveal about her and her relationship to her mother? What does the reader learn about June's mother? What was the aunties' relationship with June's mother? Why is this important? • Next ask about the setting. Question students about the differences between a natural setting and an artificial setting. Guide them to the fact that a natural setting is the natural world, nature; an artificial setting deals with the trappings of a particular culture and class. Setting also reveals time—time of year and day, as well as the era. Is the setting in the passage natural or artificial? Since much of the book takes place in China many years ago, what is important about the setting in this passage? What setting will June visit? Why is that significant? What theme can be drawn from the setting? • Though some themes have become apparent in the above questions, ask if other themes are implied by the passage. • Finally, ask students about the placement of this particular passage in the book. Use Socratic questioning to determine the author's purpose in an early passage. Guide them to see that an author is setting up the relationships between characters, the action, and/or the themes in the book. What is Tan setting up in this passage?	*Since students are already familiar with characterization, setting, action, and theme, this passage analysis will build on the skills they already have and will prepare them for the tone and style lessons to come.* *The placement of the passage refers to the fact that often in state assessments or other standardized exams, students will be given a short passage from a novel and asked to analyze it. Naturally the creators of the tests choose a passage of some importance. This passage could be a beginning passage that introduces an important conflict, characters, theme, or all of these. Another favorite choice is an ending passage that ties up conflicts and reinforces a theme. Sometimes a passage is chosen that occurs when a character has a turning point in a particular conflict or a character may have an epiphany. Once students become skilled at analyzing an important fictional passage, they can make an educated guess about the placement of that passage even if they have not read the book.* *Conduct this part of the lesson as a whole class. Some students may not be familiar with analysis of a fictional passage, and your guidance here is crucial.* *Students should note that the aunties are acting as mother figures for June, as her mother has died. June feels overwhelmed and confused by their gift of money for a plane ticket to China and the prospect of meeting two older sisters she never knew. The aunties reveal a love of their native China and its culture. June represents the newer Americanized generation and her words and actions show the age gap and the culture gap.* *The setting in the story is in San Francisco in the late 1980s; it is in sharp contrast to the flashback settings of the four mother figures in the book (1930s China). The dual settings underscore the theme of the two different cultures and time periods, the two worlds of the mothers and daughters. The fact that the aunties wish June to visit China to meet her twin sisters is indicative of the importance of Chinese culture and family, and all that it represents to them.*

Unit Sequence	Teacher Reflections
Teaching Strategies and Learning Experiences (Thirty Minutes)	

• Provide scaffolding for students who need more help.	*Students may suggests themes about mother/ daughter relationships, the Chinese viewpoint versus the American viewpoint, the hope for the future, the search for identity, and the endurance of women. Some insightful students may see others as well.* *In the passage, Tan is setting up the theme of the daughters not knowing their mother's pasts in China, and as a result, not understanding their mothers. The scene paves the way for each mother to tell her story, and in doing so to reveal her true self to her daughter.*
• Have students choose a partner and give them a passage from another book, Handout 4.2B, and ask them to follow the same procedure the class used for the *Joy Luck Club* passage. • Move from pair to pair, offering help to those who need it. ("How have the characters changed? At what section in the book does this scene take place?") • Allow time for students to work on the new passage. Tell them to finish the passage for homework. • Long-term assignment: Assign a book to be read before Lesson 4.13 is taught. The best choice of a book is one with social issues that were prevalent at the time of the book as well as in the present. Choose one that will be appropriate for your students' abilities and interests. • Interim lessons can be scheduled with the long-term book assignment so that students can discuss the book and its issues. They will also have the opportunity to use the critical analytical skills they are learning in this unit with the book. • Differentiation—Ask students to select another passage from *The Joy Luck Club* that they feel would be a key beginning passage in which the author sets the action, themes, and/or character development in motion.	*Having students work with a partner here is a good way for students to share knowledge and guide one another. You can assess their previous learning as well as their understanding of the earlier part of the lesson.* *The class work/homework passage I assigned was from* The Catcher in the Rye*. I chose an ending passage to see if students could come up with the key points in a significant concluding passage. Some suggestions for books are as follows:* Advanced or above-average classes: *The Grapes of Wrath* by John Steinbeck, *The Great Gatsby* by F. Scott Fitzgerald, *A Streetcar Named Desire* by Tennessee Williams Average classes: These classes should also respond well to *A Streetcar Named Desire* by Tennessee Williams, *A Raisin in the Sun* by Lorraine Hansberry, *Monster* by Walter Dean Myers, or *Speak* by Laurie Halse Anderson. *The differentiation activities are suggested for students who need a challenge, students who work well independently, and students who indicate a high interest level in the assignment.*

(Continued)

(Continued)

Unit Sequence	Teacher Reflections
Closure (Five Minutes)	
• Ask students how analyzing a key passage from *The Joy Luck Club* helped them to better understand the novel. • Invite students to share one piece of new information they learned.	*Asking students to share one piece of new information is a good way to assess the learning from today's lesson. Be on the lookout for students who give answers that do not reflect a clear understanding.*

HANDOUT 4.2A

Carefully read the following passage from *The Joy Luck Club*, and then answer the questions that follow on a separate piece of paper.

The aunties are all smiling at me, as though I had been a dying person who has now miraculously recovered. Auntie Ying is handing me another envelope. Inside is a check made out to June Woo for $1,200. I can't believe it.

"My sisters are sending *me* money?" I ask.

"No, no," says Auntie Lin with her mock exasperated voice. "Every year we save our mah jong winnings for big banquet at fancy restaurant. Most your mother win, so most is her money. We add just a little, so you can go Hong Kong, take a train to Shanghai, see your sisters. Besides, we all getting too rich, too fat," she pats her stomach for proof.

"See my sisters," I say numbly. I am awed by this prospect, trying to imagine what I would see. And I am embarrassed by the end-of-the-year banquet lie my aunties have told to mask their generosity. I am crying now, sobbing and laughing at the same time, seeing but not understanding this loyalty to my mother.

"You must see your sisters and tell them about your mother's death," says Auntie Ying. "But most important, you must tell them about her life. The mother they did not know, they must now know."

"See my sisters, tell them about my mother, "I say nodding. "What will I say? What can I tell them about my mother? I don't know anything. She was my mother." (Tan, 1989, pp. 39–40)

1. What is the function of the passage in the development of the characters?

2. What type of setting is used? What does it reveal?

3. What does the passage reveal about the action of the story?

4. What themes are set up or revealed in the passage?

5. What is the placement of the passage in the novel and what does that imply?

HANDOUT 4.2B

Carefully read the following passage from *The Catcher in the Rye,* and then answer the questions that follow on a separate piece of paper.

When the ride was over she got off her horse and came over to me. "You ride once, too, this time," she said.

"No, I'll just watch ya. I think I'll just watch," I said. I gave her some more of her dough. "Here. Get some more tickets."

She took the dough off me. "I'm not mad at you any more," she said.

"I know. Hurry up—the thing's gonna start again."

Then all of a sudden she gave me a kiss. Then she held her hand out, and said, "It's raining. It's starting to rain."

"I know."

Then what she did—it damn near killed me—she reached in my coat pocket and took out my red hunting hat and put it on my head.

"Don't you want it?" I said.

"You can wear it a while."

"Okay. Hurry up, though, now. You're gonna miss your ride. You won't get your own horse or anything."

She kept hanging around, though.

"Did you mean it what you said? You really aren't going away anywhere? Are you really going home afterwards?" she asked me.

"Yeah," I said. I meant it too. I wasn't lying to her. I really did go home afterwards. "Hurry up, now," I said. "The thing's starting." (Salinger, 1951, p. 274)

1. What is the function of the passage in the development of the characters?

2. What type of setting is used? What does it reveal?

3. What does the passage reveal about the action of the story?

4. What themes are set up or revealed in the passage?

5. What is the placement of the passage in the novel and what does that imply?

Lessons 4.3, 4.4, and 4.5: Character Development and Point of View (135 Minutes)

Macroconcepts

M1: Point of View/Perspective

Discipline-Specific Concepts

C6: Characterization
C9: Symbol

Principles

P3: Close scrutiny of a passage of prose reveals hints of the author's purpose in the work as a whole.
P6: Authors use a variety of tools to effect a purpose.

Skills

S1: Determine, use, and analyze text structures.
S2: Draw conclusions.
S6: Interpret author's purpose.
S7: Make and justify inferences from explicit or implicit information.
S9: Make, support, and defend judgments.
S14: Determine point of view.

Standards

SD3: Students apply knowledge of language structure, language conventions, media techniques, figurative language, and genre to create, critique, and discuss print and non-print texts.

Guiding Questions

- How does an author disclose a character?
- What does point of view reveal about the author's purpose?

Unit Sequence	Teacher Reflections
Introduction (Thirty Minutes)	
• After checking homework, break students into five groups. Assign each group one of the homework questions. Choose the students for the groups, as Questions 4 and 5 are the most challenging. • Give each group about ten minutes to share their information about their question. Have each group choose a representative to present their question and answer to the class. Give extra credit for groups that create one or more additional questions that aid in understanding the novel.	*The first question assessed if students could correctly ascertain the character development in the passage.* *The second tests their knowledge of the importance of a natural or an artificial setting.* *The third assesses their skill at interpreting the action in the story.* *The fourth tests students' insight at seeing themes that are revealed in the passage.* *The fifth looks at the placement of the passage and what that implies. This question is the most challenging as the passage yesterday was one*

(Continued)

(Continued)

Unit Sequence	Teacher Reflections
Introduction (Thirty Minutes)	
• Allow time for the group presentations. • After each group finishes, give other groups the opportunity to contribute additional information. • If necessary, scaffold questions to elicit important information that was not included. In addition, if any incorrect information was given, gently correct it. • Invite students to ask additional questions that add to understanding the passage and the novel as a whole. • Suggested answers are in the reflections column.	*that set up the action. The passage ties up the action and character development in the book.* *Guide students to the following points if they do not reach these conclusions:* • Holden has finally grown up. Phoebe has forced this decision on him by threatening to run away with him. He loves her too much to let her be in danger. • The setting is in the park at a merry-go-round, so it has trappings of a natural setting, but the merry-go-round is clearly artificial and represents childhood. • Holden does not go on the ride but sits as an adult and watches Phoebe, a child, enjoy the ride. • The action that is revealed is that Holden has finally stopped running, both literally and figuratively. He will not literally run away, and he has stopped running from responsibility. • Some of the possible themes that could be mentioned from this passage are love, taking responsibility, growing up, and accepting oneself with imperfections. • The placement of the passage is at the end and it ties up many loose ends. We know now that Holden will not run away. He has faced Phoebe; now he will face his parents and get help. Phoebe will be free to return to being a child.

• During the discussion, bring up the idea of symbols and how they can indirectly give information about a character or a theme.
• Question students about the symbols in this passage, as well as the novel as a whole, and how they help develop a character.
• Emphasize the fact that using symbols is a tool that an author can use to effect or bring about his or her purpose.
	Guide students to the merry-go-round (see above) and Holden's red hat.
	   The red hat symbolizes his individuality, as well as his impulsiveness and irresponsibility. Phoebe takes it from him, but returns it in the passage, as she feels it is safe now for Holden to be himself.
	   Scaffold for students who need help with the concept of symbolism. Ask them what the American flag represents. Remind them that a symbol represents something. Ask them what they would choose as a symbol for themselves.
	   Other important symbols that students may mention are the Museum of Natural History, the ducks in Central Park, and "the catcher in the rye."

Unit Sequence	Teacher Reflections
Teaching Strategies and Learning Experiences (Ninety-Five Minutes)	
• Begin a discussion on point of view by asking who tells the story in *The Catcher in the Rye*. Expand the answers to guide students to the conclusion that not only is it Holden's point of view, or first person, but it is actually an interior monologue, as we are privy to Holden's thoughts as well as his account of the actions in his story. Salinger takes us into Holden's mind and thoughts so that we can see what makes him tick. By using this technique, Holden becomes a real person to the reader and a sympathetic character.	*Begin the lesson on viewpoint with the class as a whole. Some students may need your guidance to grasp all of the concepts.* *Before you begin, explain clearly the difference between objective and subjective, if you have students who may need help with this concept.*
• Discuss why this type of viewpoint is subjective and then ask why that subjective view is necessary for the author's purpose in this novel. • Explain that viewpoint is another tool that a writer can use to convey to the reader the purpose of his or her book. • How would the story be different if told from the point of view of Holden's history teacher, Mr. Spencer? • Then query, "Can the first person point of view be used by a narrator who tells the story of another?"	*For students who are struggling, ask first why a person's own thoughts are subjective. Then ask students what they think was Salinger's purpose in writing this novel.* *For students who are having trouble grasping the idea of point of view, use a fairy tale. How would the story of Little Red Riding Hood differ if it were told from the point of view of the wolf?* *If the section on the different points of view is confusing to some students, simplify it; above-average and advanced students should respond well.* *You can extend this discussion further for interested students by asking for examples of first person point of view short stories or novels. Note the difference between a narrator who tells someone else's story, as in* The Great Gatsby *or* The Fall of the House of Usher, *and a first person narrator who tells his or her own story, as in* The Adventures of Huckleberry Finn. *Students will probably see that this point of view allows the reader to see an event from various points of view. While each character gives her point of view in a subjective manner, the multiple views of events give readers a more objective view of happenings. This type of viewpoint is becoming more popular in modern fiction. Louise Erdrich, a noted American writer who writes primarily about Native Americans, uses this viewpoint frequently.*

(Continued)

(Continued)

Unit Sequence	Teacher Reflections
Introduction (Thirty Minutes)	
<ul><li>Next ask about the point of view in *The Joy Luck Club*? Whose story is it? If students feel it is the story of many women, assure them they are right. It has a multiple point of view. Further probe about the advantages to using this point of view. Ask if this viewpoint is objective or subjective?</li><li>Look at the viewpoint in *The Scarlet Letter*. Guide if necessary with questions: Is this one person's story? Do we see events only from one character's point of view? Who tells the story? Students will see that this is an all-knowing or omniscient viewpoint. Is this omniscient narrator objective or subjective?</li><li>Hint if necessary: Does this storyteller (narrator) favor some characters more than others?</li><li>Finish the discussion of viewpoint by referring to third person and second person viewpoints.</li><li>Students will be familiar with the third person viewpoint, which is limited to one character's actions, thoughts, and feelings. However, again we find that the narrator can be objective or subjective. The second person viewpoint is most unusual and is rarely used. A notable exception is the short story "Journey" by Joyce Carol Oates.</li></ul>	*Be sure to note that the omniscient narrator knows information that the characters do not. This all-knowing narrator can be objective or subjective.* *The obvious sympathy toward Hester and Arthur and the lack of empathy for Chillingworth clearly make this narrator subjective.* *A good example of the third person viewpoint is* The Awakening *by Kate Chopin. Here the narrator is subjective and clearly sympathetic to the main character, Edna. Use an appropriate story or book that students have read if they have not read* The Awakening. *Students may be familiar with the second point of view from a grade school series,* Choose Your Own Adventure. *Skip this question if students are struggling.* *In* The Call of the Wild *by Jack London, the story is told from the point of view of Buck but switches to John Thornton later in the book.* *Working in a group is a good change of pace. Now that students have been given the information they need, the group format is an excellent way to share knowledge and work together.* *I assigned dynamic, major characters for this activity: Holden and Phoebe from* The Catcher in the Rye; *Suyuan Woo and June Woo from* The Joy Luck Club; *and Hester Prynne, Arthur Dimmesdale, and Roger Chillingworth from* The Scarlet Letter. *Be sure that the characters you assign are major characters who do undergo a change, making them dynamic.* *Review the rubric for this activity (at the end of this lesson) before students begin to work so they will know exactly what is being expected of them and how they will be graded.* *Obviously, adjust time as needed.*
<ul><li>Conclude the point of view discussion by asking students if there are books in which the viewpoint changes. Ask them for examples of stories or novels in which this switch happens.</li><li>Direct students to group with two or three other students, different people than they partnered with in Lesson 4.2, for an activity on characterization that uses point of view (Lesson 4.3) and symbolism (introduction to Lesson 4.3).</li><li>Tell the groups that they will use *viewpoint* and *symbolism* as they examine how *characters* are developed in the summer reading books,</li></ul>	

Unit Sequence	Teacher Reflections
Teaching Strategies and Learning Experiences (Thirty Minutes)	

The Catcher in the Rye, The Joy Luck Club, and *The Scarlet Letter.* Each group will be assigned a different character. Use Socratic questioning to come up with some general guidelines for the activity. Guide them to some points like the following: the attitude of the storyteller toward the character; the symbol(s) that represent an aspect of that character; the character's thoughts and words (look for notable quotes!); the character's actions, including body language; ways in which the character changes in the course of the book; and the attitudes toward the character as revealed by other character's actions and words. • Using these guidelines and their own insights, partners should come up with an analysis of their assigned characters and be able to support it using examples and/or quotes from the novel. Partners will then make a three to five minute oral presentation to the class in which they present their analysis of the assigned character, along with their support for this viewpoint. • Give groups a copy of the grading rubric (Handout 4.3/4.5/4.6A) for the presentation before they begin. • Let groups use the book appropriate for their particular character and give them about thirty minutes to develop their presentation. • Move from pair to pair, scaffolding where needed. • When groups have finished, tell students that the presentations will begin. This is an excellent opportunity for them to take notes while other groups are giving them valuable information about a character. • Allow sufficient time for all groups to give their presentations. Obviously the time will depend on the number of students. For seven groups, I allowed about forty-five minutes.	*While there is some latitude as to the way in which a character can be interpreted, obviously you will have to correct information that is misleading or false. Wait for a presentation to finish and for students to resume their seats. Gently add information or in some cases, correct interpretations that are obviously wrong.*
Closure (Ten Minutes)	
• Gather the class together as a group. Ask students about the ways in which an author discloses a character. • Invite students to explain one tool that a writer uses to bring about his or her purpose in a book.	*These questions are a good way to assess how much students have learned.* *If students respond with alacrity, you won't need to scaffold, but if they are confused at all, use specific examples. What does the sympathetic and admirable way in which*

(Continued)

(Continued)

Unit Sequence	Teacher Reflections
Closure (Five Minutes)	
• Next, ask what does the author's point of view, or the objective or subjective way the author portrays a character, reveal about the author's purpose? What was Hawthorne's purpose in *The Scarlet Letter*? Tan's purpose in *The Joy Luck Club* and Salinger's purpose in *The Catcher in the Rye*? • Conclude by saying that characterization is just one way that an author can reveal his or her purpose. Another way is by his or her tone. We will look at tone in the next lesson. To prepare for this lesson, your assignment is to define a list of tone words and use each in a sentence.	*Hawthorne presents Hester tell us about his purpose with* The Scarlet Letter? *Was he trying to portray the Puritan magistrates as unforgiving?*

Character Analysis Rubric

HANDOUT 4.3/4.4/4.5A

Criteria	1	2	3	4	Your Score
Content Overall insightful analysis of character	The analysis of the character is perceived incorrectly or it is not developed.	The analysis of the character is basically correct but not fully developed.	Analysis of character is accurate.	There is an excellent perception of character that shows original thinking.	1 2 3 4
Content Examples or quotes from novel that reveal character's actions, thoughts, or words, and/or the words or actions of another character that support overall character analysis	Few if any meaningful examples and/or quotes are used that show the actions, thoughts, or words of the character or another character. The character analysis lacks support.	Some examples and/or quotes are used that show actions, thoughts, or words of the character or another character. In general, the character analysis needs more solid support.	Good examples and/or quotes are used that show actions, thoughts, or words of the character or another character to support and develop the character analysis.	Notable examples and/or quotes that reveal significant actions, thoughts, or words of the character or another character are used to support and develop the character analysis.	1 2 3 4
Content Author's viewpoint/attitude toward character supports character analysis	Author's viewpoint toward character is not mentioned, or the author's viewpoint is not correctly identified. In either case, it does not support character analysis.	Perception of author's viewpoint is correct but limited.	There is good perception of author's viewpoint with support from passage.	There is excellent discernment into author's viewpoint with support from passage.	1 2 3 4

(Continued)

(Continued)

Criteria	1	2	3	4	Your Score
Content Symbols that represent an aspect of character	No symbols are mentioned or symbols are interpreted incorrectly.	One or two symbols that represent an aspect of the character are mentioned.	Several symbols are interpreted so as to give insight into the character.	A number of symbols are interpreted in a most meaningful and original manner. They add a great deal to the analysis of the character.	1 2 3 4
Group Oral Presentation Skills All members participate Delivery and eye contact Length of three to five minutes	Presentation is lacking at least two of the following: all group members participate, effective delivery and eye contact, and appropriate length.	Presentation is lacking one of the following: all group members participate, effective delivery and eye contact, appropriate length.	All group members participate, using good delivery and eye contact. Presentation is organized and is of appropriate length.	All group members participate, using excellent delivery and eye contact. Presentation is well organized and of appropriate length.	1 2 3 4

Lessons 4.6 and 4.7: Understanding Tone (Ninety Minutes)

Discipline-Specific Concepts

C10: Tone
C11: Verbal Irony
C12: Situational Irony
C13: Dramatic Irony

Principles

P4: Understanding an author's tone and use of irony reveals much of his or her true purpose and meaning in a given work.
P6: Authors use a variety of tools to effect a purpose.

Skills

S1: Determine, use, and analyze text structures.
S4: Articulate tone.

Standards

SD3: Students apply knowledge of language structure, language conventions, media techniques, figurative language, and genre to create, critique, and discuss print and non-print texts.

Guiding Questions

- Why is tone important in understanding a writer's purpose?
- Why is recognizing irony important in understanding an author's meaning?

Unit Sequence	Teacher Reflections
Introduction (Forty Minutes)	

<ul><li>Begin by reviewing the tone vocabulary words (Handout 4.6/4.7A) and asking students to read sentences using the words.</li><li>Using Socratic questioning to probe students for the reason for multiple words with somewhat similar meanings.</li></ul>
 	
<ul><li>Ask for a definition of tone. Add to it as necessary.</li></ul>
	Start the introduction with the class as a whole. This way you can assess easily the level of understanding to see if you need to scaffold for all students to understand the concepts of tone and irony.
	  Give an example if necessary of similar words with different intensities, such as disparaging *and* disdainful.
	  Tone is the way in which an author reveals his or her attitude in a particular piece of writing. Equally important to defining the writer's position is determining the intensity of the position. Having a wide variety of "tone words" allows us to specify both the attitude and the intensity of that position.

(Continued)

(Continued)

Unit Sequence	Teacher Reflections
Introduction (Forty Minutes)	
• Ask students how they detect tone in spoken words. Give them an example such as ironically stating: "I can't wait to go home and clean out the garage." • How can a reader determine tone? Guide them to see that a careful look at a writer's word choices and descriptive details combined with an overall impression will reveal his or her tone. • Why is understanding tone so important to understanding the meaning of a work? • Understanding a writer's meaning is especially important when a writer uses irony. Why? • What are the types of irony? Guide if necessary to instruct students that there are three major types: verbal irony, situational irony, and dramatic irony. • Ask for an example of verbal irony. • Give an example of situational irony and then ask them for one. • Explain dramatic irony: a situation in a story in which a character is unaware of important information that the reader knows. Ask for an example.	*Ask them what happens when we misunderstand tone in spoken words. Go back to the garage example. They will quickly see that we miss the meaning.* *Accept puns, hyperbole, understatement, and overstatement. Basically make sure they understand that verbal irony is saying one thing and meaning another.* *These are all examples: a drivers' education instructor who fears driving in heavy traffic, a librarian who dislikes reading, and a computer mogul who is awarded a new computer as a prize.* *In Oedipus the King, Oedipus is unaware that he is his father's killer. In Romeo and Juliet, the reader or viewer knows in the prologue that both young lovers will die, but the characters are unaware of their fate until the very end.* *If the tone lesson is to be taught in two separate classes of forty-five minutes each, provide closure for the first session at this point by revisiting the guiding questions at the beginning of the lesson.*
Teaching Strategies and Learning Experiences (Forty-Five Minutes)	
• Start the lesson by asking students why understanding tone and irony are important to literary analysis. What might a person miss in a writer's purpose if he or she ignored or misinterpreted tone? Irony? • Tell students that they will read a short story and then, with a partner, determine the following: 　○ Examples of verbal irony in the story 　○ Examples of situational irony in the story 　○ Examples of dramatic irony in the story 　○ Clues and details that hint at the tone 　○ Overall tone of the story	*This beginning can serve as an introduction if the tone lesson was taught on two separate days. If that is the case, then extend the questioning to be sure that students are on track. If the tone lesson is taught in one ninety-minute block, then it can be short.* *Giving students a partner at this point accomplishes three goals: it gives students a change of pace, it provides a situation where students can teach and learn from each other, and it provides an assessment tool for you as you circulate around the room and observe partners.*

Unit Sequence	Teacher Reflections
Teaching Strategies and Learning Experiences (Forty-Five Minutes)	

Unit Sequence	Teacher Reflections
• Assign partners and give students a copy of "The Open Window" by Saki (H. H. Munro). • Give students time to read the story *twice* and then work with their partners. • Scaffold as necessary for students who need help. • When pairs are ready, bring the class together to share their findings. • Why do you think you were instructed to read the story twice? What is much more evident on the second reading? • Ask for examples of verbal irony. Have students give an exact quote and explain why it is ironic. • Accept all reasonable answers.	*The story is in many short story collections. You can also access it online at http://www.classicshorts.com/bib.html.* *Emphasize that the irony in this story is much easier to see on the second reading. Vera is so good at her storytelling that many readers also believe her on the first reading.* *One good example is Vera's answer to her aunt's comment that Mr. Nuttel had "dashed off without a word of good-bye or apology when you arrived" (Saki, 1954, p. 336).* *"I expect it was the spaniel." said the niece calmly; Vera knows, of course, that it was not the spaniel that frightened Mr. Nuttel but her ghost story, complete with the "ghosts" coming through the open window.* *Another example takes place earlier in the story, after Vera has laid the groundwork for her ghost story. Upon making her appearance, Mrs. Sappleton turns to Mr. Nuttel and says, "I hope Vera has been amusing you?"* *"She has been very interesting," said Frampton (p. 335). Indeed, he does not really think Vera has been interesting; rather he has been greatly unsettled by the story of her aunt's tragedy.* *The best answer here is that Frampton Nuttel has come to the country for a "nerve cure." Instead of the quiet solicitous company he had hoped for, he has met a clever teenage girl who has played a practical joke on him.*
• Ask for examples of situational irony. Have students supply an explanation for their example. • Have pairs give examples of dramatic irony.	*The dramatic irony in this story is more evident on the second reading. Here we can see that Vera does some background work before she tells her story to Mr. Nuttel. She asks, "Do you know many of the people round here?" (p. 333). She follows this question with another: "Then you know practically nothing about my aunt?" (p. 334). Unlike Mr. Nuttel, we are dubious then about the fantastic story that Vera tells to Mr. Nuttel.* *There is another example at the end of the story. When Vera tells her aunt that Mr. Nuttel's hasty departure was due to a fear of dogs brought on by a memory of being hunted by dogs on the banks of the Ganges, we know he never told her such a story.* *In addition to the clues of Vera's careful questions, we also note that the author refers to Vera as "very self-possessed" (p. 333). Tie in the*

(Continued)

Unit Sequence	Teacher Reflections
Introduction (Forty Minutes)	

Unit Sequence	Teacher Reflections
• The examples of dramatic irony are closely intertwined with the clues and details that hint at the tone. Invite students to share their clues. Guide them to look at the way in which Saki has characterized both Vera and Frampton Nuttel. Look also for any symbols he may have used. • Point out to students that the use of irony and symbols are tools the writer uses to accomplish his purpose. • If no one mentions it, guide them to the last line of the story. It is surely the best clue of all. "Romance at short notice was her speciality" (p. 336). Ask students who is speaking here. • Finally, ask students to suggest a tone for the story as a whole and to defend their choice.	*characterization lesson and the importance of the author's attitude toward a character. On the other hand, the author tells us through Nuttel's thoughts that he "doubted more than ever whether these formal visits on a succession of total strangers would do much towards helping the nerve cure which he was supposed to be undergoing" (p. 333). He seems to doubt himself in many ways.* *Frampton Nuttel's name in itself symbolizes someone who is not fully cognizant of what is happening.* *We see that Nuttel's impressions are correct when he notes "An indefinable something about the room seemed to suggest masculine habitation" (p. 334). However, Nuttel does not have the confidence to trust his own instincts. Thus, he easily falls into the role of victim of a practical joke.* *The author speaks the last line. If some students do not understand what Saki means by romance, have them look up the word. They will see that one of the meanings of the word is a made up story.* *Many answers could be correct; accept any that are reasonable.* *The story is surely ironic, with numerous examples of irony, as well as the hint the author gives in the last line.* *The story could also be seen as humorous, especially through the eyes of Vera.*
Closure (Five Minutes)	
• Ask students what they felt Saki's purpose was in the story "The Open Window." • Query them about the tools that Saki uses in the story to develop it. • Question them about how the use of tone helps to reveal the author's purpose in a given work? • Ask how the characterization Saki develops for both Vera and Nuttel help to develop the tone. • Invite a student to explain why irony is important in the story. • End the class by assigning a second list of tone words (Handout 4.6/4.7B) for homework. Again, ask students to look up the words and use each in a sentence of their own. • Differentiation—Create a third list of tone words that would be helpful in studying literary analysis and literary criticism.	*Saki's purpose seems to be telling a clever and amusing story of a precocious young lady and a gullible and nervous man. Saki is also showing us the power of the story; good writing convinces us.* *These questions will provide a good assessment of how well students understood the concepts and principles in the lesson.* *The irony provides the humor.* *Differentiation activities are appropriate for students who need a challenge, students who work well independently, and those who have a high interest in the assignment.* *Many other tone words can be used. You can find suggested lists by going to Google and entering "tone words." AP prep books and SAT prep books also have lists of such words.*

HANDOUT 4.6/4.7A

Assignment Tone Vocabulary—List #1

The following tone words are presented in order for you to use more specific and subtle descriptions of an attitude you find in a text. Define these words and use each in a sentence of your own, using a separate piece of paper. Most importantly, make these words part of your vocabulary. Use them to describe a writer's tone when we discuss pieces of literature and nonfiction selections.

1. Allusive

2. Aloof

3. Ambivalent

4. Brusque

5. Cautionary

6. Compassionate

7. Condescending

8. Contemptuous

9. Cynical

10. Defensive

11. Detached

12. Didactic

13. Disdainful

14. Disparaging

15. Dramatic

16. Flippant

17. Frivolous

18. Grudging

19. Hollow

20. Horrific

21. Humorous

22. Hypocritical

HANDOUT 4.6/4.7B

Assignment—Tone Vocabulary—List #2

The following additional tone words are presented in order for you to use more specific and subtle descriptions of an attitude you find in a text. Define these words and use each in a sentence of your own, using a separate piece of paper. Most importantly, make these words part of your vocabulary. Use them to describe a writer's tone when we discuss pieces of literature and nonfiction selections.

1. Indifferent

2. Ironic

3. Judicious

4. Nostalgic

5. Objective

6. Optimistic

7. Pedantic

8. Pessimistic

9. Pompous

10. Prosaic

11. Provocative

12. Resigned

13. Satirical

14. Scathing

15. Sentimental

16. Skeptical

17. Subjective

18. Sympathetic

19. Thoughtful

20. Tragic

21. Vindictive

22. Whimsical

23. Witty

Lessons 4.8 and 4.9: What Is Style? (Ninety Minutes)

Discipline-Specific Concepts

C14: Style
C15: Diction
C16: Connotation
C17: Denotation
C18: Abstract
C19: Concrete
C20: Syntax
C21: Paradox

Principles

P5: An author's style provides a key to interpreting and evaluating a given work.
P6: Authors use a variety of tools to effect a purpose.

Skills

S7: Make and justify inferences from explicit or implicit information.
S5: Appraise style.
S6: Interpret author's purpose.
S11: Write with appropriate strategies to suit a purpose.

Standards

SD2: Students employ a wide range of strategies as they write and use different writing process elements appropriately to communicate with different audiences for a variety of purposes.
SD3: Students apply knowledge of language structure, language conventions, media techniques, figurative language, and genre to create, critique, and discuss print and nonprint texts.

Guiding Questions

- What is style?
- What does an author's style reveal about his or her purpose?

Unit Sequence	Teacher Reflections
Introduction (Forty Minutes)	
<ul><li>Begin by asking students what defines a person's style.</li><li>Next ask what constitutes a writer's style.</li><li>Guide if necessary to inform students that a writer's style is the way in which a writer uses words to expresses his or her thoughts.</li></ul>	*Begin with the class as a whole. You will be able to guide all students and at the same time assess how much scaffolding you need to give.* *They will probably mention such distinctions as clothing, hair, mannerisms, and so on. Tell them that while there are some generalities, each person has his or her own distinctive style.* *Guide students to see that the words a writer uses and the way he or she uses the words can*

(Continued)

Unit Sequence	Teacher Reflections
Introduction (Forty Minutes)	

• Ask students, for example, the difference between the ways a writer uses words in a second-grade chapter book and a short story in their textbook. They will probably mention differences such as the length of sentences, word choice, and the complexity of a story.
• Question students about how style is related to tone?
• Review the remaining tone words. Have students read their original sentences, scaffolding where necessary.
• Then have students partner with the student sitting in front of them and together decide on the most appropriate tone word from the two lists to describe the tone of each of the summer reading books: *The Scarlet Letter*, *The Joy Luck Club*, and *The Catcher in the Rye*. Tell them to be prepared to defend their choices.
• Discuss the choices.
	help create tone. For example, using words such as gloomy, weeping, emptiness, *and* darkness *would create a tone of sadness.*
	  Encourage students to add to the tone list.
	  You can also follow up the review of the tone words with a vocabulary quiz.
	  Here is a chance for students to put their heads together to come up with answers. It is also a chance to assess their understanding of tone.
	• *The Scarlet Letter could be described as didactic, dramatic, judicious, provocative, or tragic. Some other choices could also be accepted with good reasoning. Although the word is not on the list, one could certainly describe the tone as romantic.*
	• *The Joy Luck Club's tone could be described as nostalgic, optimistic, or sympathetic. Again, there are other choices. Accept any reasonable answer.*
	• The tone of the *The Catcher in the Rye* could be described as humorous, provocative, satirical, or skeptical. *Accept other choices that are well defended.*

Teaching Strategies and Learning Experiences (Fifty Minutes)	

• Start the lesson by asking students how the words *slender* and *skinny* are different.
• Would they rather be referred to as *confident* or *bold*?
• Emphasize the fact that in both cases the words have similar denotative or dictionary meanings. What differs is the connotation or suggested meaning. Ask how a writer could infer tone by careful choice of words.
• Have students form groups of two or three and suggest different synonyms for each of the base words on Handout 4.8/4.9A.
• Review the different synonyms and connotations for the different words.
• Then put groups together to form three large groups. Tell the first group to select at least eight words they would use if they were writing a love story. Tell the second group to do the same for a horror story, and tell the third to choose
	Bring the students back together as a class for this part of the lesson, so that you can easily see and give as much scaffolding as is needed to convey the concepts.
	  Students will probably see slender *as complimentary and* skinny *as critical. They may or may not see the difference between* confident *and* bold *as striking.*
	  Working together makes the exercise more enjoyable and helps to scaffold those students who need help.
	  Obviously the choice of words has to do with the writer's purpose. The connotative suggestions of a writer's words will suggest a tone.
	  On the board, write the three headings: love, horror, and adventure. Groups can then write the words they choose under their heading.
	  If they do not have enough words, they can create some during the activity.

Unit Sequence	Teacher Reflections

Teaching Strategies and Learning Experiences (Fifty Minutes)

words for an adventure story. Have them write the words under the appropriate heading on the board.

- Tell students that they have chosen specific words related to a purpose; this selection of carefully selected words is known as *diction*.
- Encourage students to add to the tone list. You can also follow up the tone words with a vocabulary quiz.
- Next give them two descriptions of a piece of cake.
  - ○ The cake was moist and sweet with a taste of chocolate and raspberries.
  - ○ The cake was wonderful.

- Remind them of sensory words that are concrete.
- Have them form groups of three. Give them Handout 4.8/4.9B with two passages that describe war, one by Ernest Hemingway and one by Tim O'Brien. Give them sufficient time to read and analyze the two passages for their diction. They should look for the connotative use of words, as well as the use of concrete or abstract words. Then based on their findings, they should suggest a tone and a purpose each writer had in mind in using such words.
- After they have finished, analyze the first passage as a class. Discuss not only the diction as abstract or concrete, but also invite students to suggest words that Hemingway used that had a significant connotative value.

- Ask students next about the sentences. Are they long, short, complex, or simple? Tell them that this examination of sentence structure is called *syntax*. Writers use varying types of sentences to help convey their meaning.

They will undoubtedly say that the first definition is more detailed. What you are driving at is that it is more concrete. We can imagine the moist taste of chocolate and raspberries. We can almost taste the cake. The second statement is abstract. The writer is implying an ideal, rather than using sensory details. Be sure to emphasize that one choice is not preferable to another. A writer makes a choice between abstract words and concrete words depending on his or her purpose in that statement.

This lesson should only be the beginning of a study of style; the study should be ongoing. Some students may be well versed in stylistic techniques; others may know little. Adjust your lessons accordingly.

Groups will work well here. If you have some students who are struggling, you might want to pick the groups so that they are well balanced as to ability level.

Passage #1 has many concrete, sensory words.

*In fact, Hemingway used words that convey taste (*wine, cheese*), sight (*splintered beam of wood, shells . . . float whitely*), sound (*crying, screaming, splashing*), and touch (*when I touched him . . .*). The use of these words conveys a vivid battle scene in which a soldier is jolted from his lunch of cheese and wine by enemy fire. His bodily reaction is so severe that he thinks at first that he has actually died.*

Many words have a powerful connotative meaning. Accept any that are reasonable choices. Some obvious ones are roar, *dead,* screaming, crying, torn up, *and* bombs.

Students will probably note the many short and powerful sentences. Tell them that these types of sentences are part of Hemingway's style. He uses many short simple sentences, but don't let their simplicity fool you. They often convey powerful and complex meanings.

Accept any reasonable answers. Hemingway's purpose in this passage seems to be vividly portraying the horror of war—being blasted from the everyday act of eating lunch into a frightening and life-threatening battle scene. Hemingway paints such a vivid picture that the reader feels as if he or she is almost experiencing the battle.

(Continued)

(Continued)

Unit Sequence	Teacher Reflections
Teaching Strategies and Learning Experiences (Fifty Minutes)	
• Question students about Hemingway's purpose and an appropriate tone for the passage.	*An appropriate tone could be horrific or dramatic. Again, accept any reasonable answers. There is certainly not just one right answer, but encourage students to use words from their tone lists.* *Here the author uses abstract words, and he uses them in a series of contrasts. Many words have connotative meanings, such as* hell, mystery, terror, adventure, courage, discovery, holiness, pity, despair, longing, love, forest fire, cancer, beauty, ugly, *and many more.*
• When students seem clear about Passage #1, discuss Passage #2. Again, ask about the diction as concrete or abstract, as well as key connotative words. This passage is more difficult, so you may have to do some guiding. It has both abstract and concrete words.	*O'Brien also uses some concrete words when he paints some images such as "the white phosphorous, the purply orange glow of napalm, the rocket's red glare."* *Here again, O'Brien uses a combination. He uses many short powerful sentences such as: "It fills the eye. It commands you." However, he also uses some long sentences that string a series of images together. By stringing these pictures together, he floods us with a series of images that appear to be pleasing to the eye, but we know they are horrible because they are a part of war. The effect is to make us feel confused or unsettled, which is just what O'Brien wants to convey.*
• Ask students about O'Brien's syntax. What kind of sentences does he use? Ask for examples.	*Give a gold star if anyone mentions paradox. If no one does, you introduce it.* *This passage is a great example of a paradox, an apparent contradiction that conveys a truth.*
• What is O'Brien's purpose? His tone?	*O'Brien sees war as a paradox. It can't be categorized as one thing or one idea. It is many things at many different times. The tone could be described as provocative, tragic, or thoughtful. Again, accept any reasonable answer.*

Unit Sequence	Teacher Reflections
Closure (Twenty Minutes)	

Unit Sequence	Teacher Reflections

• Ask students to describe some of the characteristics that define a writer's style.
• Invite a volunteer to explain how style can help to convey a writer's purpose.
• Ask students to explain diction.
• Tomorrow's assignment: Randomly assign numbered slips of paper to students as follows:
 	
  1. Adventure—Describe a lake from the point of view of a leading contender of an ultra sport event to be held at the lake.
  2. Drama—Describe a lake from the point of view of a person who is mourning the death of a loved one.
  3. Love—Describe a lake from the point of view of a person who has recently fallen deeply in love.
  4. Historical—Describe a lake from the point of view of someone from the early 1700s.
 	
• Tell students to write one or two paragraphs describing a lake. The focus of the paragraph(s) should be appropriate for the number they have been assigned. They should use specific details, connotative words, and careful word choice (diction) to convey the atmosphere of the appropriate scenario they have been assigned. Students should NOT indicate the scenario they have been given by any means other than their careful writing. They should limit their writing to the description, not get into plot. Paragraphs are due tomorrow.
• Review the assignment grading rubric with students.
	Prompt if necessary for connotation, concrete, or abstract words and syntax.
	
	   Students may also mention images and paradox.
	
	   The writing assignment is a good assessment to see if students understand how word choice ties into purpose.
	
	   A rubric for grading the paragraphs is included in Handout 4.8/4.9C. Be sure to review the rubric with students when you give the assignment.

HANDOUT 4.8/4.9A

In groups of two or three, suggest three or four different synonyms for each base word that follows and be prepared to explain the different connotations.

laugh				
house				
sad				
happy				
youthful				
shout				
vehicle				
cat				
teacher				
boat				

HANDOUT 4.8/4.9B

In groups of three, read and analyze the following two passages for their diction. Look for the connotative use of words, concrete words, and abstract words. Then, based on your findings, suggest the tone and purpose for each passage.

Passage #1 (from *A Farewell to Arms* by Ernest Hemingway)

I ate the end of my piece of cheese and took a swallow of wine. Through the other noise I heard a cough, then came the chuh-chuh-chuh-chuh—then there was a flash, as when a blast-furnace door is swung open, and a roar that started white and went red and on and on in a rushing wind. I tried to breathe but my breath would not come and I felt myself rush bodily out of myself and out and out and out and all the time bodily in the wind. I went out swiftly, all of myself, and I knew I was dead and that it had all been a mistake to think you just died. Then I floated, and instead of going on I felt myself slide back. I breathed and I was back. The ground was torn up and in front of me there was a splintered beam of wood. In the jolt of my head I heard somebody crying. I thought somebody was screaming. I tried to move but I could not move. I heard the machine-guns and rifles firing across the river and all along the river. There was a great splashing and I saw the star-shells go up and burst and float whitely and rockets going up and heard the bombs, all this in a moment, and then I heard close to me some one saying "Mama Mia! Oh, Mama Mia!" I pulled and twisted and got my legs loose finally and turned around and touched him. It was Passini and when I touched him he screamed. (Hemingway, 1995, pp. 54–55)

Notes:

_____

_____

_____

_____

_____

_____

_____

_____

_____

_____

_____

_____

_____

Passage #2 (from *The Things They Carried* by Tim O'Brien)

How do you generalize? War is hell, but that's not the half of it, because war is also mystery and terror and adventure and courage and discovery and holiness and pity and despair and longing and love. War is nasty; war is fun. War is thrilling; war is drudgery. War makes you a man; war makes you dead. The truths are contradictory. It can be argued, for instance, that war is grotesque. But in truth war is also beauty. For all its horror, you can't help but gape at the awful majesty of combat. You stare out at tracer rounds unwinding through the dark like brilliant red ribbons. You crouch in ambush as a cool, impassive moon rises over the nighttime paddies. You admire the fluid symmetries of troops on the move, the harmonies of sound and shape and pro portion, the great sheets of metal-fire streaming down from a gunship, the illumination rounds, the white phosphorous, the purply orange glow of napalm, the rocket's red glare. It's not pretty, exactly. It's astonishing. It fills the eye. It commands you. You hate it, yes, but your eyes do not. Like a killer forest fire, like cancer under a microscope, any battle or bombing raid or artillery barrage has the aesthetic purity of absolute moral indifference—a powerful, implacable beauty—and a true war story will tell the truth about this, though the truth is ugly. (O'Brien, 1990, pp. 80–81)

Notes:

_____

_____

_____

_____

_____

_____

_____

_____

_____

_____

_____

_____

_____

_____

_____

_____

_____

_____

_____

_____

_____

Rubric for Short Description of a Particular Scenario

Criteria	1	2	3	4	Your Score
Focus of Paragraph(s)	The paragraph(s) lack clear focus.	There is some focus on the lake description, but many other elements of plot make the focus confusing.	Focus of paragraph(s) is the lake description, but there is some extraneous plot detail.	Focus of paragraph(s) is clear and is limited to the description of the lake.	1 2 3 4
Point of View	The POV is not present or is confusing and is not consistent.	The POV is not clear and/or is not consistent.	The POV appears to be the one assigned, but it is not always consistent.	The POV is consistent and is clearly the one assigned.	1 2 3 4
Diction	Diction is weak. Word choices do not lead to the assigned scenario.	Diction is varied. There may be a few good word choices for the assignment.	Diction shows good word choices for the assignment.	Diction shows excellent word choices for the assignment.	1 2 3 4
Specific Details	Lacks specific details, or those that are present do not relate to the assigned scenario.	A few specific details add to the atmosphere of the assigned scenario.	Some good specific details add to the atmosphere of the assigned scenario.	Excellent specific details enhance the atmosphere of the assigned scenario.	1 2 3 4
Correct Mechanics	Mechanics are weak. Spelling, grammar, or punctuation errors are numerous.	Mechanics are fair. There are a number of spelling, grammar, or punctuation errors.	Mechanics are good. There may be some minor spelling, grammar, or punctuation errors.	Mechanics are flawless. Correct spelling, grammar, and punctuation are present.	1 2 3 4

Lesson 4.10: Recognizing Style (Forty-Five Minutes)

Discipline-Specific Concepts

C14: Style

Principles

P5: An author's style provides a key to interpreting and evaluating a given work.
P6: Authors use a variety of tools to effect a purpose.

Skills

S7: Make and justify inferences from explicit or implicit information.
S5: Appraise style.
S11: Write with appropriate strategies to suit a purpose.

Standards

SD2: Students employ a wide range of strategies as they write and use different writing process elements appropriately to communicate with different audiences for a variety of purposes.
SD3: Students apply knowledge of language structure, language conventions, media techniques, figurative language, and genre to create, critique, and discuss print and non-print texts.

Guiding Questions

- How can understanding style improve your writing?
- How can understanding style help a writer to achieve his or her purpose?

Unit Sequence	Teacher Reflections
Introduction (Twenty Minutes)	
<ul><li>Begin by collecting descriptive papers from yesterday.</li><li>Then pass out these papers, making sure each student gets one that is not his or her own.</li><li>Have students read papers and decide on the scenario that was the writer's intent, using the same categories from Lesson 4.8 and 4.9 (1. adventure, 2. drama, 3. love, and 4. historical). Ask students to mark the number of the category on the paper. If they can't make a reasonable guess, have them note a question mark.</li><li>Return papers to owners. Allow time for owners to make revisions, especially if the correct story genre was not correctly identified by the reader.</li><li>After allotted time, collect papers for grading.</li></ul>	*Having students read each others' papers to judge the writer's intent is one other form of assessment in addition to yours. It is also an incentive for those who need to make revisions.* *Grade papers using the rubric provided with the previous lesson.*

Unit Sequence	Teacher Reflections
Teaching Strategies and Learning Experiences (Twenty Minutes)	

Unit Sequence	Teacher Reflections
• Start the lesson by passing out a list of style words (Handout 4.10A). • Assign students to groups of two or three. Give each group access to dictionaries or a computer. • Have them look up the words they are not familiar with or do not know. • Scaffold if needed with groups that are struggling. • Review words as a class by asking different groups to use them in original sentences. • When all words have been reviewed, give each group a pad of sticky notes. • Have groups confer to decide on the style word or words that best describe the style of each of the summer reading books. Have them jot down these words on the sticky notes and then place them under the book title on the board. • Once all of the groups have placed notes with the words that best describe the style of the books, review them with the class, using Socratic questioning. ("What do you think about the fact that one note has described *The Scarlet Letter* as ornate and another note has labeled it as digressive? Can both of these be correct? Let's have the groups defend these choices.") • Go through all of the notes in this manner. Let students guide the way whenever possible to see that many answers can be correct. Let them also point out answers that are obviously incorrect.	*If most students in the class are reading below grade level, you may want to break the list into two smaller lists. Assign one this lesson and give the second one before you go on to Lesson 11.* *Group students to achieve a cross-section of ability levels.* *If students are using a computer, have them check out the site at http://dictionary.reference.com/.* *As with the tone words, you may want to reinforce this list with a vocabulary quiz.* *While groups are working on the words and their definitions, write the names of two or three books on the blackboard. For the purpose of continuity in this unit, I would write the names of the summer reading books:* The Scarlet Letter, The Catcher in the Rye, *and* The Joy Luck Club. *You could also use two or three books that students read last year or select two or three short stories.* *You could also use the two selections from Hemingway and O'Brien from Lessons 4.8 and 4.9.* *You might also look over the descriptive papers while groups are working to pick out a couple of especially effective ones. You can then ask these students if they would mind reading them at class closure.* *Having a group decide on an answer is less threatening than putting individual students on the spot; however, encourage individual students to disagree with the group if they so choose.* *Some original thinkers may come up with good style words or expressions (e.g.,* stream of consciousness*) that are not on the list. Encourage them to express their ideas and invite all students to add these words or phrases to the list.* *If students do not see that an answer is incorrect, you must guide the way by asking probing questions.*
Closure (Five Minutes)	
• Invite a student to explain how understanding style helped him or her to write the descriptive assignment. If possible, have the student read his or her paper aloud to the class. • Ask another student what tools the writer used to effect his or her purpose. • Tell students to think about the style of the book they are reading. Advise them to take notes as they are reading about the author's style, tone, and purpose.	*Having a student explain how he or she could achieve the desired purpose for the short descriptive writing assignment will reinforce the idea that understanding style helps achieve a writer's purpose.*

HANDOUT 4.10A

Below is a list of words that can be used to describe a writer's style. Define each and use each one in an original sentence on a separate piece of paper. Most importantly, use these words to describe a writer's style as we discuss different pieces of fiction and nonfiction.

1. Bizarre	12. Lyrical
2. Choppy	13. Ornate
3. Concrete	14. Philosophical
4. Conversational	15. Plain
5. Digressive	16. Polished
6. Direct	17. Ponderous
7. Explicit	18. Rambling
8. Flowery	19. Slangy
9. Graceful	20. Succinct
10. Graphic	21. Unimaginative
11. Lucid	22. Verbose

Lesson 4.11: Rhetoric and Rhetorical Devices (Sixty Minutes)

Discipline-Specific Concepts

C3: Point of View/Viewpoint
C22: Rhetoric
C23: Rhetorical Devices
C24: Rhetorical Question
C25: Allusion
C26: Repetition
C27: Parallel Structure
C28: Metaphor
C29: Hyperbole
C30: Charged words

Principles

P6: Authors use a variety of tools to effect a purpose.
P7: By recognizing and understanding literary devices, we can enhance our understanding of fiction and nonfiction.
P8: Readers and writers are influenced by personal, political, historical, social, sexual, cultural, and religious circumstances.

Skills

S1: Determine, use, and analyze text structures.
S6: Interpret author's purpose.
S7: Make and justify inferences from explicit or implicit information.

Standards

SD1: Students read a wide range of print and nonprint texts to build an understanding of texts, of themselves, and of the cultures of the United States and the world; to acquire new information; to respond to the needs and demands of society and the workplace; and for personal fulfillment. Among these texts are fiction and nonfiction, classic and contemporary works.
SD3: Students apply knowledge of language structure, language conventions, media techniques, figurative language, and genre to create, critique, and discuss print and nonprint texts.

Guiding Questions

- What is rhetoric?
- How are rhetorical devices used?

Unit Sequence	Teacher Reflections
Introduction (Five Minutes)	
• Write the word *rhetoric* on the board and ask students if they know what it means. • After reviewing the meaning with students, tell them that these lessons will focus on persuasive speeches or rhetoric. We will look at the viewpoint and purpose of the speeches, as well as some language devices, or rhetorical devices as they are called, that are effective for persuasion.	*In many ways the word* rhetoric *is similar to style. It involves the ability to use words skillfully to express one's thoughts and ideas. However, in general, rhetoric has more to do with persuasion and style has more to do with grace and beauty in using language. Rhetoric also often refers to the art of making speeches, especially persuasive speeches.*
Teaching Strategies and Learning Experiences (Forty Minutes)	
• Tell students that today they will use the same analytical tools that they have used for fiction to determine tone and style in nonfiction, specifically speeches. They will also learn about rhetorical devices that help define an author's viewpoint and purpose. • Explain that a rhetorical device is a literary technique that students may already know from poetry or fiction, such as metaphors and similes. We have already covered some, like symbols and paradox, in this unit. These same devices that we have seen describe an idea or a character can also be used to persuade. • Review allusion, repetition, metaphor, hyperbole, and rhetorical questions.	*Begin the lesson with the entire class so that you can gauge understanding of the concepts and provide scaffolding as needed.* *An allusion is a reference to something well known in history, mythology, or the Bible.* *Repetition is simply repeating. Obviously the repeating is for an effect. It may sometimes involve repeating the exact same word or words or words that are close in sound and meaning.* *A metaphor is a comparison of two things that are essentially unalike but have one important trait in common.* *Hyperbole is exaggeration for effect.* *Rhetorical questions are those that have obvious answers, but asking them reinforces the issues the speaker wishes to emphasize.* *Depending on students' familiarity with parallelism, you may want to teach a short grammar lesson on parallel structure.* *You can download a text version of Patrick Henry's speech at http://www.americanrhetoric .com/speeches/patrickhenrygivemeliberty.html.* *You can hear an audio version at http://www .history.org/Almanack/people/bios/biohen.cmf.* *At this point breaking students into groups works well. It gives them a chance to teach and learn from others.*
• Another effective rhetorical device is the use of parallel structure.	

Unit Sequence	Teacher Reflections

Teaching Strategies and Learning Experiences (Forty Minutes)

Unit Sequence	Teacher Reflections
• Distribute copies of the text of Patrick Henry's famous *Speech in the Virginia Convention*, then play an audio version of the speech. While students are listening, they should use their text copy to underline and note words and phrases that are especially effective.	*For students reading below grade level, you may have to scaffold to find some of the examples. Some notable ones follow.* *Examples and effectiveness of allusion follow:* *In the second paragraph, Henry states "We are apt to shut our eyes against a painful truth and listen to the song of that siren till she transforms us into beasts." Here, Henry is referring to the sirens from Greek mythology. They were creatures who lured sailors to their deaths with their songs.*
• Break students into six groups. Using their text copy, have one group look for allusions, one for repetition, one for metaphor, one for hyperbole, one for parallel structure, and one for rhetorical questions. In each case they should find as many examples as they can and explain what the rhetorical device means in the speech and how each is effective. Each group should also note the words that Henry used that were especially effective. These are called *charged* words. • Give groups an appropriate amount of time and then bring the class back and have each group respond. In each case, invite other groups to contribute after the main group presents its findings. As always, gently correct any mistakes.	*Another allusion in that paragraph is the following:* *"Are we disposed to be of the number of those who, having eyes, see not, and, having ears, hear not, the things which so nearly concern their temporal salvation?" Henry is alluding to the Bible.* *A third allusion is found in the third paragraph: "Suffer not yourselves to be betrayed with a kiss." Here the allusion refers to the false kiss Judas gives Jesus.* *In reminding people of other instances in the past that are similar to the present occasion, the speaker uses a powerful persuasive tool.* *All of the allusions are effective as they refer to well-known situations in which betrayal occurred. By using these, Henry is speaking indirectly about the way in which Britain is betraying the colonists in America. Sometimes an indirect reference, such as an allusion, is more effective than a direct accusation.* *Examples and efficacy of repetition are as follows:* *There are many examples of repetition, both of key points and single words. Two examples are the repetition of the words* fight *and* free *and Henry's repeated mention of God. Obviously the repetition of a word or an idea reinforces the idea in listeners.* *Examples of metaphor and its effect follow:* *One example appears in the beginning of the third paragraph: "the lamp of experience."*

(Continued)

(Continued)

Unit Sequence	Teacher Reflections
Teaching Strategies and Learning Experiences (Forty Minutes)	
	Another is in Paragraph 6, "Sir, we have done everything that could be done to avert the storm." Here, Henry compares war to a storm. In the next paragraph he states, "They are sent over to bind and rivet upon us those chains which the British ministry have been so long forging." The chains refer to taxes and the limiting of individual rights. Sometimes a figure of speech such as a metaphor can express an idea more creatively and forcefully. *Examples of hyperbole and its effect follow:* *In Paragraph 7, Henry says, "There is no retreat but in submission and slavery!" He also referred to the clanking chains that can "be heard on the plains of Boston!" His famous last line is also a hyperbole, "give me liberty or give me death!" Even though hyperbole is exaggeration for effect, its effect, if not overdone, can be most persuasive.* *Examples of parallel structure and its impact follow:* *In Paragraph 2, Henry states, "I am willing to know the whole truth; to know the worst, and to provide for it."* *In Paragraph 6, he says, "We have petitioned; we have remonstrated; we have supplicated; we have prostrated ourselves before the throne..".* *Henry uses a good deal of parallel structure, which is a smooth and powerful way of stating ideas.* *Examples of rhetorical questions and their efficacy follow:* *These questions are present in just about every paragraph of the speech. Perhaps an example of one of the most forceful comes in Paragraph 7 near the end of the speech when Henry states: "Shall we gather strength by irresolution and inaction? Shall we acquire the means of effectual resistance by lying supinely on our backs until our enemies shall have bound us hand and foot?"* *Even though the speaker and the audience know the answer to rhetorical questions, they are most forceful in making a point.*
• Once all examples have been discussed and explained, send students back into their groups and have them review the speech to determine the speaker's viewpoint and purpose, the overall tone, and the overall style. • Finally, ask what makes the speech so persuasive and powerful. How does Henry support his argument?	

Unit Sequence	Teacher Reflections
Teaching Strategies and Learning Experiences (Forty Minutes)	

• Extension—Explore the historical situation that existed when Henry made his famous speech. • Differentiation—Patrick Henry felt passionate about his purpose. Choose a political viewpoint in our world today that instills you with passion. Present a speech about your view, using some of the rhetorical devices that we have studied. • Differentiation—Compare and contrast Patrick Henry's speech to Martin Luther King's "I Have a Dream" speech. • Differentiation—Compare and contrast Martin Luther King's speech to Lincoln's Gettysburg Address. • Differentiation—Read Elizabeth Glaser's speech, 1992 Democratic National Convention Address, and identify her intent and the rhetorical devices she uses to make her speech powerful.	*Some examples of charged words are* freedom, liberty, fight, war, weak, slavery, chains, *and* death. *These are words that elicit an emotional reaction in people.* *Many answers are acceptable for the questions. Accept any that are reasonable that students can support. If necessary, guide them in these directions.* • Tone—dramatic, provocative, cautionary. • Style—lyrical, polished, lucid. • Viewpoint—political—Henry makes his speech from the Virginia House of Burgesses following a resolution he introduced to defend the colonies against England. *The speech is persuasive and powerful as Henry appeals to emotions, as seen in Paragraph 7 ("a British guard shall be stationed in every house") as well as Paragraph 6 ("An appeal to arms and to the God of hosts is all that is left us!"), and to reason, as seen in Paragraph 3 ("These are the implements of war and subjugation; the last arguments to which kings resort. I ask gentlemen, sir, what means this martial array, if its purpose be not to force us to submission?")* *Differentiation activities are designed to challenge the advanced student, but they are also appropriate for students who show a high interest level in the topic being studied. Direct students who need more challenge or those who work well on an independent project to these activities.* *King's speech can be found at the following Web site: http://www.americanrhetoric.com/speeches/mlkihaveadream.htm.* *Lincoln's address can be found at the following Web site: http://www.americanrhetoric.com/speeches/gettysburgaddress.htm.* *For students who need a more accessible speech, try Elizabeth's Glaser's 1992 Democratic National Convention Address, which can be found at http://www.americanrhetoric.com/speeches/elizabethglaser1992dnc.htm.*

(Continued)

(Continued)

Unit Sequence	Teacher Reflections
Closure (Fifteen Minutes)	
• Question students about the nature of rhetoric. • Ask them to explain how rhetorical devices aid a speaker in defining his or her purpose and persuading the audience. • Invite them to share an example of a speech or part of a speech they have heard that was powerful. • Tell students that persuasive essays are like speeches in that they too are created to persuade readers of the writer's argument or intent. Since they do not have the advantage of a powerful voice or personal presence, it is important that the writers choose their words carefully to express their opinion convincingly. • Like speeches, persuasive essays usually have a particular viewpoint along with the argument. • To guide students with the concept of viewpoint, ask them to imagine an argument concerning global warming. Use Socratic questioning to elicit examples of the argument from a political viewpoint, a historical viewpoint, a social viewpoint, a religious viewpoint, and a personal viewpoint. • Distribute a copy of the persuasive essay, "Life Is Precious, or It's Not" by Barbara Kingsolver, to each student. • Read the essay together and then ask students for their first impression of the piece. • For homework, instruct students to reread the essay carefully and analyze it, looking for the tools Kingsolver uses to express her argument. • Distribute the handout.	*Asking these questions will encourage students to review the concepts and principles in the lesson. It gives students who understand the ideas a chance to share their knowledge. It gives students who are confused or unclear about aspects of the lesson a chance to ask questions and clarify points they do not understand.* *The essay, "Life Is Precious, or It's Not" can be found in* Small Wonder *by Barbara Kingsolver (2002).* *This essay is short, powerful, and quite accessible and should be appropriate for all levels.* *While above-average students will understand viewpoint with little if any scaffolding needed, it may be difficult for some struggling students. If that is the case, focus only on the argument or purpose.* *Reading the essay together before students attempt to read and analyze it gives students a chance to capture their first impression without focusing on the details featured on the handout. You may want to adjust the handout for struggling students by listing the rhetorical devices they will find.*

HANDOUT 4.11A

"Life Is Precious or It's Not"

Carefully read the essay and then examine it carefully for the following features. Give examples from the essay for your findings.

Argument (Purpose)

Type of Support for Argument

Viewpoint

Style

Tone

Rhetorical Devices

Lessons 4.12 and 4.13: The Persuasive Essay and the Editorial (Ninety Minutes)

Discipline-Specific Concepts

C31: Persuasive Essay
C32: Editorial
C33: Thesis/Argument

Principles

P7: By recognizing and understanding literary devices, we can enhance our understanding of fiction and nonfiction.

P8: Readers and writers are influenced by personal, political, historical, social, sexual, racial, and religious circumstances.

Skills

S8: Decide and justify underlying themes.
S9: Make, support, and defend judgments.
S11: Write with appropriate strategies to suit audience and purpose.

Standards

SD2: Students employ a wide range of strategies as they write and use different writing process elements appropriately to communicate with different audiences for a variety of purposes.

SD3: Students apply knowledge of language structure, language conventions, media techniques, figurative language, and genre to create, critique, and discuss print and nonprint texts.

Guiding Questions

- What is a persuasive essay?
- What is an editorial?
- How can style, tone, and rhetorical devices help to convey a viewpoint?

Unit Sequence	Teacher Reflections
Introduction (Twenty Minutes)	
• Begin by breaking students into groups of three. Give the groups about five minutes to confer with one another about their answers for the argument, its support, and the viewpoint in Kingsolver's essay, "Life Is Precious, or It's Not." • Bring the class back together after the groups have had a chance to compare answers and reach some sort of agreement, even if they have agreed to disagree.	*Beginning with groups gives students a chance to compare and contrast answers with group members. They may decide to change their answers if they reach an understanding they did not have before, but be sure to emphasize that they can have different opinions within the group.*

Unit Sequence	Teacher Reflections
Introduction (Twenty Minutes)	
• Call on different groups for their response to the argument and also ask them where they first found it in the essay. Ask other groups if they agree. In addition, give all groups a chance to add information after the first group responds. • Question a different group about the type of support for the argument. Again, give other groups a chance to add their thoughts after the responding group finishes. • Next ask a third group about the viewpoint in the essay. Note that several answers are correct for this question. • Write the words *style, tone,* and *rhetorical devices* on the board. Give each group a piece of different-colored chalk and invite groups to go up to the board and write their answers for these categories.	*Start with the argument, its support, and the viewpoint so that you can be sure that everyone is on the right path before you proceed to the style, tone, and rhetorical devices. That way, if any students are confused, they can realign their thinking when the questions are reviewed first by the group and then by the class.* *The argument is first mentioned in the third paragraph. Kingsolver's purpose or argument is that as a society, we must stop solving problems by violent means. Children will continue the cycle of violence if we don't find peaceful means to deal with conflict.* *The type of support is basically emotional. Kingsolver hits a really emotional target when she constantly refers to the violent model that many adults provide for impressionable children. She also uses reason when she asserts that most violent acts can be traced back to society's tolerance and endorsement of guns and killing.* *The viewpoint is social, as Kingsolver talks about violence in American city streets and suburbs, in our schools, and in our own families. The viewpoint is also personal, as it is clear that these ideas are Kingsolver's personal views.* *Finally, in the last paragraph the viewpoint becomes political when Kingsolver urges the reader to demand change from our elected officials from a policy of aggression to one of diplomacy.* *Make sure that all students understand the argument, the type of support, and the viewpoints before you proceed to style, tone, and rhetorical devices.* *For Kingsolver's style, there are a number of answers that can be correct. Ask students to defend their choice and accept any that are reasonable. Her style could be described as conversational. We almost feel that she is talking to us at a coffee shop. At the same time, what she says is clear, well-organized, and powerful, so the style is also lucid. Her style is also succinct. She covers a lot of thought in nine short paragraphs.* *As with style, a number of answers are acceptable for tone. Students may feel she is*

(Continued)

(Continued)

Unit Sequence	Teacher Reflections
Introduction (Twenty Minutes)	

• After all groups have had a chance for input, use Socratic questioning to review the student responses.
• Acknowledge groups that contribute.
• Finally, review the answers for rhetorical devices. Ask for examples and try to get at least one from every student. Review any rhetorical devices that students missed or identified incorrectly.
 	
• If no one mentions it, ask students if they understand the symbolism in the columbine flower.
	judicious. Others may see that she is cautionary. Still others may see her as cynical. Their choice of tone may depend on their agreement or disagreement with Kingsolver's views. Accept both sides and the appropriate tones.
	   There is symbolism in the columbine flower in the first paragraph.
	   Kingsolver uses a lot of hyperbole, which appears in Paragraphs 1, 4, 5, 6, 7, and 8. She asks rhetorical questions in Paragraph 3. Throughout the piece Kingsolver uses repetition of words such as killing, guns, bombs, death, *and* murder. *These could also surely be called charged words as well. Finally, she uses many short powerful sentences. A good example of this is the concluding paragraph, which is just one powerful sentence.*

Teaching Strategies and Learning Experiences (Sixty-Five Minutes)	

• Begin the lesson on editorials by asking students what an editorial is. Then ask how an editorial differs from a persuasive essay and a persuasive speech?
• Stress the fact that essentially a persuasive essay, persuasive speech, and editorial are the same. The defining characteristic of an editorial is that it is published.
• Using the board, review the ways that the main argument or point of a persuasive essay or speech can be supported. Ask how Patrick Henry supported his views. How did his support differ from the support that Barbara Kingsolver used?
• How were the topics that they argued distinct?
	Guide students if necessary to see that an editorial is basically a persuasive essay that is published by a periodical or newspaper. Many are written by members of the editorial staff of that publication, but some are written by other writers.
	   Patrick Henry used logic and reason as well as emotion to support his point. Kingsolver uses some reasons and a lot of emotion to make her point. In both cases they support their reason or emotional appeal with examples.
	   If students can see that Henry is arguing for a change in the colonies' position of dealing with England while Kingsolver is arguing for a change in basic values, let them lead the way. You might follow with a comparison of Henry's point to those of some politicians concerning different strategies for the war in Iraq. These persuasive essays/editorials differ in type from those of writers who argue that the United States should not be at war with Iraq or any other nation for that matter. Note that

Unit Sequence	Teacher Reflections
Teaching Strategies and Learning Experiences (Forty Minutes)	

Unit Sequence	Teacher Reflections

• Are there other kinds of support that would be powerful? To spur their thinking, read a short segment of an editorial that uses facts and figures for support.
• Write the word *argument* on the board. Underneath it write *change in values* and *change in position or policy*. Ask student what type of support is best for each. Using Socratic questioning, ask them which type of persuasive piece would use logic and reason, which one emotion, and which one facts and figures.
• Guide them if necessary to see that all three types of support can be used with both types of arguments, although the essay calling for a change in values is more likely to appeal to emotions. The writer must decide what is most effective for his or her argument to be forceful.
• Tell students that they will write a short persuasive essay on a topic they will be given. They will have twenty-five minutes to write a draft.
• Explain that they will first develop an argument based on a viewpoint of the topic. They should imagine that the audience for this essay is the class. Then they should support their points using one or all of the following with examples:
   ○ Reason and logic
   ○ Facts and or figures
   ○ Emotional appeal
• Finally, they should end the essay with a suggested answer to the problem or a plan of action. Ask them how Patrick Henry ended his persuasive speech. Question them about how Kingsolver ended her persuasive essay.
• Pass out slips of paper with topics written on them. Explain that the topics all relate to the issues in the book they are reading for Lesson 4.14, and for purposes of this assignment, they can pretend that their books are nonfiction and that we are living in the same time period as the book. In other words, they can use incidents in the book for support in their essay.
• Give students twenty-five minutes to write a first draft.
• When the twenty-five minutes has passed, direct students to stop writing.
• Pair students and distribute a revision guide to each student. Have each student read his or her
	Kingsolver alludes to the Iraq war at the end of her essay.
	  I read the title and paragraph five of "Blessed Is the Full Plate" by Anna Quindlen, which appeared in the November 26, 2007, edition of Newsweek. *View it in its entirety at http://www.newsweek.com/id/70982.*
	
	You may give students a choice of the different topics that you have selected for this assignment.
	
	Possible topics based on the issues in the suggested books are as follows:
	
	• *A Streetcar Named Desire*—alcoholism, domestic abuse, mental illness
	• *The Grapes of Wrath*—homelessness, migrant workers, poverty, labor unions, government aid programs
	• *The Great Gatsby*—corruption, materialism, the great disparity between the "haves" and "have nots."
	• *A Raisin in the Sun*—poverty, racial prejudice, neighborhood integration
	• *Monster*—juvenile crime, peer pressure, the judicial system
	• *Speak*—date rape, peer pressure, teen depression
	
	Students who have taken the SATs or have prepared for them will be familiar with the twenty-five-minute essay. While the persuasive essay differs somewhat from the SAT essay, many of the same writing strategies apply.
	  Students will learn from carefully reading another's paper and making suggested revisions.

(Continued)

(Continued)

Unit Sequence	Teacher Reflections
Teaching Strategies and Learning Experiences (Forty Minutes)	

partner's essay and make suggestions using the revision guide.
• After partners have made suggestions on the revision guide (they should not write on the paper itself), they should sign the guide, and then return the guide and the paper to its original owner.
• Give students a chance to read over their own paper again with the suggested revisions and make changes if they wish. Students then hand in their paper along with the attached revision guide.
	They will also be graded on their revision suggestions. Stress the fact that all suggestions should be written on the revision guide, not the paper itself, as the final choice for what revisions are made must lie with the writer.
	  Give students access to dictionaries at this time, if they wish.
	  Assure students that their papers will be graded based on the fact that this was an in-class writing assignment. You can grade it holistically or use the revision guide.

• Differentiation—Write an editorial for your school newspaper about a topic that you feel passionate about. Choose a topic that is current and one that is of interest to other students. Another option is to write a letter to the editor to your local newspaper.
• Differentiation—Bring in an editorial from a newspaper or periodical that you have read and think would be interesting for the class to discuss. Before you present it to the class, determine the argument or thesis, the means of support, the viewpoint, the style, and the tone.
• Differentiation/Identity—If you enjoy writing and looking into a newsworthy topic and find the prospect of reporting intriguing, investigate the career of a famous journalist. Learn about rewards and adventure of the job, the difficulties he or she faces, the ethical values at the core of such a job, and the contributions to the world that he or she makes. Then ask yourself if such a job fits with your values, interests, and strengths. How might such a career shape your life? Prepare an oral presentation to share these thoughts with the class, or a written report.
• Differentiation—Invite a local editorial writer as a guest speaker for the class. Provide an opportunity for interested students to interview him or her.
	Suggest the differentiation projects to students who are interested in writing and those who need a challenge.
	
	If a student decides to bring in an editorial, be sure you read it carefully to determine its appropriateness for class. Check also to see that the presenting student has correctly identified the thesis, support, viewpoint, style, and tone. I found that this assignment was an excellent extra-credit project, and many of the editorials students chose were timely and provocative for the class to discuss.
	  Information about the career of journalism can be found at http://www.bls.gov/oco/ocos088 .htm. This site covers the basics about the nature of the journalistic work, the training and education needed the job outlook, and the earnings.
	  Another helpful site is the American Society of Newspaper Editors (http://www.asne.org/ index.cfm?id=5260).This site gives advice about college programs and internships and many helpful hints for getting a newspaper job.

Unit Sequence	Teacher Reflections
Closure (Five Minutes)	
<ul><li>Ask students the purpose of a persuasive essay.</li><li>Invite a student to explain the difference between a persuasive essay and an editorial.</li><li>Have other students explain how style, tone, and rhetorical devices help to convey the argument or thesis in a persuasive essay.</li><li>Give students a deadline for the book assigned in Lesson 4.2 and plan a culminating lesson on the book prior to Lesson 4.14 of this unit.</li><li>Advise students to be thinking about an aspect of the book they would like to examine in their final project, a literary analysis.</li></ul>	*This ending provides a good review of the nature of persuasive essays and editorials and the writing tools that shape them to be powerful voices.* *While a culminating lesson should include an opportunity for students to ask questions, be careful not to discuss so much of the book that students are robbed of the creativity of finding an original thesis for their culminating project.*

HANDOUT 4.12/4.13A

Revision Guide

Directions: After carefully reading your partner's paper, indicate the areas that are strengths and weaknesses. Be sure to use this guide for all of your comments; do not write comments on your partner's paper. When you have finished, sign this guide and return it and the persuasive draft to your partner. You will receive a grade for your skill at critiquing your partner's paper.

Editor's Name _____

Content:

    Argument or thesis:

    Support for thesis—reason and logic:

    Emotional appeal:

    Examples:

Structure:

    Introduction leads reader into topic and thesis:

    Effective transitions:

    Conclusion suggests an answer or plan for argument:

Expression:

    Clarity and fluency of phrasing:

    Adherence to rules of grammar, spelling, and punctuation:

Lessons 4.14 and 4.15: Writing a Literary Analysis

(105 Minutes [one class of forty-five minutes; one class of sixty minutes])

Discipline-Specific Concepts

C4: Literary Criticism
C5: Literary Analysis
C33: Thesis/Argument

Principles

P8: Readers and writers are influenced by personal, political, historical, social, racial, sexual, and religious circumstances.
P10: Sources of literary criticism need to be evaluated to authenticate their validity.

Skills

S10: Evaluate sources to authenticate validity.
S11: Write with appropriate strategies to suit audience and purpose.
S12: Research a variety of technological and informational sources.
S13: Gather appropriate critical sources for a specific purpose.

Standards

SD2: Students employ a wide range of strategies as they write and use different writing process elements appropriately to communicate with different audiences for a variety of purposes.
SD3: Students apply knowledge of language structure, language conventions, media techniques, figurative language, and genre to create, critique, and discuss print and nonprint texts.
SD4: Students conduct research on issues and interests by generating ideas and questions, and by posing problems. They gather, evaluate, and synthesize data from a variety of sources (e.g., print and nonprint texts, artifacts, people) to communicate their discoveries in ways that suit their purpose and audience.

Guiding Questions

- How do I evaluate the thesis statement for my literary analysis?
- How do I determine which pieces of literary criticism are appropriate support for my literary analysis?
- How can literary criticism enrich my literary analysis?

Unit Sequence	Teacher Reflections
Lesson 14—Introduction (Eight Minutes)	
• Assign the culminating project for this unit, a literary analysis. Go over the highlights of the assignment handout (4.14/4.15 A or B). Concentrate especially on the section of the directions that focuses on the topic of the paper:	*There are two copies of the assignment description. The first one is designed for advanced and above-average students. The second is for average students and those who*

(Continued)

(Continued)

Unit Sequence	Teacher Reflections
Introduction (Twenty Minutes)	

• The paper should examine some aspect of *The Grapes of Wrath* (or whatever book the students read. See the long-term assignment in Lesson 4.2). This scrutiny can be focused on a theme, a character, the setting, or a particular viewpoint of the novel (e.g., historical, political, social, cultural, religious). The thesis should be clearly focused so that students can cover it well in eight pages (or four pages depending on the class). On the other hand, the thesis should be broad enough so that students will have ample material for the length of the assigned paper.
• Tell students to begin with a thesis paragraph and then proceed to develop and support their point, using specific evidence from the text, and supporting ideas from critical sources.
• They should remember that a thesis states a point that they will prove. It does not merely describe. Have them note the difference between the following two statements:
  o Nathaniel Hawthorne wrote many stories about Puritan life.
  o Nathaniel Hawthorne's stories about early American life reflect a point of view that many of the Puritans were harsh and narrow-minded.
• Review the scoring rubric (4.14/4.15D) with students for the literary analysis so that they will know how they will be graded on the project.
	may be reading below grade level. The second handout, "Tips for Literary Analysis" (4.14/4.15C) can be used for all students.
	
	Example 1 merely describes Hawthorne as a writer.
	
	Example 2, an appropriate thesis statement, gives an opinion about Hawthorne's writing and establishes what the writer is going to discuss and prove.

Lesson 14—Teaching Strategies and Learning Experiences (Thirty-Five Minutes)	

• Explain to students that they will work individually today to come up with a thesis statement and at least three supporting passages from the book they've read to support this thesis.
• Tell students that before they begin to look for supporting critical sources, they need to come up with their ideas. The thesis for the paper should be their own. Then when they begin researching critical works for their papers, there will not be any question about the originality of their ideas.
• Stress the need for a thesis that is provable. It must be narrow enough to be covered in an eight- (four-) page paper but broad enough to provide ample analysis for eight (four) pages.
• Advise students that the thesis they create is a starting point, and it can be revised later as they proceed to their outline and rough draft.
	If students cannot find three supporting passages, suggest they create a different thesis.
	    The critical sources should serve as an aid for students' individual opinions, not a substitute for them. Proceeding this way will also aid students in making citation decisions when they get to their rough draft.
	    Since all students will be analyzing one book, there may be duplications of the same general topic, but the individual thesis statements should still vary.

Unit Sequence	Teacher Reflections
Teaching Strategies and Learning Experiences (Twenty Minutes)	
• Give students time to work on the project. While they are working, circulate around the room to monitor their progress and advise those students who need help.	
Lesson 14—Closure (Two Minutes)	
• Invite a student to explain how to evaluate a thesis statement. • Provide an opportunity for students to ask questions about the assignment. • Collect the assignment from those students who have finished. Tell other students that the assignment is due tomorrow. • Distribute the handout "Tips for Literary Analysis" to all students. • Be sure that all students have completed the thesis and supporting passages assignment and are ready to move to the next step before you take the class to the library to look for critical works.	*Limit the student volunteer to giving good evaluating tips for a thesis choice, not revealing his or her thesis statement.* *Read all of the thesis assignments to be sure that they are appropriate. Schedule conferences with students who need help developing a thesis.* *Be sure that you have read all of the thesis statements and supporting passages and have consulted with students who needed help.*
Lesson 15—Introduction (Ten Minutes)	

• Explain to students that today you will take them to the library where you and the librarian will show them where to find critical sources for their literary analysis. Tell them to bring their thesis statements and supporting paragraphs, as well as paper and a pen or pencil.
• Before you go to the library, explain to students that they should be searching for literary criticism that supports the thesis that they have developed. They should be discerning in their choices and make sure that the pieces they choose for support fit well with the thesis they have chosen.
• Explain to students that they will, in effect, be writing a piece of literary criticism. To strengthen their piece, they will use excerpts from other pieces of literary criticism.
• Tell them to read and copy the following guidelines they should follow for using the Internet:
 	
   ○ In general, stick to material you find from a reputable Web site.
   ○ Stay away from material that does not have an author.
   ○ Steer clear of material from another high school, as well as any site that features student papers.
   ○ Avoid sites that have grammar and spelling errors.
	Prior to students coming to class, write the Internet guidelines below on the board so they can read it and take notes before they go to the library.
	
	Before you decide to use a piece of criticism from a Web site check the following:
	
	• Is the Web site a reputable company or institution?
	• Is there an author?
	• Is the Web site run by a college or university?
	• If so, is the material you are viewing maintained by a student?
	• Is the Web site run by a private or public high school?

(Continued)

Unit Sequence	Teacher Reflections
Lesson 15—Introduction (Ten Minutes)	
○ Avoid sites (*SparkNotes*) that are the Web equivalent of *CliffsNotes.* ○ Avoid personal Web sites. ○ Emphasize that plagiarism is a very serious offense. ○ When in doubt, ask your teacher or the librarian.	
Lesson 15—Teaching Strategies and Learning Experiences (Forty Minutes)	
• Take students to the library and work with the librarian to acquaint students with the resources available to them. • Stress to students that there are excellent print sources of literary criticism, as well as nonprint sources. Encourage them to research the print sources, as well as using the computer. • Give students the remainder of the class to explore the resources available. • Circulate among students to assist those who need help and to assess their progress.	*Prior to your visit, give your librarian a copy of your assignment so he or she will know what students will be doing. Ask the librarian to show students the print resources that are available and to tell students of the nonprint resources available. The librarian may prepare a handout for your students of suitable Web sites for literary criticism. If such a sheet is not available, you can use Handout 4.14/4.15E.* *Either you or the librarian should show students how to use a book of literary criticism on a particular author before students begin their search. Many students may think they have to read the entire book. Explain that by using the index and the table of contents, they can quickly find if the topic of their thesis is covered.*
Lesson 15—Closure (Ten Minutes)	

• Ask students how to evaluate a source from the Internet.
• Invite a student who has found at least one critical source that will support his or her thesis to explain how he or she evaluated the literary criticism before deciding to use it in his or her paper.
• Invite another student to explain how his or her paper will benefit from the support of critical sources.
• Reiterate the due dates for the outline, the rough draft, and final paper.
• Following the conclusion of Lesson 4.15, administer the postassessment.
	Depending on the level of the class, you may take the class to the library again or you may leave that responsibility with the students.
	    Due dates will depend on the level of the class and the other work the class is doing.
	    Be sure to make yourself available for individual conferences with students who need help.
	    The postassessment will give you a good idea of how well students learned the concepts and principles in the unit.

HANDOUT 4.14/4.15A

Literary Analysis

Due Dates:
    Thesis statement + supporting paragraphs from *The Grapes of Wrath*—date
    Thesis statement + outline—date
    Rough draft—date
    Final paper—date

Paper Length: The final paper should be a minimum of eight pages typed, not including the title page, works cited page, or any additional supplemental pages.

Format: The paper must be typed, double-spaced. Use 1-inch margins, have a title that you create that gives a preview of your paper, and use correct MLA documentation

Sources: In addition to *The Grapes of Wrath*, students should have a minimum of three appropriate critical sources.

Content and Organization of Paper: The paper should examine some aspect of *The Grapes of Wrath*. This scrutiny can be focused on a theme, a character, the setting, or a particular viewpoint of the novel (e.g., historical, political, social, cultural, religious). Your thesis should be clearly focused so that you can cover it well in eight pages. Begin with your thesis paragraph and then proceed to develop and support your point, using specific evidence from the text, and supporting ideas from critical sources.
    Remember, a thesis states a point that you will prove. It does not merely describe. Note the difference between the following two statements:

- Nathaniel Hawthorne wrote many stories about Puritan life.
- Nathaniel Hawthorne's stories about early American life reflect a point of view that many of the Puritans were harsh and narrow-minded.

Voice and Audience: For purposes of the paper, assume that the audience is the school board. Keeping this in mind, while your voice in the paper should be as natural as possible, you should use a more formal level of phrasing than you would if you were talking to a friend.

HANDOUT 4.14/4.15B

Literary Analysis

Due Dates:
Thesis statement + supporting paragraphs from *A Raisin in the Sun*—date
Thesis statement + outline—date
Rough draft—date
Final paper—date

Paper Length: The final paper should be a minimum of four typed, not including the title page, works cited page, or any additional supplemental pages.

Format: The paper must be typed, double-spaced. Use 1" margins, and use correct MLA documentation.

Sources: In addition to *A Raisin in the Sun*, students should have a minimum of two appropriate critical sources.

Content and Organization of Paper: The paper should examine some aspect of *A Raisin in the Sun*. This scrutiny can be focused on a theme, a character, the setting, or a particular viewpoint of the novel (e.g., historical, political, social, cultural, religious). Your thesis should be clearly focused so that you can cover it well in four pages. Begin with your thesis paragraph and then proceed to develop and support your point, using specific evidence from the text, and supporting ideas from critical sources.

Remember, a thesis states a point that you will prove. It does not merely describe. Note the difference between the following two statements:

- Nathaniel Hawthorne wrote many stories about Puritan life.
- Nathaniel Hawthorne's stories about early American life reflect a point of view that many of the Puritans were harsh and narrow-minded.

Voice and Audience: For purposes of the paper, assume that the audience is the school board. Keeping this in mind, while your voice in the paper should be as natural as possible, you should use a more formal level of phrasing than you would if you were talking to a friend.

HANDOUT 4.14/4.15C

Tips for Literary Analysis

Content

Look deeply into topic; do not just describe.

Avoid needless plot summary; stick to the points that develop your thesis.

Focus on content with some universality.

Be original and creative.

Remember that a paper should be understandable even if the reader has not read the book; along that same idea, identify characters.

Structure, Coherence, and Continuity

A thesis should be present in opening paragraphs and should be a point to be proved, not just description.

Paragraphs should be carefully tied together with transitions.

A conclusion should be an evaluation, not just a repetition of the introduction.

Style and Expression

Avoid vague words such as *it, thing,* and *they.*

Avoid indefinite modifiers.

Don't switch voice; if you start with third person, keep to it; same with first person.

Don't switch voice from singular to plural.

Avoid second person voice; it lacks polish and sounds too casual.

Avoid repeating a word several times in a sentence or a short paragraph.

Don't end a sentence with a preposition.

(Continued)

(Continued)

Mechanics

Proofread carefully to avoid most errors.

When in doubt about the spelling of a word, look it up in a dictionary.

Don't hesitate to use spell check.

Avoid fragments and run-on sentences; remember a comma alone cannot separate two independent clauses.

Don't switch verb tenses.

Follow subject/verb agreement. A singular subject takes a singular verb, same with plural.

Follow pronoun-antecedent agreement. Remember *everyone, anybody,* and other words that end in *one* or *body* are singular, not plural.

Format

The title on the title page should be your title that gives a preview of your paper, not just the name of the book.

Follow correct MLA format for the title page, and the works cited page.

Come down one-third on the first page of your paper and do not number the first page.

Second and all subsequent pages should be numbered in the top righthand corner or top center of the page.

Direct quotes that are four lines or longer should be single-spaced, indented, and cited without direct quotes (unless quote is direct dialogue from story).

Follow correct MLA format for direct quotes.

Scoring Rubric for Literary Analysis

Criteria	1	2	3	4	Your Score
Thesis Clearly stated thesis or purpose	Thesis is missing or is one that does not fit the rest of the paper.	Thesis is acceptable but general.	Thesis is good with some insight.	Thesis is creative and insightful.	1 2 3 4
Content Depth of understanding Sufficiency of thought and logic Strong support using specific detail from appropriate text and critical sources Supporting details that clearly relate to thesis	There are few if any ideas. The supporting details from the text and/or critical sources are confusing or not present.	Content has some ideas but not all are developed or supported by the text and/or critical sources. There may be supporting details that do not relate to the thesis.	Content has good ideas and shows good thought and logic. There is good, developed support from both the text and critical sources that is connected to the thesis.	Content has excellent, creative ideas with depth of understanding and thought. Strong support from both text and critical sources is well developed and connects well to the thesis.	1 2 3 4
Structure, Coherence, Continuity Introduction with a preview of main points Effective transitions Conclusion restates thesis, reviews main points and makes an overall generalization or judgment.	Paper has little structure. Introduction lacks essential information. Body lacks transitions and has weak paragraph continuity. Conclusion lacks essential points or may be missing.	Paper has weak structure. Introduction may mention thesis but does not preview points. Transitions are weak or missing. Conclusion may be present but simply concludes paper and does not restate thesis or make a judgment.	Paper reflects good structure and focus. The introduction is good and previews points, as well as stating the thesis. There are transitions and an effective conclusion that makes some judgment.	Paper reflects excellent structure and focus. Introduction is strong and captures the reader's attention, previews points, and clearly states the thesis. Continuity is excellent with effective transitions. The conclusion is strong and makes an overall judgment.	1 2 3 4

(Continued)

205

(Continued)

Criteria	1	2	3	4	Your Score
Style Fluent phrasing Appropriate level of language for voice and audience Clarity of phrasing, good diction Creativity and originality Adherence to the rules of grammar, spelling, and punctuation	Style is not natural and may sound like a textbook. Little attention is paid to audience in diction or phrasing. Mechanical errors are numerous.	Language is suited for audience, but style is not natural. Phrasing is somewhat awkward, and diction is only fair. Mechanics reflect a number of errors.	Style is smooth. It is generally natural and suited for the audience. Diction and phrasing are good. The mechanics are good.	Style is creative and fluent. It is natural and well suited for the audience. Diction and phrasing are excellent. Mechanics in paper are excellent.	1 2 3 4
Format and Appearance Correct MLA format for title page and works cited page Correct format for internal citations Typed, double-spaced Appropriate length	Paper has many MLA formatting errors and/or omissions. Paper may lack some basic requirements of paper.	Paper has a number of MLA formatting errors or omissions. Most of the requirements for paper are followed.	Paper follows most MLA formatting correctly. There may be minor errors in format. All requirements for paper are followed.	Paper has excellent appearance. All MLA formatting is followed correctly, as are requirements for paper.	1 2 3 4

HANDOUT   4.14/4.15E

Web Sites for Literary Criticism

The Academy of Achievement (http://www.achievement.org/)
Questia (http://www.questia.com/Inden.jsp)
Internet Public Library. (http://www.ipl.org/) On this site, click on Art & Humanities, then on literature and then on criticism.
The Atlantic Monthly (http://wwwtheatlantic.com/)
Literary Resources on the Net (http://andromeda.rutgers.edu/~jlynch/Lit/)
New York Times Book Reviews (http://www.nytimes.com/pages/books/)
Your state library site—the Connecticut one is at http://www.iconn.org/.

Another excellent site is to look up the publisher of the book you are using. Then put that publisher's name into Google. It will come up with the publisher's Web site for you, and most publishers have some criticism and reviews on books they have published.

Unit 4 Postassessment

Administer this postassessment after students finish Lesson 4.15.

Carefully read the following passage from *The Scarlet Letter.* Then in a well-constructed essay, analyze the paragraph and explain how the author, Nathaniel Hawthorne, uses each of the elements below to develop his perspective:

- The placement of the passage in the novel and its implications
- The function of the passage in the development of action, character, setting, or a theme in the novel
- The author's tone
- The author's style
- The author's diction
- The author's viewpoint
- Any other rhetorical devices that the author uses to convey his purpose and viewpoint

But before Mr. Dimmesdale had done speaking, a light gleamed far and wide over all the muffled sky. It was doubtless caused by one of those meteors, which the night-watcher may so often observe burning out to waste, in the vacant regions of the atmosphere. So powerful was its radiance, that it thoroughly illuminated the dense medium of cloud betwixt the sky and earth. The great vault brightened, like the dome of an immense lamp. It showed the familiar scene of the street, with the distinctness of mid-day, but also with the awfulness that is always imparted to familiar objects by an unaccustomed light. The wooden houses, with their jutting stories and quaint gable-peaks; the door-steps and thresholds, with the early grass springing up about them; the garden-plots, black with freshly turned earth; the wheel-track, little worn, and, even in the market-place, margined with green on either side;—all were visible, but with a singularity of aspect that seemed to give another moral interpretation to the things of this world than they had ever borne before. And there stood the minister, with his hand over his heart; and Hester Prynne, with the embroidered letter glimmering on her bosom; and little Pearl, herself a symbol, and the connecting link between those two. They stood in the noon of that strange and solemn splendor, as if it were the light that is to reveal all secrets, and the day-break that shall unite all who belong to one another. (Hawthorne, 2003, pp. 127–128)

Description of Postassessment

The postassessment gives the teacher a good idea of how well students learned to analyze a fictional passage as to the writer's viewpoint and purpose and by what techniques this purpose and viewpoint can be discerned. This postassessment should be administered at the conclusion of the unit. It can then be compared with the preassessment to ascertain the learning that transpired. The teacher will note that the postassessment that features a passage that is a turning point in the novel is more challenging than the preassessment that presents an introductory passage.

Macroconcept

M1: Point of View/Perspective

Discipline-Specific Concepts

C3: Point of View/Viewpoint
C6: Characterization
C8: Theme
C13: Dramatic Irony
C14: Style
C15: Diction
C23: Rhetorical Devices

Principles

P1: Literary criticism is a written interpretation, analysis, and judgment of a work of fiction or nonfiction.

P2: Analyzing the content of a passage of prose imparts information about one or more of the following: characterization, conflict, setting, and theme.

P3: Close scrutiny of a passage of prose reveals hints of the author's purpose in the work as a whole.

P4: Understanding an author's tone and use of irony reveals much of his or her true purpose and meaning in a given work.

P5: An author's style provides a key to interpreting and evaluating a given work.

P6: Authors use a variety of tools to effect a purpose.

P7: By recognizing and understanding literary devices we can enhance our understanding of fiction and nonfiction.

P8: Readers and authors are influenced by personal, political, historical, social, sexual, cultural, and religious circumstances.

Skills

S1: Determine, use, and analyze text structures.
S2: Draw conclusions.
S4: Articulate tone.
S5: Appraise style.
S6: Interpret author's purpose.
S7: Make and justify inferences from explicit or implicit information.
S8: Decide and justify underlying themes.
S9: Make, support, and defend judgments.

HANDOUT 4.14/4.15D

Scoring Rubric for Literary Analysis

Criteria	1	2	3	4	Your Score
Content Placement and function of passage	Placement and function of passage are perceived incorrectly or are not mentioned.	Placement and function of passage are mentioned but not fully developed.	There is good insight as to placement and function of passage.	Excellent awareness of placement and function of passage that shows original thinking.	1 2 3 4
Content Elements of mood, tone, diction, and style to convey author's purpose	Not all elements are mentioned in analyzing the passage and/or some are perceived incorrectly.	All required elements are mentioned but their function in the passage as a whole is limited.	All required elements are mentioned as to their function in conveying the author's purpose.	All required elements are insightfully analyzed as to their role in conveying the author's purpose in the passage.	1 2 3 4
Content Author's viewpoint	The author's viewpoint is incorrect or not mentioned.	Perception of author's viewpoint is correct but limited.	There is good perception of author's viewpoint with support from passage.	There is excellent discernment into author's viewpoint with support from passage.	1 2 3 4
Content Other strategies author uses to convey purpose	No additional strategies are mentioned.	Only one other strategy is mentioned or additional strategies mentioned add little to author's purpose.	Some additional strategies are mentioned that support author's purpose.	Strategies are mentioned that add insight and push boundaries of the assignment.	1 2 3 4
Writing Skills	Writing is disordered. Mechanical errors are numerous.	Writing is adequate in organization and mechanics.	Writing is organized and relatively free of mechanical errors.	Writing has excellent organization, is coherent, and is free of any mechanical errors.	1 2 3 4

REFERENCES

Criticism. (n.d.). Dictionary.com. Retrieved December 10, 2007, from http://dictionary.reference.com/

Hawthorne, N. (2003). *The scarlet letter.* New York: Barnes & Noble.

Hemingway, E. (1995). *A farewell to arms.* New York: Simon & Schuster.

Henry, P. (1980). Speech in the Virginia convention. In F. Hodgins & K. Silverman (Eds.), *Adventures in American literature* (pp. 71–72). New York: Harcourt Brace Jovanovich.

Kingsolver, B. (2002). *Small wonder.* New York: HarperCollins.

O'Brien, T. (1990). *The things they carried.* New York: Broadway Books.

"Saki" (H. H. Munro). (1954). The open window. In R. P. Warren & A. Erskine (Eds.), *Short story masterpieces* (pp. 333–336). New York: Bantam Doubleday Dell.

Salinger, J. D. (1951*). The catcher in the rye.* New York: Little Brown.

Tan, A. (1989). *The joy luck club.* New York: Vintage Books.

Index